# First World War
and Army of Occupation
# War Diary
France, Belgium and Germany

1 CAVALRY DIVISION
9 Cavalry Brigade
Bedford Yeomanry,
1/1 Warwickshire Battery Royal Horse Artillery,
'Y' Battery Royal Horse Artillery,
9 Machine Gun Squadron and 9 Cavalry Pioneer Battalion
1 October 1914 - 9 July 1917

WO95/1116

The Naval & Military Press Ltd
www.nmarchive.com
Published in association with The National Archives

Published by

## The Naval & Military Press Ltd

Unit 10 Ridgewood Industrial Park,

Uckfield, East Sussex,

TN22 5QE England

Tel: +44 (0) 1825 749494

www.naval-military-press.com

www.nmarchive.com

*This diary has been reprinted in facsimile from the original. Any imperfections are inevitably reproduced and the quality may fall short of modern type and cartographic standards.*

**© Crown Copyright**
**Images reproduced by permission of The National Archives, London, England, 2015.**

# Contents

| Document type | Place/Title | Date From | Date To |
|---|---|---|---|
| Heading | WO95/1116/1 | | |
| Heading | ##################################################### | | |
| Miscellaneous | 1915-1918 1st Cavalry Division 9th Cavalry Brigade. 1st Bedfordshire Yeomanry Jun 1915-Feb 1918 From U.K Reorganization Machine Gun Bn | | |
| Miscellaneous | 1st Cavalry Division 9 Cav Bde 1st Bedfordshire Yeo. Vol I June & July 15-Feb. 1918 | | |
| War Diary | Stansted | 09/06/1915 | 09/06/1915 |
| War Diary | Havre | 10/06/1915 | 11/06/1915 |
| War Diary | Hazebrouck | 12/06/1915 | 12/06/1915 |
| War Diary | Ledringhem | 13/06/1915 | 31/07/1915 |
| Heading | 1st Cav Division 9 Cav Bde.Bedfordshire Yeo. Vol I From 1-31.8.15 | | |
| War Diary | Ledringhem | 01/08/1915 | 02/08/1915 |
| War Diary | Mardyck | 03/08/1915 | 03/08/1915 |
| War Diary | Ledringhem | 05/08/1915 | 31/08/1915 |
| Heading | 1st Cavalry Division 9 Cav Bde. Bedfordshire Yeo. Vol II Sep 1 15 | | |
| War Diary | Ledringhem | 01/09/1915 | 23/09/1915 |
| War Diary | Bilques | 24/09/1915 | 24/09/1915 |
| War Diary | Enquin-Les-Mines | 25/09/1915 | 25/09/1915 |
| War Diary | Vaudricourt | 26/09/1915 | 28/09/1915 |
| War Diary | Hesdigneul | 29/09/1915 | 29/09/1915 |
| War Diary | Lozinghem | 30/09/1915 | 03/10/1915 |
| War Diary | Honenghem | 04/10/1915 | 04/10/1915 |
| War Diary | Laires | 05/10/1915 | 19/10/1915 |
| War Diary | Roquetoire | 20/10/1915 | 31/10/1915 |
| War Diary | Lozinghem | 02/10/1915 | 02/10/1915 |
| War Diary | Loos | 03/10/1915 | 04/10/1915 |
| Heading | 1st Cavalry Division 9 Cav Bde Bedford Yeo Nov-1915 Vol IV | | |
| War Diary | Roquetoire | 01/11/1915 | 17/11/1915 |
| War Diary | Desires | 18/11/1915 | 30/11/1915 |
| Heading | Bedfordshire Yeo Dec 1915 Vol V 1st C.D. 9 Cav.Bde | | |
| War Diary | Desvres | 01/12/1915 | 31/12/1915 |
| Heading | Officer i/c A.'G s Office at the Base. Herewith War Diary of The Bedforshire Yeomanry for the month of January, 1916 Vol VI | | |
| War Diary | Desvres | 01/01/1915 | 06/05/1915 |
| War Diary | Ecault | 07/05/1916 | 14/05/1916 |
| War Diary | Desvres | 15/05/1916 | 12/06/1916 |
| War Diary | Ecault | 13/06/1916 | 19/06/1916 |
| War Diary | Desvres | 20/06/1916 | 24/06/1916 |
| War Diary | Dompierre | 25/06/1916 | 25/06/1916 |
| War Diary | Noeux | 26/06/1916 | 26/06/1916 |
| War Diary | St Legers Les Domart | 27/06/1916 | 27/06/1916 |
| War Diary | Querrieu | 28/06/1916 | 30/06/1916 |
| Heading | War Diary of 1/1 Bedfordshire Yeomanry From 1-7-16 To 31-7-16 Volume No. XXIV. | | |
| War Diary | Querrieu | 01/07/1916 | 05/07/1916 |

| | | | |
|---|---|---|---|
| War Diary | Longpre | 06/07/1916 | 11/07/1916 |
| War Diary | Querrieu | 12/07/1916 | 13/07/1916 |
| War Diary | Buire | 14/07/1916 | 24/07/1916 |
| War Diary | Frechencourt | 25/07/1916 | 09/08/1916 |
| War Diary | Coquerel | 10/08/1916 | 10/08/1916 |
| War Diary | Gamaches | 11/08/1916 | 06/09/1916 |
| War Diary | Bettancourt | 07/09/1916 | 07/09/1916 |
| War Diary | Daours | 08/09/1916 | 14/09/1916 |
| War Diary | Carnoy | 15/09/1916 | 17/09/1916 |
| War Diary | Daours | 18/09/1916 | 23/09/1916 |
| War Diary | Conde | 24/09/1916 | 24/09/1916 |
| War Diary | Noeux | 25/09/1916 | 25/09/1916 |
| War Diary | Oeuf | 26/09/1916 | 26/09/1916 |
| War Diary | Fillievres | 27/09/1916 | 19/10/1916 |
| War Diary | Occoches | 20/10/1916 | 20/10/1916 |
| War Diary | Naours | 21/10/1916 | 08/11/1916 |
| War Diary | Forest L'abbaye | 09/11/1916 | 09/11/1916 |
| War Diary | Douriez | 10/11/1916 | 10/11/1916 |
| War Diary | Desvres | 11/11/1916 | 31/03/1917 |
| Heading | War Diary of 1/1 Bedfordshire Yeomanry From 1-4-17 To 30-4-17 Vol XXXIII | | |
| War Diary | Desvres | 01/04/1917 | 05/04/1917 |
| War Diary | Montcavrel | 06/04/1917 | 07/04/1917 |
| War Diary | Blangy | 08/04/1917 | 08/04/1917 |
| War Diary | Aubigny | 09/04/1917 | 16/04/1917 |
| War Diary | Conchy | 17/04/1917 | 30/04/1917 |
| War Diary | Conchy-Sur Canche | 01/05/1917 | 13/05/1917 |
| War Diary | Monchy | 14/05/1917 | 14/05/1917 |
| War Diary | Labeuvriere | 15/05/1917 | 04/06/1917 |
| War Diary | Estaires | 05/06/1917 | 11/06/1917 |
| War Diary | Labeuvriere | 12/06/1917 | 16/07/1917 |
| War Diary | Neuf Berquin | 17/07/1917 | 27/08/1917 |
| War Diary | Flechin | 28/08/1917 | 28/08/1917 |
| War Diary | Rumilly | 29/08/1917 | 29/08/1917 |
| War Diary | Longvillers | 30/08/1917 | 06/10/1917 |
| War Diary | Wierre Au Bois | 07/10/1917 | 07/10/1917 |
| War Diary | Holque | 08/10/1917 | 11/10/1917 |
| War Diary | Wierre Au Bois | 12/10/1917 | 12/10/1917 |
| War Diary | Longvillers | 13/10/1917 | 10/11/1917 |
| War Diary | Aubin-St-Vaast | 11/10/1917 | 11/11/1917 |
| War Diary | Beavoir Riviere | 12/11/1917 | 12/11/1917 |
| War Diary | Querrieu | 13/11/1917 | 13/11/1917 |
| War Diary | Mericourt | 14/11/1917 | 14/11/1917 |
| War Diary | Mesnil-Bruntel | 15/11/1917 | 20/11/1917 |
| War Diary | Metz | 21/11/1917 | 21/11/1917 |
| War Diary | Marcoin | 22/11/1917 | 22/11/1917 |
| War Diary | Metz | 23/11/1917 | 23/11/1917 |
| War Diary | Flesquier | 24/11/1917 | 24/11/1917 |
| War Diary | Metz | 25/11/1917 | 27/11/1917 |
| War Diary | Chuignolles | 28/11/1917 | 30/11/1917 |
| War Diary | Roisel | 01/12/1917 | 03/12/1917 |
| War Diary | Chuignolles | 04/12/1917 | 18/12/1917 |
| War Diary | Lemesnil-Bruntel | 19/12/1917 | 31/12/1917 |
| Heading | War Diary Bedfordshire Yeomanry January 1918 Volume No. 42. | | |
| War Diary | Lemesnil-Bruntel | 01/01/1918 | 28/02/1918 |

| | | | |
|---|---|---|---|
| Heading | WO95/1116/2 | | |
| Heading | 1915-1916 1st Cavalry Division 9th Cavalry Brigade Warwick R.H.A. Jun 1915-Oct 1916 Oct 1914 To 15 Bde R H A 29 Div Troops Box 2291 | | |
| Heading | 2nd Cavalry Divisional Artillery. Disembarked Havre 1.11.14.Warwickshire Battery R.H.A. October 1914 | | |
| War Diary | At Newbury | 01/10/1914 | 16/10/1914 |
| War Diary | At Thatcham | 17/10/1914 | 30/10/1914 |
| War Diary | At Sea | 31/10/1914 | 31/10/1914 |
| Heading | 2nd Cavalry Division Artillery. Disembarked Havre 1.11.14.Warwickshire Battery R.H.A. November 1914 | | |
| War Diary | In Port-atta Havre | 01/11/1914 | 01/11/1914 |
| War Diary | At-Laheve | 02/11/1914 | 02/11/1914 |
| War Diary | In Train | 03/11/1914 | 04/11/1914 |
| War Diary | At Esquerdes | 05/11/1914 | 20/11/1914 |
| War Diary | At Esquerdes-Eblinghem Vieux-Bercquin | 21/11/1914 | 21/11/1914 |
| War Diary | Vieux Berquin | 22/11/1914 | 22/11/1914 |
| War Diary | At Vieux Bercquin | 23/11/1914 | 30/11/1914 |
| Heading | 2nd Cavalry Divisional Artillery. Warwickshire Battery R.H.A. December 1914 | | |
| War Diary | At Vieux-Bercquin | 01/12/1914 | 12/12/1914 |
| War Diary | In "T" Battery's Trenches | 13/12/1914 | 13/12/1914 |
| War Diary | In Trenches Near Fleurbaix | 14/12/1914 | 14/12/1914 |
| War Diary | Near Fleurbaix | 15/12/1914 | 15/12/1914 |
| War Diary | At Fleurbaix | 17/12/1914 | 17/12/1914 |
| War Diary | At Vieux-Bercquin | 18/12/1914 | 31/12/1914 |
| Heading | 5/2nd Cavalry Division Warwickshire R.H.A. Vol II 1-31.1.15 | | |
| Heading | War Diary of Warwickshire R.H.A. From Jan 1st 1915 To Jan 31st 1915 | | |
| War Diary | Vieux Berquin | 01/01/1915 | 08/01/1915 |
| War Diary | Vielle Chappelle | 09/01/1915 | 11/01/1915 |
| War Diary | Near Le Touret | 12/01/1915 | 24/01/1915 |
| War Diary | Guarbecque | 25/01/1915 | 25/01/1915 |
| War Diary | Dohem | 26/01/1915 | 31/01/1915 |
| Heading | 2nd. Cavalry Division Warwickshire R.H.A. Vol III 1-28.2.15 | | |
| Heading | War Diary of Warwickshire Royal Horse Artillery From February 1st To February 28th 1915 | | |
| War Diary | La Motte | 01/02/1915 | 26/02/1915 |
| War Diary | Dohem | 27/02/1915 | 28/02/1915 |
| Heading | 2nd Cavalry Division Warwickshire R.H.A. March 1915 | | |
| War Diary | Dohem | 01/03/1915 | 09/03/1915 |
| War Diary | La Motte | 10/03/1915 | 11/03/1915 |
| War Diary | Estaire | 12/03/1915 | 13/03/1915 |
| War Diary | La Motte | 14/03/1915 | 31/03/1915 |
| Heading | 5/2nd Cavalry Div Warwickshire R.H.A. Vol V 1-30.4.15. | | |
| War Diary | La Motte | 01/04/1915 | 30/04/1915 |
| Heading | 2nd Cavalry Division Warwick R.H.A. Vol VI 1-31.5.15. | | |
| War Diary | La Motte | 01/05/1915 | 17/05/1915 |
| War Diary | Worm. Hout | 18/05/1915 | 18/05/1915 |
| War Diary | Ledringham | 19/05/1915 | 23/05/1915 |
| War Diary | Vlamertinghe | 24/05/1915 | 24/05/1915 |

| | | | |
|---|---|---|---|
| War Diary | Ypres | 25/05/1915 | 28/05/1915 |
| War Diary | Ledringhem | 29/05/1915 | 31/05/1915 |
| War Diary | 2nd Cavalry Division 1st/9 Cav Bde Warwick R.H.A. Vol VII 1-30-6-15 June 1915-Oct 1916 | | |
| War Diary | Ledringhem | 01/06/1915 | 30/06/1915 |
| War Diary | 2nd Cavalry Division 1st/9 Cav Bde Warwick R.H.A. Vol VIII 1-31-7-15 | | |
| War Diary | Ledringhem | 01/07/1915 | 18/07/1915 |
| War Diary | Morbecque | 19/07/1915 | 22/07/1915 |
| War Diary | Ledringhem | 23/07/1915 | 31/07/1915 |
| Heading | 1st Cavalry Division 9 Cav Bde Warwick R.H.A. Vol IX August 15 | | |
| War Diary | Ledringhem | 01/08/1915 | 02/08/1915 |
| War Diary | Mardyck | 02/08/1915 | 03/08/1915 |
| War Diary | Ledringhem | 04/08/1915 | 30/08/1915 |
| War Diary | Wardecque | 31/08/1915 | 31/08/1915 |
| War Diary | Ledringhem | 11/08/1915 | 21/08/1915 |
| Heading | 1st Cavalry Division Warwick R.H.A. Vol X Sept 15 | | |
| War Diary | Ledringhem | 01/09/1915 | 01/09/1915 |
| War Diary | Lapugnoy | 02/09/1915 | 02/09/1915 |
| War Diary | Noeux-Les Mines | 03/09/1915 | 03/09/1915 |
| War Diary | Grenay | 04/09/1915 | 16/09/1915 |
| War Diary | Noeux-Les-Mines | 17/09/1915 | 17/09/1915 |
| War Diary | Steenbecque | 18/09/1915 | 18/09/1915 |
| War Diary | Ledringhem | 19/09/1915 | 23/09/1915 |
| War Diary | Heuringhen | 24/09/1915 | 24/09/1915 |
| War Diary | Estrees Blanches | 25/09/1915 | 25/09/1915 |
| War Diary | Vaudricourt | 26/09/1915 | 28/09/1915 |
| War Diary | Hesdigneul | 29/09/1915 | 29/09/1915 |
| War Diary | Lapugnoy | 30/09/1915 | 30/09/1915 |
| Heading Miscellaneous | Warwickshire R.H.A October 1915 Diary Missing | | |
| Heading | 1st Cavalry Division Warwickshire R.H.A. Nov 1915 Vol XII | | |
| War Diary | Cohem | 01/11/1915 | 15/11/1915 |
| War Diary | Sequieres | 18/11/1915 | 29/11/1915 |
| War Diary | Delette | 30/11/1915 | 30/11/1915 |
| Miscellaneous | D.A.G., 3rd Echelon, Base. | 10/03/1916 | 10/03/1916 |
| Miscellaneous | D.A.G. 3rd Echelon Base. | 21/03/1916 | 21/03/1916 |
| War Diary | Questrecques | 01/04/1916 | 30/04/1916 |
| War Diary | Sequieres | 01/05/1916 | 05/05/1916 |
| War Diary | Questrecques | 05/05/1916 | 31/05/1916 |
| Heading Miscellaneous | May 1916 Missing | | |
| War Diary | Ecault | 01/06/1916 | 07/06/1916 |
| War Diary | Questrecques | 08/06/1916 | 23/06/1916 |
| War Diary | Bezingham | 24/06/1916 | 25/06/1916 |
| War Diary | Prochen Estinal | 25/06/1916 | 27/06/1916 |
| War Diary | St Leger | 28/06/1916 | 28/06/1916 |
| War Diary | Querrieu | 29/06/1916 | 30/06/1916 |
| War Diary | Querrieu | 01/07/1916 | 05/07/1916 |
| War Diary | Longpre | 06/07/1916 | 11/07/1916 |
| War Diary | Querrieu | 12/07/1916 | 14/07/1916 |
| War Diary | Buire | 14/07/1916 | 24/07/1916 |
| War Diary | Querrieu | 25/07/1916 | 31/07/1916 |

| | | | |
|---|---|---|---|
| Heading | War Diary of 1/1st Warwickshire Battery Royal Horse Artillery. August 1916 | | |
| War Diary | Querrieu | 01/08/1916 | 09/08/1916 |
| War Diary | Long | 10/08/1916 | 10/08/1916 |
| War Diary | Gamaches | 11/08/1916 | 31/08/1916 |
| War Diary | Verquigneul | 21/07/1916 | 21/07/1916 |
| War Diary | Annezin | 22/07/1916 | 22/07/1916 |
| War Diary | Therouannes | 23/07/1916 | 23/07/1916 |
| War Diary | Secquires | 24/07/1916 | 29/07/1916 |
| War Diary | Gamaches | 01/09/1916 | 05/09/1916 |
| War Diary | Bettencourt | 06/09/1916 | 07/09/1916 |
| War Diary | Daours | 08/09/1916 | 14/09/1916 |
| War Diary | Carnoy | 15/09/1916 | 17/09/1916 |
| War Diary | Daours | 18/09/1916 | 23/09/1916 |
| War Diary | Conde | 24/09/1916 | 24/09/1916 |
| War Diary | Auxy-Le-Chateau | 25/09/1916 | 25/09/1916 |
| War Diary | Linzeux | 26/09/1916 | 26/09/1916 |
| War Diary | Fillievres | 21/09/1916 | 19/10/1916 |
| War Diary | Neuvillette | 20/10/1916 | 20/10/1916 |
| War Diary | Naours | 21/10/1916 | 22/10/1916 |
| War Diary | Mesnil | 23/10/1916 | 31/10/1916 |
| Heading | WO95/1116/3 | | |
| Heading | 1916-1918 1st Cavalry Division 9th Cavalry Brigade "Y" Battery R.H.A. Dec 1916 Apr 1919 | | |
| Heading | War Diary of Y Battery R H A December 1916 Volume No 1 | | |
| War Diary | Bourainville | 01/12/1916 | 01/12/1916 |
| War Diary | Verlincthun | 02/12/1916 | 06/12/1916 |
| War Diary | Verlincthun and Carly | 07/12/1916 | 07/12/1916 |
| War Diary | Carly | 11/12/1916 | 14/12/1916 |
| War Diary | Hesdin-L'abbe | 16/12/1916 | 16/12/1916 |
| War Diary | Carly | 18/12/1916 | 30/12/1916 |
| Heading | War Diary of Y Battery R.H.A. January 1917 Volume No 2 | | |
| War Diary | Carly | 01/01/1917 | 31/01/1917 |
| Heading | War Diary of Y Battery R.H.A. February 1917 Volume III | | |
| War Diary | Carly | 01/02/1917 | 28/02/1917 |
| Heading | War Diary of Y Battery R H A. For March 1917 Volume No IV | | |
| War Diary | Carly | 01/03/1917 | 31/03/1917 |
| Heading | War Diary of Y Battery R H A April 1917 Vol No V | | |
| War Diary | Carly | 01/04/1917 | 25/04/1917 |
| Heading | War Diary of Y Battery R H A May 1917 Vol No VI | | |
| War Diary | Aubrometz | 01/05/1917 | 12/05/1917 |
| War Diary | Pressy Lez Perives | 13/05/1917 | 13/05/1917 |
| War Diary | Labrouviere | 14/05/1917 | 18/05/1917 |
| War Diary | F 11 b 3.1 Ry Bethune 1/40000 | 18/05/1917 | 31/05/1917 |
| Heading | War Diary of Y Battery R H A June 1917 Vol VII | | |
| War Diary | F11 B.31 Ref Bethune 1/40000 | 01/06/1917 | 02/06/1917 |
| War Diary | Le Quesnoy | 03/06/1917 | 03/06/1917 |
| War Diary | Estaires | 04/06/1917 | 11/06/1917 |
| War Diary | Le Quesnoy | 11/06/1917 | 12/06/1917 |
| War Diary | X 24 a 11 Ref Bethune 1/40000 | 14/06/1917 | 19/06/1917 |
| War Diary | Le Quesnoy | 19/06/1917 | 19/06/1917 |
| War Diary | Rb 3 Ref Sheet 36B 1/40000 | 21/06/1917 | 21/06/1917 |

| | | | |
|---|---|---|---|
| War Diary | R 66 Ref Sheet 36B 1/40000 | 22/06/1917 | 30/06/1917 |
| Heading | War Diary of Y Battery R.H.A. July 1917 Vol. 8 | | |
| War Diary | M 21d 1-6 Ref Sheet 36C 1/40000 | 01/07/1917 | 03/07/1917 |
| War Diary | Estairs | 04/07/1917 | 04/07/1917 |
| War Diary | S6 B 1:5 | 06/07/1917 | 14/07/1917 |
| War Diary | Estairs | 15/07/1917 | 31/07/1917 |
| Heading | War Diary of Y Battery R H A For August 1917 Vol IX | | |
| War Diary | Estaires | 01/08/1917 | 26/08/1917 |
| War Diary | Cuhem | 27/08/1917 | 27/08/1917 |
| War Diary | Renty | 28/07/1917 | 28/07/1917 |
| War Diary | Carly | 29/08/1917 | 31/08/1917 |
| Heading | War Diary of Y Battery R H A Sept 1917 Vol X | | |
| War Diary | Carly | 01/09/1917 | 30/09/1917 |
| Heading | War Diary of Y Battery R.H.A. October 1917 Volume 11 | | |
| War Diary | Carly | 01/10/1917 | 07/10/1917 |
| War Diary | Bleue Maison | 08/10/1917 | 08/10/1917 |
| War Diary | Carly | 11/10/1917 | 31/10/1917 |
| Heading | War Diary of Y Battery R H A for Nov 1917 Vol No 12. | | |
| War Diary | Estree | 01/11/1917 | 14/11/1917 |
| War Diary | Le Mesnil-Bruntel | 15/11/1917 | 30/11/1917 |
| War Diary | Boursies | 01/12/1917 | 13/12/1917 |
| War Diary | Templeux-Le-Guerard | 01/01/1918 | 22/01/1918 |
| War Diary | Near Jeancourt | 23/01/1918 | 31/01/1918 |
| Heading | War Diary of "Y" Battery R.H.A. March 1918 Volume XV | | |
| War Diary | Jeancourt | 01/03/1918 | 14/03/1918 |
| War Diary | Vraignes | 15/03/1918 | 15/03/1918 |
| War Diary | Le Mesnil | 15/03/1918 | 04/04/1918 |
| War Diary | Fontaine L'Etalon | 01/06/1918 | 16/06/1918 |
| War Diary | Beauvoire-Riviere | 01/08/1918 | 10/08/1918 |
| War Diary | Camon | 11/08/1918 | 16/08/1918 |
| War Diary | Lequesnil Fm | 17/08/1918 | 21/08/1918 |
| War Diary | Amplier | 21/08/1918 | 26/08/1918 |
| War Diary | Grand-Rullecourt | 26/08/1918 | 30/09/1918 |
| War Diary | Hervilly | 01/10/1918 | 07/10/1918 |
| War Diary | In The Field | 08/10/1918 | 10/10/1918 |
| War Diary | Maretz | 11/10/1918 | 30/11/1918 |
| War Diary | | 18/11/1918 | 18/11/1918 |
| War Diary | | 17/11/1918 | 31/11/1918 |
| War Diary | Germany | 01/12/1918 | 31/12/1918 |
| War Diary | Millendorf | 01/01/1919 | 07/04/1919 |
| War Diary | Chendore | 07/04/1919 | 30/04/1919 |
| Heading | WO95/1116/4 | | |
| Heading | 1916-1918 1st Cavalry Division 9th Cavalry Brigade. 9th Machine Gun Squadron May 1916-Mar 1919 To Hussars Bde Box 1166 | | |
| War Diary | Desires | 01/01/1916 | 18/01/1916 |
| War Diary | Therouanne | 19/01/1916 | 19/01/1916 |
| War Diary | L'Eclene | 20/01/1916 | 15/04/1916 |
| War Diary | Euston Corner | 16/04/1916 | 30/04/1916 |
| War Diary | L'Ecleme | 01/05/1916 | 31/05/1916 |
| War Diary | Ecault | 01/06/1916 | 30/06/1916 |

| | | | |
|---|---|---|---|
| Heading | War Diary of 9th Machine Gun Squadron July 1916 Volume No 6 | | |
| War Diary | Querrieu | 01/07/1916 | 03/07/1916 |
| War Diary | Longpre | 04/07/1916 | 11/07/1916 |
| War Diary | Querrieu | 12/07/1916 | 12/07/1916 |
| War Diary | Buire | 13/07/1916 | 23/07/1916 |
| War Diary | Querrieu | 24/07/1916 | 31/07/1916 |
| Heading | War Diary of 9th Machine Gun Squadron August 1916 Volume No | | |
| War Diary | Querrieu | 01/08/1916 | 08/08/1916 |
| War Diary | Longuet | 09/08/1916 | 09/08/1916 |
| War Diary | Gamaches | 10/08/1916 | 31/08/1916 |
| Heading | War Diary of 9th Machine Gun Squadron September 1916 Volume No 8 | | |
| War Diary | Gamaches | 01/09/1916 | 06/09/1916 |
| War Diary | Bettencourt | 07/09/1916 | 07/09/1916 |
| War Diary | Daours | 08/09/1916 | 14/09/1916 |
| War Diary | Carnoy Valley | 15/09/1916 | 22/09/1916 |
| War Diary | Daours | 23/09/1916 | 23/09/1916 |
| Heading | Conde Folie | 24/09/1916 | 24/09/1916 |
| War Diary | Bealcourt | 25/09/1916 | 25/09/1916 |
| War Diary | Galametz | 26/09/1916 | 30/09/1916 |
| Heading | War Diary of 9th Machine Gun Squadron October 1916 Volume No | | |
| War Diary | Galametz | 01/10/1916 | 19/10/1916 |
| War Diary | Neuvillette | 20/10/1916 | 20/10/1916 |
| War Diary | Wargnies | 21/10/1916 | 28/10/1916 |
| War Diary | Havernas | 29/10/1916 | 31/10/1916 |
| Heading | War Diary of 9th Machine Gun Squadron November 1916 Volume No | | |
| War Diary | Halloy Les Pernois | 01/11/1916 | 08/11/1916 |
| War Diary | L'Heure | 09/11/1916 | 09/11/1916 |
| War Diary | Sauchoy | 10/11/1916 | 10/11/1916 |
| War Diary | Wirwignes | 11/11/1916 | 30/11/1916 |
| Heading | War Diary of 9th Machine Gun Squadron. December 1916 Volume No 1 | | |
| War Diary | Wirwignes | 01/12/1916 | 31/12/1916 |
| Heading | War Diary of 9th Machine Gun Squadron January 1917 Volume 11 | | |
| War Diary | Wirwignes | 01/01/1917 | 04/01/1917 |
| War Diary | Bourthes | 05/01/1917 | 23/01/1917 |
| War Diary | Noeux Les Mines | 24/01/1917 | 27/01/1917 |
| War Diary | Les Brebis | 28/01/1917 | 31/01/1917 |
| War Diary | In The Trenches Loos-Maroc Sector | 01/02/1917 | 28/02/1917 |
| Heading | War Diary of 9th Machine Gun Squadron March 1917 Volume No 13 | | |
| War Diary | Loos-Maroc | 01/03/1917 | 03/03/1917 |
| War Diary | Les Brebis | 04/03/1917 | 04/03/1917 |
| War Diary | Bourthes | 05/03/1917 | 31/03/1917 |
| Heading | War Diary of 9th Machine Gun Squadron April 1917 Volume No 14 | | |
| War Diary | In Billets at Bourthes | 01/04/1917 | 08/04/1917 |
| War Diary | In Bivanac at Capelle Fermont | 09/04/1917 | 16/04/1917 |
| War Diary | In Billets at Vacquerie Le Bouck | 17/04/1917 | 19/04/1917 |
| War Diary | In Billets at Rougefay | 20/04/1917 | 30/04/1917 |

| | | | |
|---|---|---|---|
| Heading | War Diary of 9th Machine Gun Squadron May 1917 Volume XV | | |
| War Diary | Rougefay | 01/05/1917 | 03/05/1917 |
| War Diary | Ligny-Sur-Canche | 04/05/1917 | 14/05/1917 |
| War Diary | Labeuvriere | 15/05/1917 | 17/05/1917 |
| War Diary | Pailosophe | 18/05/1917 | 18/05/1917 |
| War Diary | Labeuvriere | 19/05/1917 | 19/05/1917 |
| War Diary | Vermelles | 19/05/1917 | 29/05/1917 |
| War Diary | Mazingarbe | 30/05/1917 | 31/05/1917 |
| Heading | War Diary of 9th Machine Gun Squadron June 1917 | | |
| War Diary | Mazingarbe | 01/06/1917 | 02/06/1917 |
| War Diary | Annezin | 03/06/1917 | 04/06/1917 |
| War Diary | La Gorgue | 05/06/1917 | 11/06/1917 |
| War Diary | Annezin | 12/06/1917 | 13/06/1917 |
| War Diary | In The Trenches | 14/06/1917 | 21/06/1917 |
| War Diary | Hulluch | 22/06/1917 | 25/06/1917 |
| War Diary | In Action Cite Des Bureaux | 26/06/1917 | 29/06/1917 |
| War Diary | In Action Cite De Riaumont | 30/06/1917 | 30/06/1917 |
| Heading | War Diary of 9th Machine Gun Squadron July 1917 | | |
| War Diary | In The Trenches | 01/07/1917 | 02/07/1917 |
| War Diary | Les Brebis | 03/07/1917 | 04/07/1917 |
| War Diary | Annezin | 05/07/1917 | 08/07/1917 |
| War Diary | In the Trenches | 09/07/1917 | 14/07/1917 |
| War Diary | Annezin | 15/07/1917 | 16/07/1917 |
| War Diary | Estaires | 17/07/1917 | 31/07/1917 |
| Heading | War Diary of 9th Machine Gun Squadron August 1917 Volume No XVIII | | |
| War Diary | Estaires | 01/08/1917 | 27/08/1917 |
| War Diary | Pippemont | 28/08/1917 | 28/08/1917 |
| War Diary | Aix en Eigny | 29/08/1917 | 29/08/1917 |
| War Diary | Le Faux | 30/08/1917 | 31/08/1917 |
| Heading | War Diary of 9th Machine Gun Squadron September 1917 Volume No. XIX. | | |
| War Diary | Lefaux | 01/09/1917 | 30/09/1917 |
| Heading | War Diary of 9th Machine Gun Squadron October 1917 Volume 20 | | |
| War Diary | Lefaux | 01/10/1917 | 06/10/1917 |
| War Diary | Long Fosse | 07/10/1917 | 07/10/1917 |
| War Diary | Zudrove | 08/10/1917 | 11/10/1917 |
| War Diary | Long Fosse | 12/10/1917 | 12/10/1917 |
| War Diary | Lefaux | 13/10/1917 | 15/10/1917 |
| War Diary | Recques | 16/10/1917 | 16/10/1917 |
| War Diary | Montcavrel | 17/10/1917 | 31/10/1917 |
| Heading | War Diary of 9th Machine Gun Squadron Vol 20 Nov 1917 | | |
| War Diary | Montcavrel | 01/11/1917 | 13/11/1917 |
| War Diary | Le Mesnil | 15/11/1917 | 30/11/1917 |
| Heading | War Diary of 9th Machine Gun of Squadron December 1917 Volume No 22 | | |
| War Diary | Roisel | 01/12/1917 | 02/12/1917 |
| War Diary | W 24.d. (Rly Embkt.) | 03/12/1917 | 04/12/1917 |
| War Diary | Roisel | 05/12/1917 | 16/12/1917 |
| War Diary | Froissy | 17/12/1917 | 21/12/1917 |
| War Diary | Le Mesnil | 22/12/1917 | 31/12/1917 |
| Heading | War Diary of 9th Machine Gun Of Squadron January 1918 (Volume No 23) | | |

| | | | |
|---|---|---|---|
| War Diary | Le Mesnil | 01/01/1918 | 31/01/1918 |
| Heading | War Diary of 9th Machine Gun Squadron February 1918 Volume No 24 | | |
| War Diary | Le Mesnil | 01/02/1918 | 28/02/1918 |
| Heading | War Diary of 9th Machine Gun Squadron Month Of March 1918 Volume 24 | | |
| War Diary | Le Mesnil-Bruntel | 01/03/1918 | 21/03/1918 |
| War Diary | Bernes | 22/03/1918 | 22/03/1918 |
| War Diary | Hervilly | 22/03/1918 | 22/03/1918 |
| War Diary | Marchelpot | 23/03/1918 | 23/03/1918 |
| War Diary | Curchy | 24/03/1918 | 24/03/1918 |
| War Diary | Froissy | 24/03/1918 | 24/03/1918 |
| War Diary | Gerisy | 25/03/1918 | 25/03/1918 |
| War Diary | Bussy-Les-Daours | 26/03/1918 | 27/03/1918 |
| War Diary | Bonnay | 28/03/1918 | 28/03/1918 |
| War Diary | Bussy-Les-Daours | 29/03/1918 | 31/03/1918 |
| Heading | War Diary of 9th Machine Gun Squadron In The Month Of April 1918 Volume No 26 | | |
| War Diary | Bussy Les Daours | 01/04/1918 | 02/04/1918 |
| War Diary | Fouilly | 03/04/1918 | 04/04/1918 |
| War Diary | Amiens | 05/04/1918 | 09/04/1918 |
| War Diary | Resmainel | 10/04/1918 | 11/04/1918 |
| War Diary | Auchy Au Bois | 12/04/1918 | 30/04/1918 |
| Heading | War Diary of 9th Machine Gun Squadron For Month Of May 1918 Volume No 27 | | |
| War Diary | Auchy-Au-Bois | 01/05/1918 | 19/05/1918 |
| War Diary | Nedonchelle | 20/05/1918 | 21/05/1918 |
| War Diary | Monchy-Cayeux | 22/05/1918 | 22/05/1918 |
| War Diary | Le Ponchel | 23/05/1918 | 31/05/1918 |
| Heading | War Diary of 9th Machine Gun Squadron June 1918 Volume No 28 | | |
| War Diary | Le Ponchel | 01/06/1918 | 30/06/1918 |
| Heading | War Diary of 9th Machine Gun Squadron July-1918 Volume No 29 | | |
| War Diary | Le Ponchel | 01/07/1918 | 13/07/1918 |
| War Diary | Thievres | 14/07/1918 | 19/07/1918 |
| War Diary | Mezerolles | 20/07/1918 | 27/07/1918 |
| War Diary | Le Meillard | 28/07/1918 | 05/08/1918 |
| War Diary | Perois | 06/08/1918 | 06/08/1918 |
| War Diary | Longpre | 07/08/1918 | 07/08/1918 |
| War Diary | Longeau | 08/08/1918 | 08/08/1918 |
| War Diary | Guillaucourt | 09/08/1918 | 09/08/1918 |
| War Diary | Caix | 10/08/1918 | 11/08/1918 |
| War Diary | Camon Rivery | 13/08/1918 | 16/08/1918 |
| War Diary | Longuevillette Thievres | 19/08/1918 | 21/08/1918 |
| War Diary | Ampliers | 22/08/1918 | 22/08/1918 |
| War Diary | Orville | 23/08/1918 | 26/08/1918 |
| War Diary | Leincourt | 27/08/1918 | 31/08/1918 |
| Heading | War Diary of 9th Machine Gun Squadron September 1918 Volume 32 | | |
| War Diary | Leincourt | 01/09/1918 | 16/09/1918 |
| War Diary | Monchel | 17/09/1918 | 17/09/1918 |
| War Diary | Le Ponchel | 18/09/1918 | 18/09/1918 |
| War Diary | Le Quesnel Fm | 19/09/1918 | 19/09/1918 |
| War Diary | Bois Be Rgues | 20/09/1918 | 24/09/1918 |
| War Diary | St Leger-Les-Authie | 25/09/1918 | 25/09/1918 |

| | | | |
|---|---|---|---|
| War Diary | Meaulte | 26/09/1918 | 26/09/1918 |
| War Diary | Bois-St-Martin | 27/09/1918 | 29/09/1918 |
| War Diary | Hervilly | 30/09/1918 | 30/09/1918 |
| Heading | War Diary of 9th Machine Gun Squadron October 1918 Volume 33. | | |
| War Diary | Hervilly | 01/10/1918 | 07/10/1918 |
| War Diary | Buisson Gullaine Ridge | 08/10/1918 | 08/10/1918 |
| War Diary | Beaurevoir | 09/10/1918 | 09/10/1918 |
| War Diary | Maretz | 10/10/1918 | 13/10/1918 |
| War Diary | Trefcon | 14/10/1918 | 31/10/1918 |
| Heading | War Diary of 9th Machine Gun Squadron November 1918 Volume XXXIV. | | |
| War Diary | Trefcon | 01/11/1918 | 06/11/1918 |
| War Diary | Bantouzelle | 07/11/1918 | 07/11/1918 |
| War Diary | Arleux | 08/11/1918 | 08/11/1918 |
| War Diary | Pont A Marcq | 09/11/1918 | 09/11/1918 |
| War Diary | Gauram Ramecroix | 09/11/1918 | 10/11/1918 |
| War Diary | Villers St Armand | 11/11/1918 | 11/11/1918 |
| War Diary | Maffle | 12/11/1918 | 12/11/1918 |
| War Diary | La Garenne | 13/11/1918 | 17/11/1918 |
| War Diary | Bagenrieusx | 18/11/1918 | 18/11/1918 |
| War Diary | Ecaussines D'Enghien | 19/11/1918 | 21/11/1918 |
| War Diary | Mellery | 22/11/1918 | 22/11/1918 |
| War Diary | Sart D'Avril | 23/11/1918 | 24/11/1918 |
| War Diary | Huccorgne | 25/11/1918 | 27/11/1918 |
| War Diary | Esneux | 28/11/1918 | 29/11/1918 |
| War Diary | Dolhain (Liabourg) | 30/11/1918 | 30/11/1918 |
| Heading | War Diary of 9th Machine Gun Squadron December 1918 Volume XXXV | | |
| War Diary | Belgium Dolhain (Limbourg) | 01/12/1918 | 01/12/1918 |
| War Diary | Germany Rott | 02/12/1918 | 04/12/1918 |
| War Diary | Gurzenich | 05/12/1918 | 05/12/1918 |
| War Diary | Giesendorf | 06/12/1918 | 07/12/1918 |
| War Diary | St Raberg | 08/12/1918 | 09/12/1918 |
| War Diary | Pioneer Barracks Cologne | 10/12/1918 | 12/12/1918 |
| War Diary | Leverhusen | 13/12/1918 | 13/12/1918 |
| War Diary | Ohligs | 14/12/1918 | 15/12/1918 |
| War Diary | Cologne | 16/12/1918 | 16/12/1918 |
| War Diary | Kaster | 17/12/1918 | 31/12/1918 |
| Heading | War Diary of 9th Machine Gun Squadron January 1919 Volume XXXVI | | |
| War Diary | Kaster | 01/01/1919 | 29/01/1919 |
| War Diary | Duren | 30/01/1919 | 30/01/1919 |
| War Diary | Kaster | 31/01/1919 | 31/01/1919 |
| Heading | War Diary of 9th Machine Gun Squadron February 1919 Volume XXXVII | | |
| War Diary | Kaster | 01/02/1919 | 28/02/1919 |
| Heading | War Diary of 9th Machine Gun Squadron March 1919 | | |
| War Diary | Kaster | 01/03/1919 | 31/03/1919 |
| Heading | WO95/1116/5 | | |
| Heading | 1917 1st Cavalry of 9th Cavalry Brigade 9th Cav. Pioneer Battn May-Jly 1917 | | |
| War Diary | Nine Elms | 17/05/1917 | 18/05/1917 |
| War Diary | Thellus Ref Sheet 51b N W I B7a 19 to 45 Green Line | 19/05/1917 | 19/05/1917 |
| War Diary | Lear Baillenl | 19/05/1917 | 22/05/1917 |
| War Diary | Green Line | 22/05/1917 | 26/05/1917 |

| | | | |
|---|---|---|---|
| War Diary | Tommy Trench | 26/05/1917 | 28/05/1917 |
| War Diary | Green Line | 29/05/1917 | 31/05/1917 |
| War Diary | Tommy Trench | 31/05/1917 | 01/06/1917 |
| War Diary | Ecurie | 13/06/1917 | 09/07/1917 |

LD 95/1116/1

B.E.F. FRANCE & FLANDERS
1 CAVALRY DIVISION.
9 CAVALRY BRIGADE.
1 BEDFORDSHIRE YEOMANRY
1915 JUNE TO 1918 FEB.
1/1 WARWICKSHIRE ROYAL
HORSE ARTILLERY BATTER
1914 OCT TO 1916 OCT.
'Y' BATTERY ROYAL HORSE
ARTILLERY.
1916 DEC TO 1919 APR.
9 MACHINE GUN SQUADRON.
1916 MAY TO 1919 MAR.
9 CAVALRY PIONEER BN
1917 MAY TO 1917 JULY.

1116

# 1915-1918
## 1ST CAVALRY DIVISION
## 9TH CAVALRY BRIGADE.

1ST BEDFORDSHIRE YEOMANRY

JUN 1915 - FEB 1918

FROM UK

Re Organization Machine Gun On

1st Cavalry Division
9 Cav Bde

1080/121

9/7

1st Bedfordshire Yeo.
Vol I.

June & July /15 — Feb. 1918

WAR DIARY on INTELLIGENCE SUMMARY.

1st BEDFORDSHIRE YEOMANRY
Army Form C. 2118.

| Hour, Date, Place | Summary of Events and Information | Remarks and references to Appendices |
|---|---|---|
| 1915<br>June 9th STANSTED | Regiment left STANSTED in the early morning in 3 trains as follows:- 2 Sqdn. A Sqdn. Machine Gun Section, Headquarters. All had arrived SOUTHAMPTON by 3^pm and embarked by 4.30 pm. Col. Rhodes & Lt-Col the Hon. S.C. PEEL, MAJOR W. SELBY-LOWNDES, MAJOR BENNING, CAPT HEADLAM, 2LT JONES in S.S. "NORTH WEST MILLER" - the remainder of Officers & men under MAJOR S.J. GREEN in S.S. "DUCHESS OF HAMILTON." Sailed 5.30 pm. Parade state of Regiment on leaving ENGLAND was 23 Officers, 517 other ranks and 613 horses & mules. Roll of Officers who left ENGLAND with the Regiment. <br>LT-COL the Hon. S.C. PEEL in command <br>MAJOR S.J. GREEN 2nd in command <br>CAPT & ADJT. B.C.M. TYRRELL 5th (R.I.) LANCERS. <br>SURG-MAJOR M. SKELDING Medical Officer. <br>CAPT & QMR J. PEARCE } HEADQUARTERS <br>LT J. WRIGHT Veterinary Officer <br>2LT L.E. JONES Machine Gun Officer <br>2LT R.G. PAYNE Signalling Officer <br><br>MAJOR W. SELBY-LOWNDES <br>LT. W. SWANNELL <br>2LT. S.L. TREVOR <br>2LT. G.L. FOSTER <br>2LT R. SMEE } "C" Squadron. | |

WAR DIARY of 1ST BEDFORDSHIRE YEOMANRY

Army Form C. 2118.

## INTELLIGENCE SUMMARY.
*(Erase heading not required.)*

Instructions regarding War Diaries and Intelligence Summaries are contained in F.S. Regs., Part II. and the Staff Manual respectively. Title pages will be prepared in manuscript.

| Hour, Date, Place | Summary of Events and Information | Remarks and references to Appendices |
|---|---|---|
| | MAJOR J.B. WALKER. <br> CAPT. C. HEADLAM. <br> LT. G. PROBY. <br> 2LT. J.E.P. HOWEY. <br> 2LT. C. HOLLEBONE. } "D" Squadron. <br><br> MAJOR. A.C.S. BENNING. <br> CAPT. J. HOLMES. <br> LT. J.F. GORE. <br> LT. G. de la P. HARGREAVES <br> LT. A.F. LASCELLES } "A" Squadron | |
| June 10th HAVRE | Arrived HAVRE 5.a.m. Disembarkation commenced 7.a.m. Regiment camped at No.5 Rest Camp. | |
| " 11th " | Inspected at 12 noon by Commandant No 5 Rest Camp. Entrained in afternoon, 3 trains in following order A.Sqdn - C.Sqdn - D.Sqdn. Trains left 5.p.m. - 7.p.m. - 9.p.m. | |
| " 12th HAZEBROUCK | H.Q. Machine Gun Section & A.Sqdn arrived HAZEBROUCK 12.30 p.m. C. & D. Squadrons at CASSEL at 3.p.m. and 5.p.m. Trains met by CAPT. F. BULLOCH MARSHAM, Staff Captain, 9th Cavalry Brigade. Units proceeded to billets near LEDRINGHEM in 9th Cav. Brigade area. | |
| " 13th LEDRINGHEM | Rested. | |
| " 14th " | Squadron Parades. | |
| " 15th " | Regiment attended Brigade Parade, addressed by Field Marshal SIR J.D.P. FRENCH. | |

# WAR DIARY of 1st BEDFORDSHIRE YEOMANRY

Army Form C. 2118.

## INTELLIGENCE SUMMARY.

*(Erase heading not required.)*

Instructions regarding War Diaries and Intelligence Summaries are contained in F.S. Regs., Part II. and the Staff Manual respectively. Title pages will be prepared in manuscript.

| Hour, Date, Place | Summary of Events and Information | Remarks and references to Appendices |
|---|---|---|
| June 16th LEDRINGHEM. | Squadron Parades. | |
| " 17th " | " | |
| " 18th " | Regiment inspected by Brig. Gen. W.H. GREENLY. D.S.O commanding 9th CAVALRY BRIGADE. | |
| " 19th " | Route lay at CASSEL range. 2Lt HOLLEBONE & SMEE & 8 men went to ESQUELBECQ for Rifle Grenade instruction. | |
| " 20th " | Church Parade. | |
| " 21st " | Squadron Parades. All Officers & N.C.O's went to ESQUELBECQ for action on Trench Diggings by Major SANDS commanding | |
| " 22nd " | 2nd Field Squadron R.E. | |
| " 23rd " | Regimental parade and route march | |
| " 24th " | Squadron Parades. | |
| " 25th " | Brigade route march. | |
| " 26th " | Squadron Parades. Lt LASCELLES, 2Lts. HOWEY, SMEE & 16 men went to ESQUELBECQ for Trench throwing instruction. Revolver lay at CASSEL RANGE. | |
| " 27th " | Church Parades. 2Lt J.H. BRIGG rejoined from duty with Indian Cavalry. | |
| " 28th " | Squadron Parades. Inspection of "A" echelon by Brigadier. CAPT. S.P. DAVIS rejoined from duty with Indian Cavalry. | |
| " 29th " | Regimental Tactical Scheme. Lt. J.F. GORE proceeded to a Signalling course at WORMHOUDT under Brigade Signalling Officer. | See Lt Col commanding Bedfordshire Yeomanry. |
| " 30th " | Squadron Parades. CAPT. C. HEADLAM in command, + 2Lts HOWEY and FOSTER + 105 N.C.O.s & men proceeded to VLAMERTINGHE area to dig reserve Trenches. | |

# WAR DIARY 9/B Bedfordshire Yeomanry

or,

## INTELLIGENCE SUMMARY.

Army Form C. 2118.

(Erase heading not required.)

| Hour, Date, Place | Summary of Events and Information | Remarks and references to Appendices |
|---|---|---|
| July 1st LEDRINGHEM. | Squadron parades. | |
| " 2nd " | " 22Lt. H.C. RAMBAUT joined. | |
| " 3rd " | Musketry CASSEL ranges. | |
| " 4th " | Church parade. | |
| " 5th " | Squadron parade. | |
| " 6th " | " | |
| " 7th " | " LT. G. PROBY proceeded to French Division | |
| " 8th " | School for course of instruction. | |
| " 9th " | Squadron parades. | |
| " 10th " | Digging party relieved. CAPT. J. HOLMES in command of relief party with LT. HARGREAVES & 2.Lt. HOWEY. | |
| " 11th " | Rested. | |
| " 12th " | Squadron parades. CAPT. HEADLAM joined staff 9 Bry. General | |
| " 13th " | Chan. Capt. P. commanding 9th Division (Scotland Squadron) | |
| " 14th " | Squadron parades. | |
| " 15th " | "C" Squadron musketry at CASSEL RANGE. | |
| " 16th " | "C" Squadron Tactical Scheme & billeted near LA MOTTE. | |
| " 17th " | "C" Squadron swam horses over canal near LA MOTTE. Machine Gun Section musketry at CASSEL RANGE. 2Lt. J.H. BRIGG went to WISQUES for Machine Gun Course. All officers attended lecture by A.D.M.S. on general scheme of medical arrangements to secure Sanitary Conditions in the Field. | |
| " 18th " | Church parade. | |
| " 19th " | Digging party returned. Lt. A.R. LASCELLES in command Relief party with 2Lts TREVOR and SMEE. MAJOR SJ GREEN in command of Brigade digging party. | |

Army Form C. 2118.

# WAR DIARY of 1st Bedfordshire Yeomanry
## or
## INTELLIGENCE SUMMARY.

(Erase heading not required.)

Instructions regarding War Diaries and Intelligence Summaries are contained in F. S. Regs., Part II. and the Staff Manual respectively. Title pages will be prepared in manuscript.

| Hour, Date, Place | Summary of Events and Information | Remarks and references to Appendices |
|---|---|---|
| July 19th LEDRINGHEM. | 2 LT. P.G.S. PAYNE proceeded to G.H.Q. 1st Arch Appointed 1st of Regiment. | |
| " 20th " | LT. J. F. GORE appointed Regimental Signalling Officer. | |
| " 21st " | Squadron parades. | |
| | The C.O. v Squadron Leaders attended Staff Ride under Brigadier. | |
| | LT. G. PROBY appointed Regimental Trench Mortar Officer v 2 LT. | |
| | as Brigade Trench Mortar Officer. 2 LT. R. SMEE appointed | |
| | Regimental Grenade Officer. | |
| " 22nd W | Squadron parades. Machine Gun Section had a Tactical Scheme. | |
| " 23rd Th | D Squadron Tactical Scheme. Infantry near LA MOTTE. | |
| " 24th F | D Squadron swam horses over Canal near LA MOTTE. | |
| | Machine Gun Team shoots at CASSEL range. | |
| " 25th S | Church Parade. | |
| " 26th M | Regiment took part in Brigade Tactical Scheme. | |
| " 27th T | All Officers attended Lecture by Brigadier on Trench Warfare. | |
| " 28th W | Regiments did Dismounted exercise in Entering over Trenches | |
| | at night from the 15th HUSSARS. LT. J.F. GORE appointed 2nd | |
| | Regimental Intelligence Officer. | |
| " 29th Th | Squadron parades. | |
| " 30th F | Digging party returned. S.S.M. PENZELOW appointed 2 LT on probation | |
| " 31st S | Bigger Trench Scheme. | |

Sd/ Lt-Col
commanding
Bedfordshire Yeomanry.

1st Cav. Division
9 Cav Bde.

121/6607

Bedfords'nre Geo:
Vol I
From 1-3. 8. 15

Army Form C. 2118.

# WAR DIARY
## or
## INTELLIGENCE SUMMARY.
(Erase heading not required.)

1/1 Bedfordshire Yeomanry

August 1915

| Hour, Date, Place | Summary of Events and Information | Remarks and references to Appendices |
|---|---|---|
| Aug 1st LEDRINGHEM | Advanced parties left at 3.15 P.M at tactical scheme to MARDYCK | |
| " 2nd " | Regiment had tactical scheme to MARDYCK | |
| | 2nd LT. L.J.C. Southam joined the Regiment. | |
| " 3rd MARDYCK | Brigade drill on the sands in the morning & had tactical scheme back to LEDRINGHEM in the afternoon. with Capt Davis. | |
| " 5th LEDRINGHEM | Digging parties of 9 Officers & 275 other ranks proceeded to ELVERDINGHE to dig under the orders of 6th Corps. | |
| " 7th " | 2nd Lt G H. Briggs rejoined from Machine Gun School | |
| | LT S. Posty bro. temp. Captain 11.7.15. | |
| | 2nd Lt Trevor to temp. Lieutenant 11.7.15. | |
| " 8th " | LT A. F. Loockes rejoined from Tunnel Howitzer Course. | |
| " 9th " | 2nd Lt F. B. Harper joined from 2/1 Bn Beds Yeomanry. | |
| " 13th " | Relief digging party consisting of 3 Officers & 94 other ranks proceeded to ELVERDINGHE. | |
| " 14th & 19th " | Nothing to report. | |
| " 20th " | Relief digging party under Major Selby Lowndes consisting of 4 Officers & 135 other ranks proceeded to ELVERDINGHE. | |

**Army Form C. 2118.**

# WAR DIARY
## or
## INTELLIGENCE SUMMARY.
*(Erase heading not required.)*

| Hour, Date, Place | Summary of Events and Information | Remarks and references to Appendices |
|---|---|---|
| Aug 25th LEDRINGHEM | One man (The Robinson) was wounded in the arm by a shell at the dressing camp. | |
| " 26th | Regiment under Major BENNING proceeded to 15th Hussars HQRS to attend a tactical demonstration, on return, asphyxiating gases. | |
| | CAPT & ADJ. G.C.M TYRRELL was struck off station, & rejoined the 5th (R.I) LANCERS. | |
| " 28th | LT. ADJ. J.C. CRABBE, ROYAL SCOTS GREYS joined the Regiment. A draft of 14 men & 4 horses joined the Regiment. LT. COL TO HON ST. PAUL took command. D. Bgde Dispatch. | |
| " 29th | LT. J.E.P. HOWEY went to the Royal Flying Corps on probation. Draft of 9 men joined the Regiment | |
| " 31st | Dessay Relief under Major Walker covering king 4 officers & 120 other ranks proceeded to ELVERDINGHE. | |

S. P. Green Major Commanding
Bedfordshire Yeomanry

121/7050

1st Cavalry Division
9 Cav. Bde.

Bedfordshire Yeo:
Vol II
Sep 1-15.

22.10.15

**WAR DIARY** of 1st Bedfordshire Yeomanry

Army Form C. 2118.

or

**INTELLIGENCE SUMMARY.**

(Erase heading not required.)

Instructions regarding War Diaries and Intelligence Summaries are contained in F.S. Regs., Part II. and the Staff Manual respectively. Title pages will be prepared in manuscript.

| Hour, Date, Place | Summary of Events and Information | Remarks and references to Appendices |
|---|---|---|
| Sept 1st LEDRINGHEM. | Lt. SWANNELL went to the Officers Hospital at ST OMER. | |
| " 2nd " | Very wet. First lines had to be changed. | |
| " 3rd " | Some heavy rain. Digging party were made to dig. | |
| " 4th " | Cleaned out the billets. | |
| " 5th " | Digging party returned to billets. | |
| " 6th " | Squadron parades. | |
| " 7th " | Regimental parade with 1st & 3rd Bedfordshire. Lecture by the Brigadier on Tactical Scheme. | |
| " 8th " | Brigade Route March & practiced hasty organization. Brigadier afternoon. Both CO's Squadron leaders for a staff ride. | |
| " 9th " | Squadron Parades. Instruction to all subaltern officers in the use of employment given by Staff Officers 9 Horse Bde. Brigade Tactical Scheme. | |
| " 10th " | Squadron Parades. 2/L TREVOR admitted to Hospital. | |
| " 11th " | Church Parade. | |
| " 12th " | Divisional Route March. | |
| " 13th " | Squadron practice dismounted attack. | |
| " 14th " | Squadron Parade. | |
| " 15th " | Regimental dismounted scheme. | |
| " 16th " | Brigade dismounted scheme. Two extra Vickers Guns arrive. | |
| " 17th " | Remote Party to draft at CASSEL RANGE. | |
| " 18th " | Church Parade. Officers went to ESQUELBEC to see Fridges constructed by the 1st Field Squadron R.E. | |
| " 19th " | | |

Army Form C. 2118.

# WAR DIARY
or
## INTELLIGENCE SUMMARY.

9th Bn Bedfordshire Regiment

*(Erase heading not required.)*

Instructions regarding War Diaries and Intelligence Summaries are contained in F. S. Regs., Part II. and the Staff Manual respectively. Title pages will be prepared in manuscript.

| Hour, Date, Place | Summary of Events and Information | Remarks and references to Appendices |
|---|---|---|
| Sept 20th LEDRINGHEM | Musketry for Regiment at CASSEL range. | |
| " 21st " | Squadron Parades. | |
| " 22nd " | " | |
| " 23rd " | Brigadier inspected Machine Guns. | |
| " 24th BILQUES | Billeting party left at 10am. Regiment paraded 9.45pm & marched to new area. Arrived BILQUES at 3am went into billets at 11am. Billeting party left for new area. Party of 20 men went to AIRE to take over 20 machine B. Regiment paraded 6.40pm, marched to ENQUIN-LES-MINES arriving at 10.30pm. | |
| " 26th ENQUIN-LES-MINES | Overhauled & echelon & left some of the surplus stores with the MAIRE. Regiment paraded at 12 noon & marched via ESTREE BLANCHE — FERFAY — BRUAY to VAUDRICOURT where the Regiment bivouaced in the CHATEAU grounds about 12 pm in a deluge of rain. | |
| " 26th VAUDRICOURT | After a very wet night the Regiment was ready to move at 10 am in the morning but stood there all day. Weather much better. | |
| " 27th " | Orders came after midnight for ready to move at 5 am. So Regiment paraded 4.45 am at 6.30 am this was cancelled. Regiment remained there for the rest of day. Started again in rain at 5-4 pm. | |

(9 29 6) W 4141—463 100,000 9/14 H W V Forms/C. 2118/10

Army Form C. 2118.

# WAR DIARY 1st BEDFORDSHIRE YEOMANRY
## or
## INTELLIGENCE SUMMARY.
*(Erase heading not required.)*

Instructions regarding War Diaries and Intelligence Summaries are contained in F.S. Regs., Part II. and the Staff Manual respectively. Title pages will be prepared in manuscript.

| Hour, Date, Place | Summary of Events and Information | Remarks and references to Appendices |
|---|---|---|
| Sept 28th VAUDRICOURT | After another very hot night, Regiment paraded at 7 a.m. & went back for a word near HESDIGNEUL when it bivouaced. Still very wet. | |
| " 29th HESDIGNEUL | At 12 noon Regiment moved back to good billets at LOZINGHEM. Horses put in the fields but all the men under cover. | |
| " 30th LOZINGHEM. | Remained in billets. To Gun howitzer attached to Field Ambulance & 115 Howitzer moved their tents. | |

Sgd/ Lt Col
commanding
1st BEDFORDSHIRE YEOMANRY

WAR DIARY OF 1/1 BEDFORDSHIRE YEOMANRY
Army Form C. 2118.

127/1435

1915

## INTELLIGENCE SUMMARY.
(Erase heading not required.)

| Hour, Date, Place | Summary of Events and Information | Remarks and references to Appendices |
|---|---|---|
| Oct 1st LOZINGHEM | Rested in billets. | Diary of the working party attached. |
| " 2nd " | A party of 4 Officers & 110 men under Capt Davis proceeded to NOVELLES-LES-VERMELLES to help the XI Corps to clear the battlefield. | |
| " 3rd " | Moved to new billeting area at 8.30 a.m to make room for the IV Corps who were coming out of the trenches to rest. Arrived in new billets at HONENGHEM near FEBVIN-PALFART about 11.30 a.m. | |
| " 4th HONENGHEM | At 2.30 p.m the Regiment changed billets to LAIRES. Party returned from the trenches after midnight having had 2 men wounded. | |
| " 5th LAIRES | Rest. | |
| " 6th " | Squadron Drill. Machine Gun practice. | |
| " 7th " | " " | |
| " 8th " | Baths at a leather works ESTRÉE BLANCHE. Grenade practice. | |
| " 9th " | Church Parade. | |
| " 10th " | Squadron Drill & Grenade practice. | |
| " 11th " | " " | |
| " 12th " | " " | |
| " 13th " | Baths. | |
| " 14th " | Regimental Trench Scheme. | |
| " 15th " | Squadron Parades. | |
| " 16th " | Church Parade. | |
| " 17th " | Squadron Parades. | |
| " 18th " | Brigade Trench Scheme. | |

# WAR DIARY of 1st BEDFORD YEOMANRY

## INTELLIGENCE SUMMARY

Army Form C. 2118.

(Erase heading not required.)

Instructions regarding War Diaries and Intelligence Summaries are contained in F.S. Regs., Part II. and the Staff Manual respectively. Title pages will be prepared in manuscript.

| Hour, Date, Place | Summary of Events and Information | Remarks and references to Appendices |
|---|---|---|
| Oct 19th LAIRES | Billeting party left at 7am. Regiment paraded at 10.30am & moved to new billeting area, | |
| " 20th ROQUETOIRE | ROQUETOIRE, LIGNE & CAUCHIE D'ECQUES. Regiment went into numbers Billets; all horses under cover except one troop of A Sqdn. Billets very dirty & insanitary. | |
| " 21st " | Cleaned Billets | |
| " 22nd " | " | |
| " 23rd " | " | |
| " 24th " | Church Parades | |
| " 25th " | Squadron Parades & classes for young signallers, shoeing smiths, bomb throwers etc started | |
| " 26th " | Squadron Parades  2Lt. E.W. WOODHAMS joined | |
| " 27th " | " | |
| " 28th " | The Regiment from the Base. | |
| " 29th " | Squadron Parades " CAPT DAVIS admitted to Hospital | |
| " 30th " | " | |
| " 31st " | Church Parades. | |

S.J. Greenhalgh Lt Col
(i. Cmd)
Bedfordshire Yeomanry

Army Form C. 2118.

# WAR DIARY OF 1ST BEDFORD YEOMANRY
## or
## INTELLIGENCE SUMMARY.
(Erase heading not required.)

Instructions regarding War Diaries and Intelligence Summaries are contained in F.S. Regs., Part II. and the Staff Manual respectively. Title pages will be prepared in manuscript.

| Hour, Date, Place | Summary of Events and Information | Remarks and references to Appendices |
|---|---|---|
| Oct 2nd LOZINGHEM | A detachment of 110 men & 4 officers (CAPT DAVIS, LT LASCELLES, 2LT HOLLEBONE, 2LT SOUTHERN) left LOZINGHEM at 1.15 p.m. to join a Brigade looking party. These parties under the command of LT-COL F. PILKINGTON XV HUSSARS were taken in motor lorries to a point on the BETHUNE — LENS road near where the COURANT DE BULLY cuts it. From there we marched, as soon as it got dark about 4 P.M. to the foot of the ridge above LOOS. But the proof of the hill itself top (where tunnels kept hounded & marched) over a mile along a french memory roughly NE, in line with the top by several very deep communication trenches, immediately under. At about 10 A.m. a section of the french was allotted to the BEDFORD YEOMANRY. Work was begun at once on the hospital, in removing the dead from the trench, 1 Class-oxb.1 clearing of generally. At 11 P.m. a party was sent back so much water as possible, FOSSE 7, & form back so much water as possible, at 3.45 a.m. the Regiment turned in, trenches dry but reply. |  |
| Oct 3rd " | Work was begun at 12 noon; no man was allowed to leave the trench, so work was confined to digging a fire step on the S.E. side of the trench. At 8am the fire |  |

# WAR DIARY of 1/1 BEDFORD YEOMANRY

Army Form C. 2118.

or

## INTELLIGENCE SUMMARY.

*(Erase heading not required.)*

Instructions regarding War Diaries and Intelligence Summaries are contained in F.S. Regs., Part II. and the Staff Manual respectively. Title pages will be prepared in manuscript.

| Hour, Date, Place | Summary of Events and Information | Remarks and references to Appendices |
|---|---|---|
| Oct 4th<br>LOOS | Changed to a section of trench about 250 yards long Opposite the centre was about 1/4 mile N.W. of the Fosse bridge of LOOS. A heavy artillery duel went on the whole day, many of the German's shells burst near our trench. About 10pm PTE BARTLETT was wounded in both hands by a splinter. That evening a shell burst on the parapet of our salient, partly on the LENS road, killing an A.S.C. driver incoming by PTE SAWYER in the shoulder. Work was continued till 11pm. Snipers harrased somebody were carried up from the dumping ground, the shelling of the parapet was completely + a number of German + English dead were found. Very violent rifle fire was heard in the direction of HULLOCH at intervals all though the night. It was a bright + starlight night but cold. Fire began at 9.15 a.m., the Forms Coy was thrown forward. He was again shelled intermittently all day. He returned to the wailer trench after sunset. | |

Forms/C. 2118/10

1st Cavalry Division / 9 Cav Bde

Bethune Nov 1915 / Vol IV

149/4 / 121

**WAR DIARY** of **1st BEDFORD YEOMANRY**

or

**INTELLIGENCE SUMMARY**

Army Form C. 2118.

*(Erase heading not required.)*

Instructions regarding War Diaries and Intelligence Summaries are contained in F.S. Regs., Part II. and the Staff Manual respectively. Title pages will be prepared in manuscript.

| Hour, Date, Place | Summary of Events and Information | Remarks and references to Appendices |
|---|---|---|
| Nov 1st ROQUETOIRE | 2 hrs by 40 men under CAPT HOLMES proceeded to RENESCURE area to dig a reserve line of trenches. Squadron Parades. | |
| " 2nd " | " " " " " " | |
| " 3rd " | " " " " " " | |
| " 4th " | " " " " " " | |
| " 5th " | Diggers party increased to 50. | |
| " 6th " | CAPT J. DAVIS struck off strength. | |
| " 7th " | Regiment found 2 exhibit pools of 3 men each to guard the BLARINGHEM & WITTES bridges. | |
| " 8th " | 2Lt BRIGG takes charge of the diggers party vice CAPT J. HOLMES. Squadron Parades. | |
| " 9th " | Lecture at BDE HQRS by CAPT PATTERSON LONDON SCOTTISH on trench warfare etc. 2Lt THOWER att R.F.C. captioned & struck off strength. | |
| " 10th " | Squadron Parades | |
| " 11th " | " " | |
| " 12th " | 2nd LT PENTELOW H. arrived from base. Church Parades. Returned party left for new billeting area near DESVRES. | |
| " 13th " | " " | |
| " 14th " | " " | |

Army Form C. 2118.

# WAR DIARY of 1st BEDFORD YEOMANRY
## or
## INTELLIGENCE SUMMARY.
*(Erase heading not required.)*

Instructions regarding War Diaries and Intelligence Summaries are contained in F.S. Regs., Part II. and the Staff Manual respectively. Title pages will be prepared in manuscript.

| Hour, Date, Place | Summary of Events and Information | Remarks and references to Appendices |
|---|---|---|
| Nov 15 ROQUETOIRE | Squadron Billeting parties went to DESVRES. | |
| " 16 " | Digging party & control posts rivalled. | |
| " 17 " | Regiment prepared to move. | |
| | Regiment paraded at 7.30 a.m. & reached DESVRES at 2 p.m. & went on to new billets. HQ, Machine Gun Section & A squadron in DESVRES, B Sqd" in | |
| " 18 DESVRES | LONGFOSSE. C Squadron near MANROY. Inoculated New drafts. | |
| " 19 " | Digging party under CAPT PROBY started to 10 | |
| " 20 " | REMESCOURE area. | |
| " 21 " | C. Sqd" changed from billets near MANROY to N.W. | |
| " 22 " | Church parades. Regiment (dismounted) paraded at 10.30 a.m at CURSOT on the new infantry organisation. | |
| " 23 " | 265 SOOTHERN L.C. promoted to Lance Horporal School at BERTHEN. | |
| " 24 " | Squadron parades. Baths at CEMENT WORKS | |
| " 25 " | LT HARGREAVES. G. proceeded as to French Morning Jen School at BERTHEN | |

Army Form C. 2118.

# WAR DIARY of 1st BEDFORD YEOMANRY
## INTELLIGENCE SUMMARY.
*(Erase heading not required.)*

Instructions regarding War Diaries and Intelligence Summaries are contained in F.S. Regs., Part II. and the Staff Manual respectively. Title pages will be prepared in manuscript.

| Hour, Date, Place | Summary of Events and Information | Remarks and references to Appendices |
|---|---|---|
| Nov 26th DESVRES | Squadron Parades. | |
| " 27th " | " " | |
| " 28th " | 1 5th HUSSARS (S.R.) 2Lt J.M. LOTTMAN-JOHNSON Church Parade confirmed as attached | |
| " 29th " | Squadron Parades " | |
| " 30th " | " " | |

Sgd H.W.L.
Bedford Yeomanry
Comm.

Besfonsgivne Jao:
Dec 1915
vol V

**WAR DIARY** or **INTELLIGENCE SUMMARY**

Army Form C. 2118.

1/1st BEDFORDSHIRE YEOMANRY

(Erase heading not required.)

| Hour, Date, Place | Summary of Events and Information | Remarks and references to Appendices |
|---|---|---|
| Dec 1st DESVRES | Squadron Parades. | |
| " 2nd " | Regimental Route March. MAJOR SELBY-LOWNDES & 2LT JONES attached to 1st ARMY for instruction. | |
| " 3rd " | Squadron Parades. | |
| " 4th " | " | |
| " 5th " | Church Parade. | |
| " 6th " | Squadron Parades. | |
| " 7th " | Regimental Route March. | |
| " 8th " | Baths. 2LT CRAIG joined from 2nd Regiment. | |
| " 9th " | MAJ-GEN MULLENS inspected the 9th Bde on arm (?) | |
| " 10th " | Battalion. Major BENNING & 2LT GORE attached to 1st ARMY for instruction. MAJOR SELBY LOWNDES & 2LT JONES rejoined. | |
| " 11th " | Squadron Parades. | |
| " 12th " | Church Parades. 2LT M.A.C. HALLIDAY joined from 2nd Regiment. | |
| " 13th " | Squadron Parades. | |
| " 14th " | Regimental Route March. | |
| " 15th " | Baths. 2LT JONES gave a lecture to the Officers. | |
| " 16th " | MAJOR BENNING & 2LT GORE rejoined. MAJOR GREEN & CAPT HOLMES attached 1st ARMY for instruction | |

WAR DIARY 91/1st BEDFORDSHIRE YEOMANRY Army Form C. 2118.
or
INTELLIGENCE SUMMARY.
(Erase heading not required.)

| Hour, Date, Place | Summary of Events and Information | Remarks and references to Appendices |
|---|---|---|
| Dec 17th DESVRES. | Squadron Route Marches. | |
| " 18th " | Squadron Parades. 2Lt HARPER rejoined from Hospital | |
| " 19 " | Church Parade. 2Lt WOOD HAMS admitted to Hospital | |
| " 20 " | Horse Inspection by ADVS, 1st CAV DIV | |
| " 21 " | Baths. | |
| " 22nd " | Squadron Parade. MAJOR GREEN & CAPT HOLMES rejoined. | |
| " 23rd " | Squadron Parades. | |
| " 24th " | " " Digging Party returned. | |
| " 25th " | " | |
| " 26th " | Holiday. | |
| | Church Parade. Service taken by Right Rev. the Lord Bishop of OXFORD. Digging Party under Lt HARGREAVES returned to RENESCURE. | |
| " 27th " | Squadron Parades | |
| " 28th " | Digging Party returned. Preparation for move. | |
| " 29th " | The 5th Dismounted Battalion left for the Trenches, 10 Officers + 368 other ranks under command of MAJOR GREEN. | |
| " 30th " | BEDFORD YEOMANRY COMPANY | |
| " 31st " | | Bedford Yeomanry |

Confidential.

B. 1082.

Officer i/c
    A.G's Office at the Base.
---------------------------------

        Herewith War Diary of the Bedfordshire Yeomanry for the month of January, 1916.
        Please acknowledge receipt.

5/5/16.                                  Captain,
                          Brigade Major, 9th Cav. Brigade.

Army Form C. 2118.

# WAR DIARY of 1/1 BEDFORD YEOMANRY
## INTELLIGENCE SUMMARY.
*(Erase heading not required.)*

| Hour, Date, Place | Summary of Events and Information | Remarks and references to Appendices |
|---|---|---|
| Jan 1st DESVRES | Exercise | |
| " 2 " | Church Parade. | |
| " 3 " | Exercise | |
| " 4 " | " | |
| " 5 " | " | |
| " 6 " | " | |
| " 7 " | " | |
| " 8 " | " | |
| " 9 " | " | Lt PRIESTLEY & 6 O.R. joined from England |
| " 10 " | Church Parade | |
| " 11 " | Exercise | |
| " 12 " | " | |
| " 13 " | " | |
| " 14 " | " | |
| " 15 " | " | |
| " 16 " | " | |
| " 17 " | Church Parade | |
| " 18 " | " | |
| " 19 " | Exercise | Headquarters went up to 1st Brigade |
| " 20 " | " | |

Army Form C. 2118.

# WAR DIARY 1/1 Bedford Yeomanry
## or INTELLIGENCE SUMMARY.
*(Erase heading not required.)*

Instructions regarding War Diaries and Intelligence Summaries are contained in F. S. Regs., Part II. and the Staff Manual respectively. Title pages will be prepared in manuscript.

| Hour, Date, Place | Summary of Events and Information | Remarks and references to Appendices |
|---|---|---|
| Jan 21 DEVIZES | Exercise | |
| " 22 " | " | |
| " 23 " | Church Parade | |
| " 24 " | Exercise | |
| " 25 " | " | |
| " 26 " | " | |
| " 27 " | " | |
| " 28 " | " | |
| " 29 " | " | |
| " 30 " | Church Parade | |
| " 31 " | Exercise | |

See T/Col
Bedford Yeomanry.

Army Form C. 2118.

# WAR DIARY of 1/1 BEDFORD YEOMANRY
## or
## INTELLIGENCE SUMMARY.

*(Erase heading not required.)*

Instructions regarding War Diaries and Intelligence Summaries are contained in F. S. Regs., Part II. and the Staff Manual respectively. Title pages will be prepared in manuscript.

| Hour, Date, Place | Summary of Events and Information | Remarks and references to Appendices |
|---|---|---|
| Feb 1st DESVRES. | Euvise. | |
| " 2 | " | |
| " 3 | " | |
| " 4 | " | |
| " 5 | " | |
| " 6 | " | |
| " 7 | " | |
| " 8 | " | |
| " 9 | " | |
| " 10 | " | |
| " 11 | " | |
| " 12 | " | |
| " 13 | 8 to noon Co. Company returned from to Tireches | |

# WAR DIARY 9/11 BEDFORD YEOMANRY
## INTELLIGENCE SUMMARY.

Army Form C. 2118.

*(Erase heading not required.)*

Instructions regarding War Diaries and Intelligence Summaries are contained in F.S. Regs., Part II. and the Staff Manual respectively. Title pages will be prepared in manuscript.

| Hour, Date, Place | Summary of Events and Information | Remarks and references to Appendices |
|---|---|---|
| 7.6.12. D1. 7.30 am | Lorbery was joined by 7th Royal Sussex | |
| | Marched to BOURSE | |
| 7.6.13. LA BOURSE | Marched to FOUQUEREUIL and found | |
| 7.6.14. DESVRES | BILLETS at NOEUX | |
| " 15 " | Inspected men, equipment etc | |
| " 16 " | Batts. | |
| " 17 " | Troop Training. Brigadier inspected Horse Trooping. | |
| " 18 " | " " | |
| " 19 " | Church Parade. | |
| " 20 " | Troop Training. 2Lt SHANNELL. 2Lt HOARE. 2Lt ANDERSON arrived. | |
| " 21 " | " " | |
| " 22 " | Baths. | |
| " 23 " | Troop Training. Lt HARGREAVES attached to 2nd Army. | |
| " 24 " | " " Lt JONES. 2Lt HALL.DAY. 267 Ptes. | |
| " 25 " | Ranks transferred to the Machine Gun Squadron. | |
| " 26 " | Troop Training | |
| " 27 " | Church parade. | |
| " 28 " | Troop Training | |
| " 29 " | Regimental Route March. | |

Sgd ?? ??
Bedfordshire Yeomanry.

Army Form C. 2118.

# WAR DIARY of 1/1 BEDFORD YEOMANRY.
## INTELLIGENCE SUMMARY.
*(Erase heading not required.)*

Instructions regarding War Diaries and Intelligence Summaries are contained in F.S. Regs., Part II. and the Staff Manual respectively. Title pages will be prepared in manuscript.

| Hour, Date, Place | Summary of Events and Information | Remarks and references to Appendices |
|---|---|---|
| March 1st DESVRES | Baths. 247 WOODHAMS rejoined from Hospital | |
| " 2nd " | Troop Training | |
| " 3rd " | " | |
| " 4th " | " | |
| " 5th " | Church Parade | |
| " 6th " | Troop Training  LT HARGREAVES rejoined from HQ 1st Army | |
| " 7th " | " | |
| " 8th " | Baths | |
| " 9th " | Troop Training | |
| " 10th " | " | |
| " 11th " | " | |
| " 12th " | Divisional Pole Jump. MAJOR S.T. GREEN on week end leave | |
| | Territorial Decoration | |
| | Church Parade. LT. SWANNELL admitted to Hospital | |
| | 247 WILTSHIRE & 13 other ranks joined from 3/1 | |
| | BEDFORD YEOMANRY | |
| " 13th " | Troop Training. LT. FOSTER admitted to Hospital | |
| " 14th " | " | |
| " 15th " | Baths | |
| " 16th " | Troop " | |
| " 17th " | Troop Training  MAJ. BENNING admitted to Hospital | |
| " 18th " | " | |

Army Form C. 2118.

# WAR DIARY 9/11 BEDFORD YEOMANRY
## INTELLIGENCE SUMMARY.
*(Erase heading not required.)*

Instructions regarding War Diaries and Intelligence Summaries are contained in F.S. Regs, Part II. and the Staff Manual respectively. Title pages will be prepared in manuscript.

| Hour, Date, Place | Summary of Events and Information | Remarks and references to Appendices |
|---|---|---|
| March 19th DES VRES | Church Parade. 2 LT H.V.W. FIELDS CLARKE joined for 3/1 BEDFORD YEOMANRY. | |
| 20th " | Troop Training. LT BRIGG & LT PENTELOW proceeded to 1st CAV. DIV. H.Q. Tr Hotchkiss Course. | |
| 21st " | Troop Training. | |
| 22nd " | Battn. LT SHANNELL discharged Hospital. | |
| 23rd " | Troop Training | |
| 24th " | " " | |
| 25th " | S.O.C. 9th CAV. BDE Inspected "B" Echelon. LT BRIGG & LT PENTELOW rejoined from Hotchkiss course. | |
| 26th " | Church Parade. MAJ BENNING discharged Hospital | |
| 27th " | Troop Training. LT CRABBE & 2 LT RAMSBOT proceeded to HQ 1st CAV DIV Tr Hotchkiss course. | |
| 28th " | Troop Training. LT SHANNELL transferred to Remount Dept. CAPT. GORE attached to Signal School | |
| 29th " | " " | |
| 30th " | 1st Orang. LT HOLLEBONE rejoined from England. CAPT HOLMES. 2 LT WILTSHIRE & 83 other ranks invalided to Base to IV CORPS area to dis. | |
| 31st " | Troop Training. | |

Sgd. J.L.K.
Bedford Yeomanry

2.4.16.

# WAR DIARY 1/1 BEDFORD YEOMANRY
## or
## INTELLIGENCE SUMMARY.

*(Erase heading not required.)*

Army Form C. 2118.

| Hour, Date, Place | Summary of Events and Information | Remarks and references to Appendices |
|---|---|---|
| April 1st DESYRES | Squadron Parades. CAPT. BORE admitted | |
| " 2nd | to Hospital. | |
| " 3rd | Church Parade. 30 men arrived from 3/1 | |
| " 4th | BEDS YEO. Squadron Parade | |
| " 5th | Squadron Parade " | |
| " 6th | Baths. | |
| " 7th | Squadron Parades. | |
| | Inspection of 1st Cav. Div. on SANDS by | |
| | G.O.C. 1st CAV. DIV. | |
| " 8th | Squadron Parades. CAPT. BORE discharged | |
| " 9th | Church Parade | |
| " 10th | Inspection of Regimental Transport by | |
| | O.C. 1st CAV. DIV. | |
| " 11th | Squadron Parades. 267 Cook and 2 men | |
| | joined from 3/1 BEDS. YEO. | |
| " 12th | Baths. | |
| " 13th | Squadron Parades. | |
| " 14th | Brigade Tactical Scheme & Divisional Cavalry. | |

WAR DIARY 2/1 BEDFORD YEOMANRY
or
INTELLIGENCE SUMMARY.

Army Form C. 2118.

(Erase heading not required.)

Instructions regarding War Diaries and Intelligence Summaries are contained in F. S. Regs., Part II. and the Staff Manual respectively. Title pages will be prepared in manuscript.

| Hour, Date, Place | Summary of Events and Information | Remarks and references to Appendices |
|---|---|---|
| April 15th DES VRES | Squadron Parades | |
| " 16th | Church Parade. | |
| " 17th | Inspection on sands of 1st Cav Div by G.O.C. 1st Army. | |
| " 18th | Squadron Parades | |
| " 19th | Bde Hd. G.O.C. & right. 2Bde inspected all Squadron Officers on the following. | |
| " 20th | Support party relieved | |
| " 21st | Horsing Parade | |
| " 22nd | Squadron Parade | |
| " 23rd | Church Parade. | |
| " 24th | Holiday | |
| " 25th | Regimental Exercise. 2nd & 3rd CR&15 mounted & dismounted | |
| " 26th | Bde. Officers Staff ride. | |
| " 27th | Regimental Exercise. | |
| " 28th | Squadron Parades | |
| " 29th | " " | |
| " 30th | Church Parade. | |

Sgd J.L.K
Bedford Yeomanry.

Army Form C. 2118
IC&
G.E.B.

# WAR DIARY
of 1/1 BEDFORD YEOMANRY
or
INTELLIGENCE SUMMARY.

May 1916

Vol 10

(Erase heading not required.)

Instructions regarding War Diaries and Intelligence Summaries are contained in F. S. Regs., Part II. and the Staff Manual respectively. Title pages will be prepared in manuscript.

| Hour, Date, Place | | Summary of Events and Information | Remarks and references to Appendices |
|---|---|---|---|
| DESVRES | May 1st | Squadron Parades. | |
| " | 2nd | Regimental Scheme | |
| " | 3rd | Baths. | |
| " | 4th | Regimental Scheme | |
| " | 5th | Squadron Parades. | |
| " | 6th | Moved into camp at ECAULT. | |
| ECAULT | 7th | Exercise | |
| " | 8th | Squadron Drill | |
| " | 9th | " | |
| " | 10th | Regimental Drill | Lt PRIESTLY admitted to Hospital |
| " | 11th | " | |
| " | 12th | " | |
| " | 13th | Instruction by G.O.C. 1st CAV. DIV. | |
| " | 14th | Regiment returned to billets. | |
| DESVRES | 15th | Squadron Parades. | |
| " | 16th | Regimental Scheme | |
| " | 17th | Baths. Staff ride for officers. Lt PRIESTLY rejoined. | |
| " | 18th | Squadron Parades. | |
| " | 19th | Divisional Scheme | |
| " | 20 | Squadron Parades. | |

Army Form C. 2118.

# WAR DIARY of 1/1 BEDFORD YEOMANRY
## or
## INTELLIGENCE SUMMARY.

(Erase heading not required.)

Instructions regarding War Diaries and Intelligence Summaries are contained in F. S. Regs., Part II. and the Staff Manual respectively. Title pages will be prepared in manuscript.

| Hour, Date, Place | Summary of Events and Information | Remarks and references to Appendices |
|---|---|---|
| DESVRES May 21st | Church Parades. CAPT PROBY & 83 O.R. Returned | |
| " 22nd | Gissing Party. | |
| " 23rd | Squadron Parades. | |
| " 24th | Regimental Scheme. | |
| " 25th | Inspection by G.O.C. RESERVE CORPS. | |
| " 26th | Tactical Scheme for Officers | |
| " 27th | Squadron Parades. 2Lt WOODHAMS to 1st ARMY SIGNAL SCHOOL (course) | |
| " 28th | Squadron Parades. | |
| " 29th | Church Parades. | |
| " 30th | Regimental Scheme for evening bivouacs. | |
| " 31st | Brigade Tactical Exercise | |
| | Horse Clothing. Baths. | |

S. Green Dixon
Bedford Yeomanry

IC8/9 C.B.

# WAR DIARY of 1/1 BEDFORDSHIRE YEOMANRY

Army Form C. 2118

## INTELLIGENCE SUMMARY
*(Erase heading not required.)*

June 1916

| Hour, Date, Place | Summary of Events and Information | Remarks and references to Appendices |
|---|---|---|
| June 1st DESVRES | Squadron Parades | |
| " 2nd " | Regimental Scheme | |
| " 3rd " | Squadron Parades | |
| " 4th " | Church Parades | |
| " 5th " | Squadron Parades | |
| " 6th " | — | |
| " 7th " | Battn. Divisional Tactical Scheme for Officers | |
| " 8th " | Divisional Scheme. Lt. Woodhams from 1st Army | |
| | Signal School | |
| " 9th " | Brigade schemes. G.O.C. 1st Army. | |
| " 10th " | Divisional Horse Show at HOBERSENT | |
| " 11th " | Regiment moved into Camps at ECAULT | |
| " 12th " | Lt. CRAIG discharged Hospital | |
| | Regimental Drill. Lt CRAIG admitted to Hospital | |
| " 13th ECAULT | " " | |
| " 14th " | " " | |
| " 15th " | " " | "CAPT J GORE attached to 9.M.G.B as sig. officer |
| " 16th " | " " | CAPT HOLMES & 20 OR attended |
| " 17th " | Church Parade | Field Marshal Lord |
| " 18th " | Memorial Service to the late Kitcheners ones at SAMER. | |

Army Form C. 2118.

# WAR DIARY or INTELLIGENCE SUMMARY.

9th BEDFORDSHIRE YEOMANRY

(Erase heading not required.)

Instructions regarding War Diaries and Intelligence Summaries are contained in F.S. Regs., Part II. and the Staff Manual respectively. Title pages will be prepared in manuscript.

| Hour, Date, Place | Summary of Events and Information | Remarks and references to Appendices |
|---|---|---|
| June 19th ECAULT | 35 O.R. joined from 9th BEDFORD YEOMANRY. Regiment returned to Billets at DESVRES. 2 & F. CRAIG discharged Hospital | |
| " 20th DESVRES | Baths. Squadron Parades | |
| " 21st " | B echelon paraded at 7.30 pm & marched to BEZINGHEM | |
| " 22nd " | Regiment paraded at 7.30 pm Strength 23 Officers & 437 O.R. & marched 31 miles to DOMPIERRE where it billeted | |
| " 23rd " | at 4 A.M. Dismounted party under CAPT PROBY 2 nd Lt | |
| " 24th " | by train. | |
| " 25th DOMPIERRE | Paraded at 11.30 am & marched 10 miles via AUXI LE-CHATEAU to NOEUX where it billeted at 6 a m | |
| " 26th NOEUX | Paraded at 7.30 pm & marched via BERNAVILLE to | |
| " 27th ST LEGERS LES DOMART | ST LEGERS LES DOMART, where it billeted at 1 a m 23 horses & 20 O.R. arrived. Paraded at 10 h m & marched 15 miles to QUERRIEU, going into | |
| " 28th QUERRIEU | bivouac at 6 a m in a wood. Very wet. CAPT HOLMES & 16 O.R. attached F.A.P.M. | |
| " 29th " | 9th Corps. Rest d) | |

Forms/C. 2118/10

Army Form C. 2118.

# WAR DIARY
## or
## INTELLIGENCE SUMMARY.

9/Y, BEDFORDSHIRE YEOMANRY.

*(Erase heading not required.)*

Instructions regarding War Diaries and Intelligence Summaries are contained in F. S. Regs., Part II. and the Staff Manual respectively. Title pages will be prepared in manuscript.

| Hour, Date, Place | Summary of Events and Information | Remarks and references to Appendices |
|---|---|---|
| June 30th QUERRIEU. | Rec'd. Lt LASCELLES & 4 O.R. attached 2nd Indian Cav. Div. as Liaison Officer. | Sgd. H. H. [?] Bedfd Yeomanry. |

Forms/C. 2118/10

WAR DIARY
of
1/1 BEDFORDSHIRE YEOMANRY
from 1-7-16 to 31-7-16
VOLUME No. XXIV

Confidential

Army Form C. 2118

WAR DIARY of 1 BEDFORD YEOMANRY.
or
INTELLIGENCE SUMMARY.

(Erase heading not required.)

Instructions regarding War Diaries and Intelligence Summaries are contained in F.S. Regs., Part II. and the Staff Manual respectively. Title pages will be prepared in manuscript.

July 1916   Volume No.

| Hour, Date, Place | Summary of Events and Information | Remarks and references to Appendices |
|---|---|---|
| July 1st QUERRIEU | Paraded 3.10am & moved to BRESLE; no-5pm moved back to QUERRIEU. Remained in bivouac. | |
| " 2nd " | " | |
| " 3rd " | " | |
| " 4th " | " | |
| " 5th " | 1 & 7 O.R. sent up mounted to the XV Corps to clear the battlefield. MAJOR BENNING, LT. BRIGGS Paraded at 6am & marched via AMIENS to LONGPRÉ a distance of 26 miles. MAJOR GREEN CAPT PROBY 1 2 & 7 WILTSHIRE & 37 O.R. proceeded by train to STILL. Coyped on to train from 5, by train to STILL. Coyped on to train from 5, 2 LT PROCTOR joined from 3/1 BEDFORD YEO | |
| " 6th LONGPRÉ | Remained in billets. | |
| " 7th " | Stood to from 6am to 9 a.m. at 1 hours notice. Remained in billets. | |
| " 8th " | " | |
| " 9th " | " | |
| " 10th " | " | |

# WAR DIARY of 1/1 BEDFORD YEOMANRY
## INTELLIGENCE SUMMARY

Army Form C. 2118.

(Erase heading not required.)

| Hour, Date, Place | Summary of Events and Information | Remarks and references to Appendices |
|---|---|---|
| July 11th LONGPRÉ | Paraded at 8 h.m. & marched via AMIENS to QUERRIEU, arriving in Bivouac at 5.30 a.m. | |
| " 12th QUERRIEU. | Remained in Bivouac. The Adjutant reconnoitred roads etc to CARNOY and MONTAUBAN. 2LT WILTSHIRE severely wounded bringing Yeomans dead body into BECOURT. He died at 2 a.m. Went morning to DERNANCOURT. | |
| " 13th QUERRIEU | Paraded at 6 a.m. & marched via BRESLE to BUIRE-SOUR-ANCRE, arriving in Bivouac about 9.30 h.m. | |
| " 14th BUIRE | Stood to at 1½ hours notice from 3.30 a.m. & remained in Bivouac. LT LASCELLES attached to 7th DIV as Liaison Officer. | |
| " 15th " | Same as July 14th. | |
| " 16th " | Church Parades. MAJOR GREEN rejoined from digging party. 2LT CRAIG proceeded to DIEPPE. Party under 3rd INF. DIV. | |
| " 17th " | Remained in Bivouac. | |

Army Form C. 2118.

# WAR DIARY
## or
## INTELLIGENCE SUMMARY.
(Erase heading not required.)

OF BEDFORD YEOMANRY. JULY 1916
VOLUME Nº XXIV

Instructions regarding War Diaries and Intelligence Summaries are contained in F.S. Regs., Part II. and the Staff Manual respectively. Title pages will be prepared in manuscript.

| Hour, Date, Place | | Summary of Events and Information | Remarks and references to Appendices |
|---|---|---|---|
| July 18th | BUIRE | Remained in Bivouac | |
| " 19th | " | " | |
| " 20th | " | " LT. LASCELLES returned from 7th INF. DIV. | |
| " 21st | " | " | |
| " 22nd | " | " | |
| " 23rd | " | " Church Parades | |
| " 24th | " | Paraded at 9a.m. & marched to FRECHENCOURT arriving 12.30 p.m. 2 LT WOODHAMS & 6 O.R. proceeded to FRICOURT on Digging fatigue for XIII corps. CAPT. HOLMES ??? CAPT PROBY. 1 O.R. killed & 3 O.R. wounded with Digging Party at MARICOURT. | |
| " 25th | FRECHENCOURT | Remained in Bivouac. | |
| " 26th | " | Squadron Parades. | |
| " 27th | " | " | |
| " 28th | " | " | |
| " 29th | " | " 36 O.R. arrived from 3/1 BEDS. YEO. | |
| " 30th | " | Church Parades. CAPT HOLMES returned from Digging Party. | |
| " 31st | " | Squadron Parades. | |

Sgd/ H.Col.
Bedfordshire Yeomanry.

# WAR DIARY of 1/1 BEDFORDSHIRE YEOMANRY

## INTELLIGENCE SUMMARY

Army Form C. 2118.

AUGUST 1916.

| Hour, Date, Place | Summary of Events and Information | Remarks and references to Appendices |
|---|---|---|
| Aug 1st FRECHENCOURT | Squadron Parades | YM/3 |
| " 2nd " | " LT PRIESTLEY & 40 O.R. rejoined 2LT CRAIG & 40 O.R. with the Diss'ns Party. | |
| " 3rd " | Bde. Staff ride for C.O. & adjt. & 2nd in C. | |
| " 4th " | Squadron Parades | |
| " 5th " | " Practised signalling to R.F.C. | |
| " 6th " | Church Parade | |
| " 7th " | C.O. attended Divisional Staff Ride. | |
| " 8th " | Bde Staff Ride for O.C. Squadrons & 2nds in C. | |
| | 2LT. FIELDS-CLARKE & 300 O.R. rejoined. 2LT WOODHAMS | |
| | 1.30. O.R. with the Diss'ns Party. | |
| " 9th " | Paraded 4.30 a.m. & marched to COQUEREL-SUR-SOMME | |
| " 10th COQUEREL | Paraded 8.30 a.m. & marched to GAMACHES | |
| " 11th GAMACHES | Remained in Bivouac. | |
| " 12th " | " | |
| " 13th " | Church Parade. 2LT CAVALIER joined from 3/1. BEDS. YEO. | |
| " 14th " | Remained in Bivouac. | |

Army Form C. 2118.

# WAR DIARY of BEDFORDSHIRE YEOMANRY
## or INTELLIGENCE SUMMARY.
*(Erase heading not required.)*

Instructions regarding War Diaries and Intelligence Summaries are contained in F.S. Regs., Part II. and the Staff Manual respectively. Title pages will be prepared in manuscript.

| Hour, Date, Place | Summary of Events and Information | Remarks and references to Appendices |
|---|---|---|
| Aug 15th–15th CAMACHES | Holiday. Small parties of men were permitted to visit the sea-side. | |
| " 19th | CAPT C.F.M. RUSSELL joined. | |
| " 20th | Church Parade. | |
| " 21st | CAPT HOLMES, 2LT PROCTOR & 35 O.R. returned. LT PRIESTLEY & 30 O.R. with the Dissmy. Party. 2LT WHITE, 2LT WOOLF, 2LT WOOD & 200 O.R. joined. | |
| " 22nd | from 3/1 BEDS. YEO. Squadron Parades. | |
| " 23rd | " | |
| " 24th | Horse inspection by the G.O.C. 1st CAN. DIV. | |
| " 25th | Squadron Parades. | |
| " 26th | " CAPT. G.R. BOXTON. NORFOLK YEOMANRY joined attached | |
| " 27th | Church Parade. | |
| " 28th | Squadron Parades. | |
| " 29th | " | |
| " 30th | " | |
| " 31st | " | |

31.8.16

Sgd [signature]
Lt Col
Beds. Yeomanry

Confidential

# WAR DIARY 1/1 BEDFORDSHIRE YEOMANRY
## INTELLIGENCE SUMMARY
### SEPTEMBER 1916
### VOLUME XXVI

Army Form C. 2118

(Erase heading not required.)

Instructions regarding War Diaries and Intelligence Summaries are contained in F.S. Regs., Part II. and the Staff Manual respectively. Title pages will be prepared in manuscript.

| Hour, Date, Place | Summary of Events and Information | Remarks and references to Appendices |
|---|---|---|
| Sept 1st GAMACHES | Squadron Parades | Vol 14 |
| " 2nd " | 2Lt CRAIG proceeded to ENGLAND | |
| " 3rd " | CAPT RUSSELL " " 2Lt WHITE " | |
| " 4th " | Attached to 1/1 ESSEX YEOMANRY | |
| " 5th " | Hotchkiss guns near CAYEUX | |
| " 6th " | at 7 pm received orders to the ready to move at 4am 6/9/16. 2Lt COOK to Hospital | |
| " 7th BETTANCOURT | Rose at 9.15 am to BETTANCOURT arriving 3.30. Paraded at 11.0 am & moved to THIEVRES nr E 9 Pt | |
| " 8th DAOURS | HALLUE RIVER 1 M 9 DAOURS. Remained in THIEVRES | |
| " 9th " | Squad Parades | |
| " 10th " | Practised crossing trenches under rifle on payments | |
| " 11th " | C.O. inspected hacks & 2nd Côte Emont | |
| " 12th " | Adjutant & 2Lt HARGREAVES marched via BRESLES to aeroplane near BRESLES | |
| " 13th " | Remained in THIEVRES | |

JSC

Army Form C. 2118.

# WAR DIARY of 1/1 BEDFORDSHIRE YEOMANRY
## INTELLIGENCE SUMMARY.
*(Erase heading not required.)*

Instructions regarding War Diaries and Intelligence Summaries are contained in F. S. Regs., Part II. and the Staff Manual respectively. Title pages will be prepared in manuscript.

| Place | Date | Hour | Summary of Events and Information | Remarks and references to Appendices |
|---|---|---|---|---|
| DAOURS | 14.9.16 | | Paraded 7.30 a.m. & moved via BONNAY to MORLANCOURT. Where Rest rested for 3 hours. Arrived area W of CARNOY at 5.30 p.m. | |
| CARNOY | 15.9.16 | | Stood to at 20 min. notice from 8 a.m. CAPT HOLMES slightly wounded near GUILLEMONT. | |
| " | 16.9.16 | | Stood to at 20 min. notice from 9 a.m. LT HARGREAVES to E.H.Q. in C.M. Duty. | |
| " | 17.9.16 | | Paraded 1 p.m. & moved back to former area N of DAOURS | |
| DAOURS | 18.9.16 | | Very wet. | |
| " | 19.9.16 | | " | |
| " | 20.9.16 & 21.9.16 | | " | |
| " | 22.9.16 | | Divisional aeroplane scheme. S.S.M. ANDREW. M. 1/1 BEDS. YEO received a reminder in the 1/1 BEDS YEO. | |
| " | 23.9.16 | 7.50 a.m. | Paraded & marched via AMIENS to CONDÉ. | |
| CONDÉ | 24.9.16 | 10 a.m. | " " DOMQUEUR to NOEUX. | |
| NOEUX | 25.9.16 | 9 a.m. | " " GALAMETZ to OEUF. Dismounted Party rejoined | |
| OEUF | 26.9.16 | | Changed billets in the afternoon 30 O.R. from 3/1 BEDS YEO. to FILLIÈVRE. | |
| FILLIÈVRE | 27.9.16 | | | |

WAR DIARY of 1/1 BEDFORDSHIRE YEOMANRY
or
INTELLIGENCE SUMMARY.

Army Form C. 2118.

| Place | Date | Hour | Summary of Events and Information | Remarks and references to Appendices |
|---|---|---|---|---|
| FILLIEVRE | 28.9.16 | | Squadron Work. | |
| " | 29.9.16 | | " " Very wet. | |
| " | 30.9.16 | | Tactical Exercise for 2nd in C. & Squadron Leaders by G.O.C. 2nd CAV. BDE. | W. |

Sd/ Lt Col
Beds Yeomanry.

30.9.16.

Army Form C. 2118.

# WAR DIARY 9 1/1 BEDFORDSHIRE YEOMANRY

## or

## INTELLIGENCE SUMMARY

OCTOBER 1916

(Erase heading not required.)

Instructions regarding War Diaries and Intelligence Summaries are contained in F. S. Regs., Part II. and the Staff Manual respectively. Title pages will be prepared in manuscript.

| Place | Date | Hour | Summary of Events and Information | Remarks and references to Appendices |
|---|---|---|---|---|
| FILLIEVRES | Oct 1st | | Church Parades. | |
| " | " 2nd | | Baths. | |
| " | " 3rd | | Very wet. 2Lt SLATTER +14 O.R. joined from 3/1 BEDS. YEO. | |
| " | " 4th | | Bde "Gym" Scheme for G.O.C. CAV. CORPS. Returned home at 10 a.m. owing to rain. | |
| " | " 5th | | Inspection of horses by A.D.V.S. 1st CAV. DIV. Lecture by C.R.H.A. for Senior Officers. | |
| " | " 6th | | Squadron Work. | |
| " | " 7th | | Staff Ride for Troop Leaders by G.O.C. 9th CAV. BDE. | |
| " | " 8th | | Church Parades. CAPT PRUDBY, 2Lt MOORE + 75 O.R. proceeded by train to Div. | |
| " | " 9th | | Baths. CAPT. HARGREAVES rejoined from C.M. duty G.H.Q. | |
| " | " 10th | | Lecture by C.R.H.A. for Senior Officers. | |
| " | " 11th | | Squadron Work. | |
| " | " 12th | | Divisional Scheme in the neighbourhood of HOMIERES — BLANGY. | |
| " | " 13th | | Inspection of Regimental Transport by O.C. A.S.C. 1st CAV. DIV. | |
| " | " 14th | | Divisional Scheme 9th against 2nd CAV. BDE | |
| " | " | | Divisional Scheme 9th against 1st CAV. BDE | |

T2134. Wt. W708—776. 500000. 4/15. Sir J. C. & S.

Army Form C. 2118.

# WAR DIARY
## or
## INTELLIGENCE SUMMARY.

(Erase heading not required.)

9/11 BEDFORDSHIRE YEOMANRY

Instructions regarding War Diaries and Intelligence Summaries are contained in F. S. Regs., Part II. and the Staff Manual respectively. Title pages will be prepared in manuscript.

| Place | Date | Hour | Summary of Events and Information | Remarks and references to Appendices |
|---|---|---|---|---|
| FALLIEVRES | 15th | | Church Parade | |
| " | 16th | | Sqdn Work | |
| " | 17th | | " | |
| " | 18th | | V. Wet. D sqdn changed to HAUT MAISNIL | |
| " | 19th | | Paraded 7.30 a.m. & marched via PREVENT to OCCOCHES | |
| OCCOCHES | 20th | | 8.50 a.m " " DOULLENS to NAOURS | |
| NAOURS | 21st | | 2 L.T. COOK rejoined from Hospital. W.O.R. joined from 3/1 BEDS. YEO. | |
| " | 22nd | | Church Parade. | |
| " | 23rd | | Sqdn Work. 8.O.R. to 1st CAV. DIV. as dispatch Riders. | |
| " | 24th | | " " } weather very wet. | |
| " | 25th | | " " | |
| " | 26th | | " " | |
| " | 27th | | " " | |
| " | 28th | | " " | |
| " | 29th | | Church Parade | |
| " | 30th | | Sqdn work | |
| " | 31st | | " " | |

Self 2/Lt
Beds. Yeomanry

Army Form C. 2118.

# WAR DIARY
## of
## 1/1 BEDFORDSHIRE YEOMANRY
## INTELLIGENCE SUMMARY.
### VOLUME XXVIII

(Erase heading not required.)

Instructions regarding War Diaries and Intelligence Summaries are contained in F. S. Regs., Part II. and the Staff Manual respectively. Title pages will be prepared in manuscript.

9916

| Place | Date | Hour | Summary of Events and Information | Remarks and references to Appendices |
|---|---|---|---|---|
| NAOURS | NOV 1st | | Sqdn Work. CAPT R.G. BUXTON to Hospital. | |
| " | 2nd | | " | |
| " | 3rd | | " | |
| " | 4th | | Staff ride by G.O.C. 9th CAV BDE for 2nd in C. & 2nd in E.O. Sqdns. | |
| " | 5th | | Church Parade | |
| " | 6th | | Lecture by MAJOR SETTLE on Tactical Handling of Machine Guns. | |
| " | 7th | | V. W.L. 17. O.R joined from 3/1 Beds Yeo. | |
| " | 8th | | Paraded at 8.30 a.m. & marched to FOREST L'ABBAYE. | |
| FOREST L'ABBAYE | 9th | | " at 10 a.m. " marched via CRECY to DOURIEZ. | |
| DOURIEZ | 10th | | " at 8 a.m. " marched via MONTCAVRIL to DESVRES. | |
| DESVRES | 11th | | HQ & A Sqdn billeted in DESVRES. B Sqdn SACRIQUIER D Sqdn LONGFOSSE. | |
| " | 12th | | Church Parade. CAPT. PROBY & 247 HORSE & 62 O.R. on Digging Party. | |
| " | 13th | | | |
| " | 14th | | Inspection of HH & G by G.O.C. 9 Horse BDE. | |
| " | 15th | | Lecture to Subaltern Officers by Th Adjutant on Troop Training. | |
| " | 16th | | | JSC |

# WAR DIARY or INTELLIGENCE SUMMARY.

Army Form C. 2118.

1/1 BEDFORDSHIRE YEOMANRY

*(Erase heading not required.)*

| Place | Date | Hour | Summary of Events and Information | Remarks and references to Appendices |
|---|---|---|---|---|
| DESYRES | Nov 7 18 | | LT BRIGG appointed Assistant Adjutant. CAPT. McBRIDE (AVC) attached. | |
| " | " 19 | | Church Parades. Troop Training. | |
| " | " 20 | | Troop Training. | |
| " | " 21 | | 2/LTs RAMBAUT, ANDERSON & ANDREWS visited Div School. Troop Training. | |
| " | " 22 | | Foot looking Parade. | |
| " | " 23 | | "A" sqdn depart for Div'l School. Troop Training. | |
| " | " 25 | | Troop Training. | |
| " | " 26 | | Church Parades. | |
| " | " 27 | | CAPT. PROBY, LTS BRIGG, FOSTER, 2/LTs SOUTHERN, HOARE & HARRIS to Veterinary Lecture Bde HQ. | JL |
| " | " 28 | | CAPT HARGREAVES T.C.M duty 5th Can Div. Inspected by HP & Asst Ins. H.D.V.S. | |
| " | " 29 30 | | " C. V Dgdm " " | |

S. Stuart Mayne
Bde. Yeomanry

**WAR DIARY** 9/14 BEDFORDSHIRE YEOMANRY

Army Form C. 2118.

VOLUME *** VOL 17

| Place | Date | Hour | Summary of Events and Information | Remarks and references to Appendices |
|---|---|---|---|---|
| DESVRES | Dec 1 | | Troop Training. CAPT HARGREAVES from C.M. duty 5th Cav. Div. | |
| " | " 2 | | Lecture by Rev. H.G. GIBBON at Bde. HQ on "Envy". 2 Lt CAVALIER | |
| | | | to the Bttn. 2 Lt MUNCKTON joined from 3/1 Beds. Yeo. | |
| " | " 3 | | Church Parade. Capt HARGREAVES to Hospital | |
| " | " 4 | | Baths & Troop Training | |
| " | " 5 | | " | |
| " | " 6 | | " | |
| " | " 7 | | " | |
| " | " 8 | | " | |
| " | " 9 | | Church Parades. | |
| " | " 10 | | Bde. Vet. came for 6 M.C.Os & Signalling came for 2 Lt WOOD MBBS | |
| " | " 11 | | J.O.R. | |
| " | " 12 | | Troop Training | |
| " | " 13 | | " | |
| " | " 14 | | " | |

Army Form C. 2118.

# WAR DIARY
## or
## INTELLIGENCE SUMMARY.
(Erase heading not required.)

WAR DIARY OF 2/1 BEDFORDSHIRE YEOMANRY VOLUME VOL II

| Place | Date | Hour | Summary of Events and Information | Remarks and references to Appendices |
|---|---|---|---|---|
| DENVRES | Dec 1 | | Troop Training CAPT HARGREAVES from C.M. duty 5th Cav. Div. | |
| " | " 2 | | Lecture by Rev. H.E. GIBSON at Bde. HQ on "Envy". 2LT COURIER to the BDE. | |
| " | " 3 | | 2LT MUNCKTON joined from 3/1 Beds Yeo. | |
| " | " 4 | | Church Parade. CAPT HARGREAVES to Hospital. | |
| " | " 5 | | Baths & Troop Training. | |
| " | " 6 | | " | |
| " | " 7 | | " | |
| " | " 8 | | " | |
| " | " 9 | | " | |
| " | " 10 | | Church Parade. | |
| " | " 11 | | Bde. Vet. Course for 6 N.C.O's & 1 Sgn ellmg course for 2LT WOOD HEAMS & 3.O.R. | |
| " | " 12 | | Troop Training | |
| " | " 13 | | " | |
| " | " 14 | | " | |

# WAR DIARY 1/1 BEDFORDSHIRE YEOMANRY

Army Form C. 2118.

| Place | Date | Hour | Summary of Events and Information | Remarks and references to Appendices |
|---|---|---|---|---|
| DESVRES | Dec 16 | | | |
| " | " 17 | | Regt Training | |
| " | " 18 | | Church | |
| " | " 19 | | Regt Training & Baths | |
| " | " 20 | | " " & " | |
| " | " 21 | | D.D.V.S. Cos. Cpts inspected Horse D troop | |
| " | " 22 | | G.O.C. "CAV-DIV" inspected D sqdn & billets D 4 & G sqdn | |
| " | " 23 | | Regt Training | |
| " | " 24 | | Church Parade | |
| " | " 25 | | Holiday | |
| " | " 26 | | Regt Training & Baths | |
| " | " 27 | | " " " | |
| " | " 28 | | 267 horses to HQ in cipher officer | J.S. |
| " | " 29 | | " Baths | |
| " | " 30 | | Church Parade. | |
| " | " 31 | | | Sgt [signature]<br>Beds Yeomanry |

Army Form C. 2118.

# WAR DIARY
## or
## INTELLIGENCE SUMMARY.
(Erase heading not required.)

1/1 BEDFORDSHIRE YEOMANRY.

Vol 18

| Place | Date | Hour | Summary of Events and Information | Remarks and references to Appendices |
|---|---|---|---|---|
| DESVRES | JAN 1 | | Troop Training and Baths | |
| " | 2 | | Instruction of Horses by V.O. 2nd Field Works on 12 W. Regt Intelligence Course Setw A Battalion. Capt Forby Lieut Foster, Rough Riders Sergt Churchill Sqdrn 2nd Horse Singleton | |
| " | 3 | | Troop Training | |
| " | 4 | | do | |
| " | 5 | | Instd Lt J.G. Barthrop attached Regt. Relinted Divisional Staff Inspection of Regiment Standards by G.O.C. of the Bde. Returned to Divisionals Maj R Kelly Command | |
| " | 6 | | Capt C.M. Meredam Capt J.E. Jones Lt W.G. Dowler | |
| " | 7 | | Troop Training | |
| " | 8 | | Church Parade | |
| " | 9 | | Baths. Lt Col Grigor D.S.O. 2nd in Command allowed us Regimental attached | |
| " | 10 | | Baths | |
| " | 11 | | 2nd Lt Proctor to CAUMARTIN for Intelligence Course. Regt Raymond Argent 16th Eng for Officers Commission | |
| " | 12 | | Troop Training | |
| " | 13 | | do | |
| " | | | do | |

Army Form C. 2118.

# WAR DIARY
## or
## INTELLIGENCE SUMMARY.
### 1/1 BEDFORDSHIRE YEOMANRY.
*(Erase heading not required.)*

Instructions regarding War Diaries and Intelligence Summaries are contained in F. S. Regs., Part II. and the Staff Manual respectively. Title pages will be prepared in manuscript.

| Place | Date | Hour | Summary of Events and Information | Remarks and references to Appendices |
|---|---|---|---|---|
| DESVRES | JAN 14 | | Church Parade | |
| " | 15 | | Baths Lt Col Grigg DSO struck off | |
| " | 16 | | Do 2nd Lt E.R. Rothera to Divisional Signalling Course | |
| " | 17 | | Troop Training. Lt L.J.G. Butler member of Field General Court Martial wounded at BOURTHES | |
| " | 18 | | Do | |
| " | 19 | | Do | |
| " | 20 | | Do | |
| " | 21 | | Church Parade 2nd Lt Platts to 2nd Signalling Service School HQ | |
| " | 22 | | Squadron training. Maj I. Spicer 42nd Lt H.J. Bosh attached 2nd Indian Mounted Rifles | |
| " | 23 | | Baths | |
| " | 24 | | Maj K. Pelly Jones Presided at a F.G.C.M. Lieut H.R. 15th Hussars | |
| " | 25 | | Squadron Training | |
| " | 26 | | Do Capt D.K. Pitts Franks Yeo attached | |
| " | 27 | | Do | |
| " | 28 | | Church Parade | |
| " | 29 | | G.O.C. 4th Cav Bde inspected D Squadron at Squadron Training | |

Army Form C. 2118.

# WAR DIARY
## or
## INTELLIGENCE SUMMARY.

1/1 BEDFORDSHIRE YEOMANRY

(Erase heading not required.)

Instructions regarding War Diaries and Intelligence Summaries are contained in F. S. Regs., Part II. and the Staff Manual respectively. Title pages will be prepared in manuscript.

| Place | Date | Hour | Summary of Events and Information | Remarks and references to Appendices |
|---|---|---|---|---|
| DESVRES | JAN 30 | | Baths | |
| " | 31 | | Squadron Training | |

Sgd. Lt Colonel,
Commg 1st Beds. Yeomanry.

# WAR DIARY
## or
## INTELLIGENCE SUMMARY

*(Erase heading not required.)*

Army Form C. 2118.

1/1 BEDFORDSHIRE YEOMANRY

Vol/9

| Place | Date 1917 | Hour | Summary of Events and Information | Remarks and references to Appendices |
|---|---|---|---|---|
| DESVRES | FEB: 1 | | 2nd Course Gun Sir School. 595 Sergt E. Elms 1069 Sergt R.J. Andrews 492 Sergt W Chapman proceed on First Second & Third | |
| " | 2 | | Squadron Training. 2nd Lt E.K.P. Rootham from 1st Gun Sir Signalling Course. 1601 Sdl. McRevie 1778 Pte Vincent 9 | |
| " | | | 664 2/Cpl W Raybrow to 1st Gun Sir Gas School | |
| " | 3 | | Squadron Training 1814 2/Cpl W. Davies to England for Commission | |
| " | 4 | | Church Parade | |
| " | 5 | | Baths | |
| " | 6 | | Squadron Training. 2nd Lt Hoare. Lt Poulton. 2/Lt Cook Sergt Puel. Sergt W. a Knight Flint to go to France as Divisional Patrol. | |
| " | 7 | | Squadron Training. 2nd Lt Rattlins attached 2nd Dragoon Mounted Regiment | |
| " | 8 | | Squadron Training. Pte Lechfield 2nd Dragoon Mounted Regiment attached. | |
| " | 9 | | Lectural Steward to HQ 4th army for Intelligence Course. Capt White Hants Yeo Struck off | |
| " | 10 | | Squadron Training | |
| " | 11 | | 2660 S.S.M.T. Mellington. 4th Hussars attached Beds Yeomanry awarded the Crow de Guerre. | |
| " | 12 | | Baths | |
| " | 13 | | Squadron Training | |

Army Form C. 2118.

# WAR DIARY
## or
## INTELLIGENCE SUMMARY
1/1 BEDFORDSHIRE YEOMANRY

(Erase heading not required.)

Instructions regarding War Diaries and Intelligence Summaries are contained in F. S. Regs., Part II. and the Staff Manual respectively. Title pages will be prepared in manuscript.

| Place | Date 1917 | Hour | Summary of Events and Information | Remarks and references to Appendices |
|---|---|---|---|---|
| DESVRES | FEB. 14 | | Squadron Training. Capt. S.P. Davis from Base. Major P.J. Green rejoined from 2nd Id gac Mounted Regt. | |
| " | 15 | | Tactical Scheme with D Squadron 2nd Id gac Mounted Regt. | |
| " | 16 | | Squadron Training | |
| " | 17 | | Colt Party attached 2nd Id gac Mounted Regt | |
| " | 18 | | Church Parade | |
| " | 19 | | Baths. 2nd Lt. E.P. Woodlands to A.Q. Gas School for General Signalling | |
| " | 20 | | Squadron Training | |
| " | 21 | | Squadron Training | |
| " | 22 | | Squadron Training | |
| " | 23 | | Lt Col P.L. Peel presided Maj P. Green member of Board of Inquiry which assembled H.Q. 9th Cav Field Ambulance COURSET. Major W.E. Benning President of Field General Court Martial at A.Q. 15th Hussars | |
| " | 24 | | Lecture by Divisional Gas Officer with use & fitting of small Box Respirator | |
| " | 25 | | Voluntary Church Services | |
| " | 26 | | Squadron Training | |
| " | 27 | | Baths and disinfecting of Billets | |
| " | 28 | | Baths and disinfecting of Billets | |

Sully
Lt Colonel
Comndg. Beds. Yeomanry

# WAR DIARY or INTELLIGENCE SUMMARY

Army Form C. 2118.

1/1 BEDFORDSHIRE YEOMANRY. MARCH 1917. VOLUME XXXII.

| Place | Date | Hour | Summary of Events and Information | Remarks and references to Appendices |
|---|---|---|---|---|
| DESYRÊH | Mar 1 | | Regimental Tactical Scheme. | |
| " | " 2 | | Sqdn Training. 2Lt WOODD rejoined from Gas School | |
| " | " 3 | | Horse inspection by G.O.C. 1st CAV. DIV. | |
| " | " 4 | | Church Parade. 2LT SLATTER attached to 1st Signal Sqdn. | |
| " | " 5 | | Sqdn Training. | |
| " | " 6 | | " Lecture by C.R.H.A. 1st MR. DIV. LT. LASCELLES rejoined. | |
| " | " 7 | | " 2Lt WING & 2Lt EDIS joined from 2/1 BEDS. YEO. | |
| " | " 8 | | " MAJOR GREEN & MAJOR BENNING to DIV. SCHOOL | |
| " | " 9 | | Regimental Exercise. | |
| " | " 10 | | Sqdn Training. | |
| " | " 11 | | Church Parade. | |
| " | " 12 | | Sqdn Training. G.O.C. 9th CAV. BDE inspected Regiment. Lecture. | |
| " | " 13 | | " MAJOR SELBY LOWNDES from Hospital. | |
| " | " 14 | | " | |
| " | " 15 | | " 2LT BARLOW VILOR. as sword cutting Inst. | |
| " | " 16 | | Hotchkin competition. MAJOR GREEN & MAJOR BENNING from DIV. SCHOOL | |

Army Form C. 2118.

# WAR DIARY
## or
## INTELLIGENCE SUMMARY.
(Erase heading not required.)

1/1 BEDFORDSHIRE YEOMANRY.

Instructions regarding War Diaries and Intelligence Summaries are contained in F.S. Regs., Part II. and the Staff Manual respectively. Title pages will be prepared in manuscript.

| Place | Date | Hour | Summary of Events and Information | Remarks and references to Appendices |
|---|---|---|---|---|
| DESVRES | Jan 17 | | Sqdn Training. | |
| " | " 18 | | Church Parade. | |
| " | " 19 | | Sqdn Training & Baths. | |
| " | " 20 | | Inspection of Horses by G.O.C. 9th Cav. Bde. 2 Lt WOODHAMS from Cav. Corps. | |
| " | " 21 | | Sqdn Training. Lt SMEE rejoined from Hospital. | |
| " | " 22 | | Fitted with smalls box respirators. | |
| " | " 23 | | Sqdn Training. | |
| " | " 24 | | " " | |
| " | " 25 | | Church Parade. 2Lt FIELDS CLARKE, 2Lt WING & 7O.R. proceeded to VI | |
| " | " 26 | | Corps area to dig. 2Lt SLATTER from 1" Signal Sqdn. | |
| " | " 27 | | D.D.R. Cav Corps. inspected horse for casting. | Y.M. |
| " | " 28 | | Sqdn Training & Baths. | |
| " | " 29 | | " " | |
| " | " 30 | | " " Capt KIRK A.V.C. joined. | |
| " | " 31 | | " " Lt CRABBE rejoined from HQ. 9th Cav Bde. | Sgd. Lt Col Beds. Yeomanry |

War Diary
of
1/1 BEDFORDSHIRE YEOMANRY
from 1-4-17 to 30-4-17

VOL XXXIII

Army Form C. 2118.

# WAR DIARY 1/1 BEDFORDSHIRE YEOMANRY
## or
## INTELLIGENCE SUMMARY

(Erase heading not required.)

Instructions regarding War Diaries and Intelligence Summaries are contained in F.S. Regs., Part II. and the Staff Manual respectively. Title pages will be prepared in manuscript.

Vol 21

| Place | Date | Hour | Summary of Events and Information | Remarks and references to Appendices |
|---|---|---|---|---|
| DESVRES | April 1st | | Church Parades. | |
| " | " 2nd | | Field Firing & Baths. | |
| " | " 3rd | | Sqdn Training & Baths. | |
| " | " 4th | | " | |
| " | " 5th | | Paraded at 9.45am & marched via PARENTY to MONTCAVREL | |
| MONTCAVREL | " 6th | | Remained in billets. | |
| " | " 7th | | Paraded at 8.30am & marched via FRUGES to BLANGY-SUR-TERNOISE. | |
| BLANGY | " 8th | | MAJOR SELBY LOWNDES to HQ. 1st CAV DIV as A.D.C. | |
| AUBIGNY | " 9th | | Paraded at 11.30am & marched via ST POL to TINQUES S.E. of AUBIGNY | |
| " | " 10th | | Stood to at 1 hours notice after 7am. 2LT MUNCKTON to Hospital. | |
| " | " 11th | | " " 2 " " 7am. ⎫ | |
| " | " 12th | | Remained in TINQUES ⎬ very cold & deep snow. | |
| " | " 13th | | " " " ⎭ 2LT SLATTER to R.F.C. Two shells landed near | |
| " | " 14th | | TINQUES | |
| " | | | Changed camp to a drier field. | |

JC

Army Form C. 2118.

# WAR DIARY
## or
## INTELLIGENCE SUMMARY.

of 1/1 BEDFORDSHIRE YEOMANRY.

(Erase heading not required.)

| Place | Date | Hour | Summary of Events and Information | Remarks and references to Appendices |
|---|---|---|---|---|
| AUBIGNY | April 15th | | In Bivouac. | |
| " | " 16th | | Marched via MARGNICOURT & FREVENT to CONCHY-SUR-CANCHE. | |
| CONCHY | " 17th | | Cleaned up. | |
| " | " 18th | | " | |
| " | " 19th | | Training. | |
| " | " 20th | | Inspection of Horse Lines by G.O.C 9th CAV. BDE. | |
| " | " 21st | | — | |
| " | " 22nd | | Church Parades. | |
| " | " 23rd | | Horse casting by A.D.V.S.   46 horses cast. | |
| " | " 24th | | Dismounted Scheme. | |
| " | " 25th | | Training | |
| " | " 26th | | " | |
| " | " 27th | | Regimental Route March.  CAPT SHAW A.V.C joined | |
| " | " 28th | | "                         CAPT KIRK A.V.C departed | JW |
| " | " 29th | | 24 O.R. joined from 3/1 BEDS.YEO | |
| " | " 30th | | Dismounted scheme.  Regiment at Horse Stunt. | Sel Lt Col |
| | | | | Beds. Yeomanry |

Army Form C. 2118.

# WAR DIARY
or
# INTELLIGENCE SUMMARY.

1/1 BEDFORDSHIRE YEOMANRY

Vol 2

(Erase heading not required.)

Instructions regarding War Diaries and Intelligence Summaries are contained in F. S. Regs., Part II. and the Staff Manual respectively. Title pages will be prepared in manuscript.

| Place | Date | Hour | Summary of Events and Information | Remarks and references to Appendices |
|---|---|---|---|---|
| CONCHY-SUR- | May 1st | | | |
| CANCHE | " 2nd | | LT FOSTER to Hospital. | |
| " | " 3rd | | Inspection of Billets by G.O.C. 9th CAV. BDE. Route March. | |
| " | " 4th | | Staff ride. 22 horses arrived. | |
| " | " 5th | | | |
| " | " 6th | | Church Parades. | |
| " | " 7th | | LT HOLLEBONE & 2LT BOWEN joined from ENGLAND. | |
| " | " 8th | | | |
| " | " 9th | | 60 horses arrived | |
| " | " 10th | | CAPT. HARGREAVES joined from ENGLAND. | |
| " | " 11th | | | |
| " | " 12 | | CAPT HOLMES, LT HOLLEBONE & 2LT HOARE & 83 O.R. proceeded as Advance to a Pioneer Batt" to XIII Corps Area. | |
| " | " 13th | | Marched to MONCHY CAYEUX. | |
| MONCHY | " 14th | | Marched via PERNES to LABEUVRIÈRE. | |
| LA BEUVRIÈRE | " 15th | | LONDON GAZETTE May 15th mentioned in Despatches. | |

Army Form C. 2118.

# WAR DIARY
## or
## INTELLIGENCE SUMMARY.

1/1 BEDFORDSHIRE YEOMANRY

(Erase heading not required.)

| Place | Date | Hour | Summary of Events and Information | Remarks and references to Appendices |
|---|---|---|---|---|
| LABEUVRIERE | May 16 | | LT-COL HON: C.C. PEEL. MAJOR S.J. GREEN T.D. CAPT. J.F. GORE. N°P/6732 Sgt MARSON L. | |
| " | " 17 | | CAPT. HARGREAVES. LT SOUTHERN. 2LT COOR v. DIS. v. 189. O.R. Went to | |
| " | " 18 | | ECURIE as a company of 6th PIONEER Batt under XIII Corps. | |
| " | " 19 | | Horse Casting Parade by D.D.R. 1st ARMY. | |
| " | " 20 | | " " " " " | |
| " | " 21 | | " " " " " | |
| " | " 22 | | Inspection of Horses by A.D.V.S. 1st CAV. DIV. | |
| " | " 23 | | | |
| " | " 24 | | | |
| " | " 25 | | | |
| " | " 26 | | LT. SMEE to 9th Batt". LT FOSTER rejoined from Hospital. | W. |
| " | " 27 | | Church Parade. | |
| " | " 28-31 | | Casualties during month 6. O.R. wounded. | Sgt Lt-bt ——— Beds. Yeomanry. |

# WAR DIARY or INTELLIGENCE SUMMARY.

Army Form C. 2118.

**BEDFORDSHIRE YEOMANRY**  Vol 23

| Place | Date | Hour | Summary of Events and Information | Remarks and references to Appendices |
|---|---|---|---|---|
| LABEUVRIERE | June 1 | 2ᵖ | Every Pioneer Battⁿˢ returned to their respective Units | |
| " | " 2 | 3ᵖ | Church Parade. 2ᵈᵗ Woodhams L.G.T.M. BDE as acting Signalling Officer. | |
| " | " 4 | | Marched to Avenue joint H.E.D.ESTAIRES. LT-COL 7ᵗʰ Sc. PEEL Command D.S.O. | |
| ESTAIRES | " 5 | | | |
| " | " 6 | | LT C.G.E. RUSSELL Assumed Captain. | |
| " | " 7 | | | |
| " | " 8 | | | |
| " | " 9 | | Inspection of horses by G.O.C. 1ˢᵗ Cav. Div. | |
| " | " 10 | | Church Parades | |
| " | " 11 | | Marched back to LABEUVRIERE. Digging party of Capt HARGREAVES + LT RAMBAUT + 84 O.R. to Composite Battⁿ | |
| LABEUVRIERE | " 12 | | | |
| " | " 13 | | BEDS YEO. COY ᵖ H.Q (MAJOR GREEN. OC. LT LASCELLES ADJT. LT BRIGG QM. CAPT DAVIS, LT SMEE. 2ᴸᵗ PENTELOW, 2ᴸᵗ WOODD, 2ᴸᵗ BOWEN) T/199.O.R to XIII Corps as GHQ party 8ᵗʰ Pioneer Battⁿ | |

Army Form C. 2118.

# WAR DIARY
## or
## INTELLIGENCE SUMMARY.
of BEDFORDSHIRE YEOMANRY

(Erase heading not required.)

| Place | Date | Hour | Summary of Events and Information | Remarks and references to Appendices |
|---|---|---|---|---|
| LABEUVRIÈRE | June 14th | | 2LT HOARE to 1st CAV. DIV. as Gas Officer (on probation) | |
| | -15th-23rd | | General duties. | |
| | -24 | | LT A.F. LASCELLES to be Captain. 2LT WOODHAMS rejoined | |
| | -25 | | | |
| | -26 | | Inspection of horses for working by DDR 1st ARMY | |
| | -27 | | | |
| | -28 | | | |
| | -29 | | | |
| | -30 | | | |

Sd/ H.H.
Beds Yeomanry

# WAR DIARY or INTELLIGENCE SUMMARY

**BEDFORDSHIRE YEOMANRY**

Army Form C. 2118.
(Erase heading not required.)

Vol 24

| Place | Date | Hour | Summary of Events and Information | Remarks and references to Appendices |
|---|---|---|---|---|
| LABEUVRIÈRE | July 1st | | Church Parades | |
| " | " 2nd | | Horses of No 2 Troop "A"sqdn inspected | |
| " | " 3rd | | — | |
| " | " 4th | | Inspection of Sanitary Arrangements by A.D.M.S. 2nd Div. | |
| " | " 5th | | Visit from the Listening Officer | |
| " | " 6th | | 25 Horses arrived from Base | |
| " | " 7th | | 1st Hotchkiss party of 4 officers (Capt Holmes, 2Lt S Andrew, Anderson & Bowen) v 28 O.R. of Cameras for Shooting practice | |
| " | " 8th | | Church Parades | |
| " | " 9th | | The Pioneer Batt's attached to VIII Corps reported (11 officers & 267 O.R.) | |
| " | " 10th | | — | |
| " | " 11th | | A party of 5 officers & 200 O.R. under Capt Hargreaves attend the Proxy by King George V. "C" Sqdn marching order parade. Regt v Transport (two o'sqdn) marching order parade. 2nd Hotchkiss Brigade Route March. Party relieved No 1st Party | |
| " | " 12th | | | |
| " | " 13th | | | |
| " | " 14th | | | |

# WAR DIARY
## or
## INTELLIGENCE SUMMARY.

*(Erase heading not required.)*

Army Form C. 2118.

**BEDFORDSHIRE YEOMANRY**

| Place | Date | Hour | Summary of Events and Information | Remarks and references to Appendices |
|---|---|---|---|---|
| LABEUVRIERE | July 15th | | Church Parade. | |
| " | " 16th | | Marched to NEUF BERQUIN. | |
| NEUF BERQUIN | " 17 | | 2nd Hotchkiss Party reported. A "Sqdn" was 1st in the Division. | |
| " | " 18 | | | |
| " | " 19th | | G.O.C. 9th Cav. Bde. V.A.D.V.S. inspected horses of the Regiment. | |
| " | " 20th | | Sqdn Training | |
| " | " 21st | | " | |
| " | " 22nd | | Church Parade | |
| " | " 23rd | | Sqdn Training. 20 remounts arrived from Base. | |
| " | " 24/25th | | " | |
| " | " 26th | | Parade of Dismounted Battn. | |
| " | " 27th | | Sqdn Training | |
| " | " 28th | | " Signalling Scheme with aeroplanes. | W.L. |
| " | " 29th | | Church Parade. | |
| " | " 30th | | Major S.J. GREEN. 16" 1st CAV. BDE as Liaison Officer | |
| " | " 31st | | Sqdn Training | |

S.J.L. BC
Beds. Yeomanry.

Army Form C. 2118.

# WAR DIARY / 1 BEDFORDSHIRE YEOMANRY
## INTELLIGENCE SUMMARY
*(Erase heading not required.)*

Instructions regarding War Diaries and Intelligence Summaries are contained in F. S. Regs., Part II. and the Staff Manual respectively. Title pages will be prepared in manuscript.

Vol 25

| Place | Date | Hour | Summary of Events and Information | Remarks and references to Appendices |
|---|---|---|---|---|
| NEUF — BERQUIN | Aug 1 | | | |
| " | " 2 | | MAJOR S.J. GREEN from 3rd ARMY. | |
| " | " 3 | | | |
| " | " 4 | | Lecture to Gas Officers & NCOs by D.G.O. "C" Sqdn musketry at Morbecque Range | |
| " | " 5 | | MAJOR J.B. WALKER rejoined from England. Church Parades. CAPT J. HOLMES & 3rd ARMY Co joined Regt from | |
| " | " 6 | | MAJOR S.J. GREEN, 2Lt C. WOODHAMS & Lt J.O. attended "ARMY Service 2Lt CROZIER visit on promoted to fly 2nd Dinghs and R.H. Army | |
| " | " 7 | | D" Sqdn musketry at MORBECQUE RANGE | |
| " | " 8 | | | |
| " | " 9 | | | |
| " | " 10 | | | |
| " | " 11 | | A Sqdn musketry at MORBECQUE RANGE | |
| " | " 12 | | Church Parades | |
| " | " 13 | | Sqdn Training | V.C |

Army Form C. 2118.

# WAR DIARY
## BEDFORDSHIRE YEOMANRY
## or INTELLIGENCE SUMMARY.
(Erase heading not required.)

Instructions regarding War Diaries and Intelligence Summaries are contained in F.S. Regs., Part II. and the Staff Manual respectively. Title pages will be prepared in manuscript.

| Place | Date | Hour | Summary of Events and Information | Remarks and references to Appendices |
|---|---|---|---|---|
| NEUF BERQUIN | May 14th | | Sqdn Training. | |
| " | " 15th | | " | |
| " | " 16th | | " | |
| " | " 17th | | Brigade Tactical Exercise. | |
| " | " 18th | | Inspection of horses by A.D.V.S. | |
| " | " 19th | | Church Parades. | |
| " | " 20th | | Sqdn Training. | |
| " | " 21st | | " | |
| " | " 22nd | | " | |
| " | " 23rd | | " | |
| " | " 24th | | Visit from D.G.O. & Sanitary Inspection by A.D.M.S. | |
| " | " 25th | | Sqdn Training. | |
| " | " 26th | | Church Parades. | |
| " | " 27th | | Paraded 8am & marched via MERVILLE, STVENANT, BERGUETTE, LINGHEM to FLECHIN. | |
| FLECHIN | " 28th | | Paraded 9.30am & marched via MAERINGHEM to ROMILLY | JK |

Army Form C. 2118.

# WAR DIARY
## or
## INTELLIGENCE SUMMARY.

BEDFORDSHIRE YEOMANRY.

(Erase heading not required.)

Instructions regarding War Diaries and Intelligence Summaries are contained in F. S. Regs., Part II. and the Staff Manual respectively. Title pages will be prepared in manuscript.

| Place | Date | Hour | Summary of Events and Information | Remarks and references to Appendices |
|---|---|---|---|---|
| RUMILLY | Aug 29th | | Paraded at 8.30am & marched via HURDCELLERS to LONGVILLERS ("HQ" & "C" sqdn LONGVILLERS. "A" sqdn MARESVILLE "D" sqdn BREXENT) | |
| LONGVILLERS | " 30 | | | |
| | " 31 | | | |

W.M. L. F.F.
Bed Yeomanry

**WAR DIARY** or **INTELLIGENCE SUMMARY.**

1 BEDFORDSHIRE YEOMANRY.

Army Form C. 2118.

Vol 26

| Place | Date | Hour | Summary of Events and Information | Remarks and references to Appendices |
|---|---|---|---|---|
| LONGVILLERS | Sept 1 | | Squadron work | |
| " | " 2 | | Church Services | |
| " | " 3 | | Sqdn work | |
| " | " 4 | | CAPT LASCELLES attached to 9th Cav Bde for instruction | |
| " | 5–8 | | CAPT SWEETNAM. RAMC joined the Regiment | |
| " | 9 | | Sqdn work | |
| " | 10–14 | | Church Services | |
| " | 15 | | Sqdn work | |
| " | 15 | | Regimental Athletic Sports | |
| " | 16 | | Horse coolies by D.D.R. Cav. Corps. 11 hors. ent. | |
| " | | | Church Services. MAJOR S.J. GREEN to ENGLAND. | |
| " | 17 | | Majors Sqdn work | |
| " | 18 | | " | |
| " | 19 | | " | |
| " | 20 | | " LT BRIGG promoted CAPTAIN. | |
| " | 21 | | 1st CAV. DIV. Sports | |

# WAR DIARY or INTELLIGENCE SUMMARY.

**Army Form C. 2118.**

of **BEDFORDSHIRE YEOMANRY.**

(Erase heading not required.)

| Place | Date | Hour | Summary of Events and Information | Remarks and references to Appendices |
|---|---|---|---|---|
| LONGVILLERS | Sept 23 | | Sqdn work | |
| " | " 24 | | Church Service | |
| " | " 25 | | Sqdn work | |
| " | " 26 | | Brigade Tactical Exercise | |
| " | " 27 | | Sqdn work | |
| " | " 28 | | Brigade Rifle Shooting (1" in hops Competition. Gained 1st in Snipers & 2nd in section comp.) | |
| " | " 29 | | Sqdn work | |
| " | " 30 | | LT WOODHAMS & CAN. CORPS SIGS. IN COURSE | |
| | | | CAPT LASCELLES rejoined | |
| | | | ~~T. Reinf. of.... BDE~~ | |
| | | | Donald hasty rejoined from VI H ARMY. | |

Sgd. J K Noel
Beds Yeomanry

# WAR DIARY or INTELLIGENCE SUMMARY.

Army Form C. 2118.

of BEDFORDSHIRE YEOMANRY

1/10/17 to 31/10/17

Vol 27

| Place | Date | Hour | Summary of Events and Information | Remarks and references to Appendices |
|---|---|---|---|---|
| LONGVILLERS | Oct 1st | | Troop Musketry Competition. | |
| " | " 2nd | | " | |
| " | " 3rd | | Regimental Tactical Exercise. | |
| " | " 4th | | Troop Musketry Competition. | |
| " | " 5th | | — | Showers. |
| " | " 6th | | Paraded 11 am & marched to WIERRE-AU-BOIS | Heavy rain for 4 hrs |
| WIERRE-AU-BOIS | " 7th | | " 6 am & marched to HOLQUE. | " " 7 hrs |
| HOLQUE | " 8th | | Remained in billets. | V. windy. |
| " | " 9th | | " | Rain for 8 hrs. |
| " | " 10th | | " | Showers. |
| " | " 11th | | Paraded 8 am & marched to WIERRE-AU-BOIS | Fine till 7 pm. |
| WIERRE-AU-BOIS | " 12th | | Paraded 9 am & marched to LONGVILLERS. | Rain till 11 am. |
| LONGVILLERS | " 13th | | Lt. C.F. HOLLEBONE struck off (sick). Lt. AC. HOARE to 1st Cav. Div. as Claims Officer | |
| " | " 14th | | Church Parade. | |
| " | " 15th | | Troop Training | |
| " | " 16th | | " | |

# WAR DIARY or INTELLIGENCE SUMMARY.

Army Form C. 2118.

BEDFORDSHIRE YEOMANRY

| Place | Date | Hour | Summary of Events and Information | Remarks and references to Appendices |
|---|---|---|---|---|
| LONGVILLERS | Oct 17th | | Troop Training | |
| " | " 18th | | 5/5 2nd LIFE GUARDS. 33 BEDS YEO. 1 GLASGOW YEO. joined from BASE. | |
| " | " 19th | | Training | |
| " | " 20th | | CAPT PROBY, 2LT FIELDS CLARKE + 74 O.R. proceeded to join PIONEER BATT.(CAVALRY) | |
| " | " 21st | | Church Parade | |
| " | " 22nd | | Troop Training | |
| " | " 23rd | | " " | |
| " | " 24th | | GOC 1st CAV. DIV. inspected the section holders of "D" Sqdn | |
| " | " 25th | | Troop Training | |
| " | " 26th | | 2LT F.N. SHARPE. 2LT E.A. BUTLER. 2LT N.H. CLARKE. 2LT W.S. LUMSDEN joined from ENGLAND | |
| " | " 27th | | Despatch Riders Competition | |
| " | " 28th | | Church Parade | |
| " | " 29th | | Training. Capt g. de L. R. Hargreaves to H.Q. 2nd army as Court Martial Officer. | J/L |
| " | " 30th | | Brigadier inspected D Squadron on Squadron Drill. | |
| " | " 31st | | Training | MB |

Mosley Maj
to 2i-tc
Beds Yeomanry

**WAR DIARY of Bedfordshire Yeomanry**

**INTELLIGENCE SUMMARY**

Army Form C. 2118.

Vol 28

| Place | Date | Hour | Summary of Events and Information | Remarks and references to Appendices |
|---|---|---|---|---|
| LONGVILLERS | 1st Feb | | Inspection of Horses by the Brigadier A.D.V.S. | |
| | 2nd | | Training. Regimental Tactical Scheme. | |
| | 3rd | | " | |
| | | | Seven Remounts & Mule Charger for E.O. arrived. 3009 L/Cpl. Richardson wounded with 1st Bristol Bantry River Battn. Capt. E.G.E. Russell detailed as member of F.G.C.M. whilst serving with 1st Bristol Bantry River Batt. | |
| | 4th | | Church Parade. 2nd/Lt H.P. Fields-Lyon of 1st Bristol Bar. River Batt. | |
| | 5th | | Refitting of Small Box Respirators. Medical Y.G. Battn. H.Q. 1st Cav Div. | |
| | 6th | | Training | |
| | 7th | | 2nd/Lt Bowie & Butler. 30197 Sergt Rusher. 30338 L/Cpl Edwards 30482 L/Cpl Stephen to go to Boures les Samer. | |
| | 8th | | Brigade Route March. Quartermaster Capt. J. Pearce gazetted Major July 1st. | |
| | 9th | | Capt. J. de la P. Hargreaves struck off effective strength | |
| | 10th | | Paraded 10.30 am & marched to AUBIN-ST-VAAST | AUBIN-ST-VAAST |
| AUBIN-ST-VAAST | 11th | | Paraded at 8.45 am & marched to BEAUVOIR-RIVIERE billeted there, via LA PAIX-FAITE-MARENLA-BEAURAINVILLE | |
| MARESQUEL | | | | |
| BEAUVOIR-RIVIERE | 12th | | Paraded at 9.15 am & marched to QUERRIEU billeted there, via MARCONELLE-HESDIN-REGNAUVILLE-TOLLENT-HAVERNAS-FLESSELLES-VILLERS-BOCAGE-ST GRATIEN. | |
| QUERRIEU | 13th | | Paraded at 3.50 pm & marched to MERICOURT billeted there, via DADOURS-FOUILLOY-VAIRE-HAMEL-CERISY. | |
| MERICOURT | 14th | | Paraded at 2.30 pm & marched to MESNIL-BRUNTEL billeted there in huts, via FOUCAUCOURT-VILLERS-CARBONEL-BRIE. | |
| MESNIL-BRUNTEL | 15th | | Consolidating huts & erecting stables. | |

# WAR DIARY
## or
## INTELLIGENCE SUMMARY.

Army Form C. 2118.

| Place | Date | Hour | Summary of Events and Information | Remarks and references to Appendices |
|---|---|---|---|---|
| MESNIL-BRUNTEL | 16th Oct. | | Erecting huts in huts & stabling | |
| | 17th | | Erecting stabling & consolidating huts. Lt. J.G. Brathe M.C. rejoined from 1st Cav. Div. H.Q. | JWB. |
| | 18th | | Church Parade. | |
| | 19th | | Sunday Spare kit & getting ready for move. Lt. J.G. Brathe M.C. attached 1st Cav Div H.Q. as G.S.O.3. 15th Hussars Major Pilkington D.S.O. attached to command the regiment. | |
| METZ | 20th | | Marched 1.45 a.m. to FINS, arrived FINS, 6.15 a.m. off saddled watered & fed, saddled up at 10 a.m. & marched by short stages to METZ, arrived METZ 3.30 p.m. 2000 German Prisoners locked forward through Prisoners bay by 3.30 p.m. Off saddled 11 p.m. Night 20/21st very wet. | |
| METZ | 21st | | Marched via RIBENCOURT to MARCOING, arrived MARCOING 6 p.m. left horses S.E. MARCOING, spent rear of the day saddled up & waiting at RIBENCOURT. Bois de Neuf at 8 p.m. Relief carried over under perfectly quiet conditions. 4th D.Gs. by the 10 centuries broke his arm whilst visiting an advanced post. | |
| MARCOIN | 22nd | | Pte Lancaster killed whilst cooking in empty house. Dismounted party returned to horses at now 9 regiment marched back to bivouac at METZ | |
| METZ | 23rd | | Marched at 8.30 a.m. to FLESQUIERES & took to all day, could see Tanks manoeuvring W of BOURLON WOOD. Went into bivouac 6 p.m. Regiment sent up dismounted party of C & D Squadrons. | JWB. |

**Army Form C. 2118.**

# WAR DIARY
## or
## INTELLIGENCE SUMMARY.
(Erase heading not required.)

Instructions regarding War Diaries and Intelligence Summaries are contained in F. S. Regs., Part II. and the Staff Manual respectively. Title pages will be prepared in manuscript.

| Place | Date | Hour | Summary of Events and Information | Remarks and references to Appendices |
|---|---|---|---|---|
| | NOV | | | |
| | 23rd | | To Suffort 119th Bde at 8 p.m. after marching to GRANDCOURT, the Bde gave dismounted party was placed under the command of Lt. Col. Franks D.S.O. Maj Pilkington D.S.O. q headquarters returning to horses. | |
| FLESQUIER | 24th | | Led horses taken back to METZ at 6.15 p.m. dismounted party sent up at BOURLON WOOD. | |
| METZ | 25th | | Dismounted party still up at BOURLON WOOD, were relieved after dark 9 spent night 25/26th at FLESQUIERES. Capt. A.G. LASCELLES 1st run deg 9 shell shock 2/Lt N.F. Blanks mortally wounded. | |
| | 26th | | Dismounted party returned to METZ. Total casualties 2 officers & 20 O.R. wounded 10 O.R. killed. | |
| | 27th | | Marched at 8.30 a.m via FINS – NURLU – DOMPIERRE to CHUIGNOLLES ? | |
| CHUIGNOLLES | 28th | | Cleaning up all equipment. | |
| | 29th | | do. Maj Pilkington D.S.O. 15th Hussars rejoined his regiment. | MR |
| | 30th | | do. | |
| | | | do. | MR |

W.Henning Major.
Comm g. Regt. Petmoungt.

Army Form C. 2118.

# WAR DIARY
# or
# INTELLIGENCE SUMMARY.

Bedfordshire Yeomanry

(Erase heading not required.)

Instructions regarding War Diaries and Intelligence Summaries are contained in F. S. Regs., Part II. and the Staff Manual respectively. Title pages will be prepared in manuscript.

| Place | Date | Hour | Summary of Events and Information | Remarks and references to Appendices |
|---|---|---|---|---|
| ROISEL | Dec 1st | | Stood to at 30 mins notice from 7 a.m. to 5 p.m. 24th Div Train accommodated officers & O.Rs in Winter quarters for the night 1st/2nd. | |
| | 2nd | | Stood to at 30 mins notice from 6.30 a.m. 5.15 p.m. Sent up a dismounted company of 7 officers & 215 O.Rs under Major A.C.S. Browning. 19th Hussar Headquarters commanding the dismounted companies of the Bde. Dismounted company went into support at REVELON FARM. | |
| | 3rd | | Led horses of regiment returned to CHUIGNOLLES under command of Capt. S. Price Davies. Maj. J.R. Walker remaining at ROISEL as reinforcement. | |
| CHUIGNOLLES | 4th | | Dismounted party came into rest at ROISEL. 2 O.Rs killed. 2 O.Rs wounded. Horses H.Q. at CHUIGNOLLES. | |
| " | 5th | | Horses at CHUIGNOLLES. Dismounted party resting at ROISEL. | |
| " | 6th | | Dismounted party at ROISEL joined into 9th Cav: Dismounted Batt: confined of 19th Hussar boy. 15th Hussar boy. Bedsyes boy. Regimental Headquarters provided by boy 15 ROISEL & relieved 19th Hussars after 48 hours. Maj J.R. Walker commanding 9th Cav dismounted Batt. Capt I.H. Brigg adjutant. Lt R.Price quartermaster. Lt E.W.P.Woodham signal officer. | |
| " | 7th | | Capt. G. Pooley relieved Major M.C.S. Browning commanding Bedsyes Coy. Led Horses at CHUIGNOLLES. 9th Cav Batt dug trenches N of GUYENCOURT 5-8 p.m. Capt Goodman | |
| " | 8th | | 15th Hussars Lt. had 16th Hussars joined 9th Cav dismounted Batt as second-in-command and intelligence officer. | MB |

T2134. Wt. W708-776. 500000. 4/15. Sir J. C. & S.

# WAR DIARY
## of
## INTELLIGENCE SUMMARY. Bedfordshire Yeomanry

Army Form C. 2118.

| Place | Date | Hour | Summary of Events and Information | Remarks and references to Appendices |
|---|---|---|---|---|
| CHUIGNOLLES | Dec: 8th | | Led Horses at CHUIGNOLLES. 9th Cav Dismounted Batt dug trenches as on 7th | |
| " | 9th | | Do. 9th Cav Dismounted Batt: relaid, orders were given later. | |
| " | 10th | | Do. Do. Do. dug trenches as in 8th, 2 companies went up at 99 a.h - 1/2 n. | |
| | | | Casualties caused by enemy aerial bombardment by 15th Hussar Cortrays Batt: Head quarters | |
| | | | Lt Rootham & 3 O.R.s wounded. 16th Hussars Lt Lillyson & 4 O.R.s wounded | |
| " | 11th | | Led Horses at CHUIGNOLLES. Party of 300 hr from 9th Cav Dismounted Battalion worked No 7 GUYENCOURT. | |
| | | | Lt Rootham died of wounds. | |
| " | 12th | | Do. 9th Cav Dismounted Batt: rested | |
| " | 13th | | Do. Do dug trenches No 7 GUYENCOURT. | |
| " | 14th | | Do. Major W.C.S. Binning reported in Richelieu. Do. | |
| " | 15th | | Do. 9th Cav Dismounted Batt: rested | |
| " | 16th | | Do. 9th Cav Dismounted Batt relieved by train to BRAY, en-route to | |
| | | | joining their regiments | |
| " | 17th | | The day spent getting the horses & equipment etc cleaned | |
| " | 18th | | Marched via FOUCAUCOURT. VILLERS CARBONNEL. BRIE to LE MESNIL BRUNTEL | MB |
| | | | roads covered with frozen snow, led horses all the way. Found huts at MESNIL BRUNTEL | |

Army Form C. 2118.

# WAR DIARY
## INTELLIGENCE SUMMARY

Bedfordshire Yeomanry

(Erase heading not required.)

Instructions regarding War Diaries and Intelligence Summaries are contained in F. S. Regs., Part II. and the Staff Manual respectively. Title pages will be prepared in manuscript.

| Place | Date | Hour | Summary of Events and Information | Remarks and references to Appendices |
|---|---|---|---|---|
| | Dec. | | | |
| MESNIL- BRUNTEL | 19th | | Badly knocked about, very bad accomodation for officers/men | |
| | 20th | | Working in camp, erecting stabling, latrines etc. Mr. J. G. Crabbie M.C. gazetted out whilst employed as adjutant | |
| | 21st | | Do | |
| | 22nd | | Do | |
| | 23rd | | Do | |
| | 24th | | Do | |
| | 25th | | Church Services | |
| | 26th | | Nothing in camp, erecting stabling latrines etc. D Squadron had Xmas dinner in marquee lent by Y.M.C.A. | |
| | 27th | | Do     C. Squadron had Xmas dinner | |
| | 28th | | Do     A  Do  Do  Do | |
| | 29th | | Do     H.Q Do  Do  Do | |
| | 30th | | Do | |
| | 31st | | Do | |

Mowbray Lt Col
Commanding Bedfd Yeo

JMB.

CONFIDENTIAL.
=============

WAR DIARY

BEDFORDSHIRE YEOMANRY

JANUARY

1918.

Volume No. 42.

Army Form C. 2118.

# WAR DIARY
## or
## INTELLIGENCE SUMMARY. BEDFORDSHIRE YEOMANRY
*(Erase heading not required.)*

Instructions regarding War Diaries and Intelligence Summaries are contained in F. S. Regs., Part II. and the Staff Manual respectively. Title pages will be prepared in manuscript.

| Place | Date | Hour | Summary of Events and Information | Remarks and references to Appendices |
|---|---|---|---|---|
| | 1918 Jan. | | | |
| LE MESNIL-BRUNTEL | 1 | | Working on Camp, erecting Stables and Latrines etc. | |
| | 2 | | do | |
| | 3 | | do | |
| | 4 | | do Capt. C.M. Kadlow awarded D.S.O. | |
| | 5 | | do 3 Officers & 12 O.R. proceeded to Cav. School at DROURS | |
| | 6 | | Medical Inspection by M.O. of Horses & Repines. Church Service. Capt. J. Holmes struck off effective strength on appointment as A.P.M. 1st Cav. Divn. | |
| | 7 | | Working in Camp, erecting Stables and Stablements etc. | |
| | 8 | | do Parade for all Signallers | |
| | 9 | | do | |
| | 10 | | do Major Pearce granted 1 months leave to England | |
| | 11 | | do | |
| | 12 | | do the Regiment provided a guard of honour at a presentation of Medal Ribbons by the Corps Commander in LE MESNIL-BRUNTEL Church Service. Major J.B. Walker promoted A/Lt. Col. while Commanding the Regt. | MJR |
| | 13 | | | |

Army Form C. 2118.

# WAR DIARY
## or
## INTELLIGENCE SUMMARY.
(Erase heading not required.)

BEDFORDSHIRE YEOMANRY

| Place | Date | Hour | Summary of Events and Information | Remarks and references to Appendices |
|---|---|---|---|---|
| LE MESNIL BRUNTEL | 1918 Jan 14. | | 9th Dismounted Brigade relieved part of the 3rd Dismounted Division at VADENCOURT. 15th Hussars Head Quarters Commanding. Beds. two Coy formed as under:— Capt Ruindl in command — Lt Foster 2nd in command — Lt Andrew 2nd Lt Chapin Maton commander. Lr Souton Transport Officer (on H.Q.) 212 O.R. † 15 Horses Jarton in Clergy Transferred to 2nd Cav. Bgde Hd. † Interpreter Gerard Nakin on Strength from 2nd Car. Bde H.Q. Capt. C.F.W. Russell transferred to T.F. Reserve | |
| | 15. | | Work in Camp. Dismounted Party been killed 2nd Lt Andrew severely wounded 3 O.R. Killed 4 O.R. died of wounds and 120 O.R. wounded Capt J.G. Gatte M.C. att'd to G.S.O. 3rd grade and Struck of strength. Capt J.E.D. Holland M.C. 5th D.G. appointed 2nd in command of 15 Regt. 1 O.R. died of Pneumonia in hospital | |
| | 16. | | Work in Camp. | |
| | 17. | | Work in Camp. Baths for men at BUIRE. | |
| | 18. | | do do do and at LEMESNIL-BRUNTEL. | |
| | 19. | | do do do | ACR |
| | 20. | | Voluntary Church Services. 3 O.R.'s returned from course of Sanitation. | ACR |
| | 21st | | Work in Camp. Capt. J.W. Roig appointed adjutant with effect from 9th Jan/18 and Lt(a/Capt) J.G. Gratle M.C. appointed B.S.O.3 for tear Div with effect from 9th Jan/18 | JWB |

# WAR DIARY
## or
## INTELLIGENCE SUMMARY
(Erase heading not required.)

BEDFORDSHIRE YEOMANRY

Army Form C. 2118.

| Place | Date | Hour | Summary of Events and Information | Remarks and references to Appendices |
|---|---|---|---|---|
| LE MESNIL-BRUNTEL | 1918 JAN. 22nd | | Work in Camp. 3 first class signallers to 1st Dismounted Div. H.Q. | |
| | 23rd | | " " " | |
| | 24th | | " " " Major ct C.S. Benning president of Board of Inquiry as to the finding of a German Balloon. | |
| | 25th | | " " " | |
| | 26th | | " " " | |
| | 27th | | Church Parade. Lieut. P.W. Priestly to England. Strength off. Dismounted party returned 7 Officers 1900 R & 1517 horses. Lieut Penton from Cav. Corps Equitation School. | |
| | 28th | | Baths at BUIRE & disinfection of clothing. | |
| | 29th | | Work in Camp. Revetting of huts | |
| | 30th | | G.O.C. 1st Cav Div inspected stretcher of the regiment. | |
| | 31st | | G.O.C. 9th Cav Bde inspected Equitation. Blanco, N.C.O.s & Kitchen in Camp. G.O.C. 9th Cav Bde also addressed Officers & N.C.O.s on the subject of Gen: Sir H de la P Gough's letter. | MB |

Russell Capt
for Major Commanding
Beds Yeomanry

# WAR DIARY
## or
## INTELLIGENCE SUMMARY.

Army Form C. 2118.

BEDFORDSHIRE YEOMANRY

| Place | Date 1918 Feb | Hour | Summary of Events and Information | Remarks and references to Appendices |
|---|---|---|---|---|
| LE MESNIL-BRUNTEL | 1 | | 150 O.R.s proceeded to near JEANCOURT for digging returned same day. Capt Swetenham R.A.M.C. to No. 3 C.F.A. and Lieut Feldman R.A.M.C. from 3rd C.F.A. joined the regiment. | |
| | 2 | | 150 O.Rs proceeded to near JEANCOURT for digging returned same day. W.O.CL. 1 6 aw Sn vacated on arrival of the regiment. 300003 S.Q.M.S. Tregey 93010 Lock Barlow awarded Belgian Croix de Guerre. | |
| | 3 | | 150 O.R.s proceeded to near JEANCOURT for digging returned same day. 30146 Pte Wainwright awarded Pte wts | |
| | 4 | | Voluntary Church Service. 200 O.R.s proceeded to near JEANCOURT for digging returned same day. | |
| | 5 | | 150 O.R.s proceeded to near JEANCOURT for digging returned same day. Capt. C.G.E. Pearce attached to 35th Squadron R.F.C. as Intelligence Officer. | |
| | 6 | | 150 O.R.s proceeded to near VADENCOURT for digging returned same day. | |
| | 7 | | 4 Officers and 1650 O.R.s 98 mules proceeded to join the 9th Pioneer Regt. 80.R.s attached to 258 Tunnelling Coy | |
| | 8 | | 10 R.s to Baw Cords Gas School. Resetting of Hubs. | |
| | 9th | | Work in camp. Resetting of Hubs. | |
| | 10th | | Voluntary Church Services | |
| | 11th | | Work in camp. 2nd Lieut R.S. Knight rejoined regiment for duties. 2nd Lt J Thacker Rb joined from England. | yrs. |

# WAR DIARY or INTELLIGENCE SUMMARY

Army Form C. 2118.

BEDFORDSHIRE YEOMANRY

| Place | Date 1918 | Hour | Summary of Events and Information | Remarks and references to Appendices |
|---|---|---|---|---|
| LE MESNIL BRUNTEL | Feb. 12 | | Rotn in Camp. 2nd Lieut P.I. Hartigan, 2nd Lieut J.B. Stair, 2nd Lieut A. Ireland, 2nd Lieut J.G. Livingstone joined the regiment from England | |
| | 13 | | 4 Officers & 162 O.R.s.& horses rejoined from 4th Pioneer Regt. Rotn in Camp | |
| | 14 | | Rotn in Camp | |
| | 15 | | 8 Officers & 198 O.R.s. & 12 horses proceeded with 9th Bn Devons Bde to VADENCOURT | |
| | 16 | | Voluntary Church Services | |
| | 17 | | Rotn in Camp | |
| | 18 | | do | |
| | 19 | | do | |
| | 20 | | do | |
| | 21 | | do. Lieut R.W. Lawrence resigns his commission on account of ill health | |
| | 22 | | do | |
| | 23 | | do | |
| | 24 | | do. Voluntary Church Services | |
| | 25 | | do. Commenced ploughing up land for potatoes & vegetables | |
| | 26 | | do. Continued ploughing | WB |

Army Form C. 2118.

# WAR DIARY
## or
## INTELLIGENCE SUMMARY.
*(Erase heading not required.)*

BEDFORDSHIRE YEOMANRY

Instructions regarding War Diaries and Intelligence Summaries are contained in F. S. Regs., Part II. and the Staff Manual respectively. Title pages will be prepared in manuscript.

| Place | Date | Hour | Summary of Events and Information | Remarks and references to Appendices |
|---|---|---|---|---|
| | 1918 Feb | | | |
| LE MESNIL | 27 | | Working party. Continued ploughing | |
| BRUNTEL | 28 | | do. do. 2 Officers & 8 O.R.s for Divisional School rejoined | MB |

JWalker Lieut Colonel
commanding Bedfordshire Yeomanry

10045/1116/2

## 1915-1916
## 1ST CAVALRY DIVISION
## 9TH CAVALRY BRIGADE

I/I  WARWICK R.H.A.
~~SHIRE~~
~~JUN 1915~~-OCT 1916
OCT 1914

To 15 BDE R H A
29 DIV TROOPS
Box 2294

2nd Cavalry Divisional Artillery.
----------

Disembarked Havre 1.11.14.

WARWICKSHIRE BATTERY R. H. A.

OCTOBER 1914.

Army Form C. 2118.

# WAR DIARY
## or
## INTELLIGENCE SUMMARY.

*(Erase heading not required.)*

Instructions regarding War Diaries and Intelligence Summaries are contained in F. S. Regs., Part II. and the Staff Manual respectively. Title pages will be prepared in manuscript.

| Hour, Date, Place | Summary of Events and Information | Remarks and references to Appendices |
|---|---|---|
| At Newbury. Oct 1st/14 | | Fine |
| At Newbury. Oct. 2nd/14 | | Fine |
| At Newbury. Oct. 3rd/14 | | Overcast. |
| At Newbury Oct 4th/14. | Church parade 9.30. | Fine, warmer. |
| At Newbury. Oct 5/14 | An armourer-artificer arrived from Ho. C. Camp at Churn to adjust sights re- During rifle-horse no 34 bolted and owing to fractured tibia, destroyed. O.C. and Adjutant proceeded to Thatcham to inspect proposed billets there | Fine |
| At Newbury Oct. 6th/14. | | Fine |
| At Newbury Oct-7th/14. | Field day. Scheme to resist an attack from Churn & Streatly | Fine. |

(9-29 6) W 2794 100,000 8/14 H W V Forms/C. 2118/11.

Army Form C. 2118.

# WAR DIARY
## or
## INTELLIGENCE SUMMARY.
*(Erase heading not required.)*

Instructions regarding War Diaries and Intelligence Summaries are contained in F. S. Regs., Part II. and the Staff Manual respectively. Title pages will be prepared in manuscript.

| Hour, Date, Place | Summary of Events and Information | Remarks and references to Appendices |
|---|---|---|
| At Newbury Oct. 8/14 | Inspection by H.M. the King at Churn Camp. H.M. His Majesty was previously pleased to issue a statement congratulating the Troops inspected on their appearance. | Very Cold, fine later. |
| At Newbury, Oct 9th/14 | The Brigadier inspected horses of Battery & Amm. Column and recommended that Horses Nos 97, 178 be drafted for Territorial training and that Horse No 215 be Cast as unfit for Artillery duty. | Cold, fine. |
| At Newbury Oct. 10th/14 | About 10.25 Brigadier called with reference to men's clothing. | Fine |
| At Newbury Oct 11/14 | Church parade 9.30 a.m. Foot inspection 11.15 a.m. | Fine |
| At Newbury Oct 12th/14 | About 10.30 a.m. the I.G.M. and D.A.D.O.S called and inspected harness & saddlery of Battery both the crew of replacing cast stuff with serviceable Equipment | Fine |

(signature)

Army Form C. 2118.

# WAR DIARY
## or
## INTELLIGENCE SUMMARY.
(Erase heading not required.)

Instructions regarding War Diaries and Intelligence Summaries are contained in F. S. Regs., Part II. and the Staff Manual respectively. Title pages will be prepared in manuscript.

| Hour, Date, Place | Summary of Events and Information | Remarks and references to Appendices |
|---|---|---|
| At Newbury Oct 13/14 | About 7.45 pm Cap'n Lindsay, R.H.A. Staff Officer to 2nd Newbury H.A.C. called with reference to Equipment and transport for foreign service. | Broken weather. Wet. |
| At Newbury Oct 14/14 | At 11 am General Clayton inspected Ammn Column together with other units of the Brigade. | Cold, raw. |
| At Newbury Oct 15/14 | Inspection by Gen'l Payton in Newbury Common 9 am | Perfect |
| At Newbury Oct 16/14 | At 8 am Battery proceeded to Thatcham Villa's, the Battery billeting at Hartshill farm house, the Columns in the village's guns, horses, loads being parked in an adjacent field. | Dull, cold |
| At Thatcham Oct 17/14 | — | Dull |
| At Thatcham Oct 18/14 | — | Fine, cold |

Army Form C. 2118.

# WAR DIARY
or
## INTELLIGENCE SUMMARY.
(Erase heading not required.)

Instructions regarding War Diaries and Intelligence Summaries are contained in F. S. Regs., Part II. and the Staff Manual respectively. Title pages will be prepared in manuscript.

| Hour, Date, Place | Summary of Events and Information | Remarks and references to Appendices |
|---|---|---|
| At Thatcham Oct 19th/14 | The OC proceeded to Goring Street - Genl. Paton & other ORs at 3 pm. | Fine. |
| At Thatcham Oct 20/14 | About 4.30 pm a call from the Brigadier | Fine. |
| At Thatcham Oct 21st/14 | Twenty (20) heavy horses proceeded to Reading and were delivered to OC Remounts by Lieut Felden A.V.C. Lieut. Woodhouse & R.Q.D. with 2 men proceeded to Woolwich. Arrived with horses. Works for conversion. Horse No 18 died. Cause of death, suffocation | Fine. |
| At Thatcham Oct 22/14 | — | Heavy rain. |
| At Thatcham Oct 23/14 | — | Dull. |
| At Thatcham Oct 24/14 | — | Very wet. |

(9 29 6) W 2794 100,000 8/14 H W V Forms/C. 2118/11.

Army Form C. 2118.

# WAR DIARY
## or
## INTELLIGENCE SUMMARY.
*(Erase heading not required.)*

Instructions regarding War Diaries and Intelligence Summaries are contained in F. S. Regs., Part II. and the Staff Manual respectively. Title pages will be prepared in manuscript.

| Hour, Date, Place | Summary of Events and Information | Remarks and references to Appendices |
|---|---|---|
| At Hatcham Oct 25/14 | Church Parade 9.30 am. The Rev Canon Robotte officiating | Rainy, dull. |
| At Hatcham Oct 26/14 | During morning Lieut Loo-Thorne proceeded to Remount depot at Reading. In the afternoon Major Maclure, Capt Rawdon, & Capt Sinclair RFA called at 6 pm. (The Brigadier met all officers of the Brigade at Worcester Nursery H.Q.) | Dull |
| At Hatcham Oct 27/14 | At 10.30 am Battery proceeded to Hampstead Norris to take over guns firing Bk pop no 5. In the afternoon Capt Sinclair & H.A. C. the Adjutant-foring also. Capt Hodgkinson called in afternoon. | Fine |
| At Hatcham Oct 28/14 | The Brigadier called at 4.30. Some amounts for Officers charges received were afterward | Colder |

# WAR DIARY
## or
## INTELLIGENCE SUMMARY.
*(Erase heading not required.)*

Army Form C. 2118.

Instructions regarding War Diaries and Intelligence Summaries are contained in F. S. Regs., Part II. and the Staff Manual respectively. Title pages will be prepared in manuscript.

| Hour, Date, Place | Summary of Events and Information | Remarks and references to Appendices |
|---|---|---|
| At Thatcham Oct 29/14 | Woolwich artificers who had arrived 28th inst. completed their tank on guns. Blankets, Medical stores, iron stores, cardigan jackets, woolwear issued. A Staff Superintendent Woolwich Arsenal arrived by motor. Col. Munro A.D.D. arrived & inspected Horse Hooks. Capt Sinclair called also our A.S.C. Officer about 2.30 & take over Civilian wagons. Col. Butler, 2nd in 1st Div. called at 10.30 also Col. Brown, A.P.C. about 2.30. | Collier |
| At Thatcham Oct 30/14 | At 6am a party under the Captain went to Newbury Station Wet, variable. Were 12 Service wagons & two water carts were drawn; also five armoured stores, including 3 bicycles from Woolwich. Progress towards departure was made and at 2 pm the Rt Section under OC proceeded to Newbury to entrain leaving for Southampton at 3.45 pm. Two other trains with left Section and Amm. Col. left later. On arrival at Southampton |  |

Army Form C. 2118.

# WAR DIARY
## or
## INTELLIGENCE SUMMARY.
*(Erase heading not required.)*

Instructions regarding War Diaries and Intelligence Summaries are contained in F. S. Regs., Part II. and the Staff Manual respectively. Title pages will be prepared in manuscript.

| Hour, Date, Place | Summary of Events and Information | Remarks and references to Appendices |
|---|---|---|
| At Chatham. Oct 30/14 (Continued). | The Battery boarded H.M. Transport "Victorian" the last load getting aboard about 11.0 p.m. Previous to starting five horses were cast on the quay by the Inspecting Veterinary Officer. These were not replaced. | |
| At Sea. Oct 31st/14. | The Transport "Victorian" left for Havre about 1.30 a.m. arriving in the Estuary about 1 p.m. Going to port of Havre the troops on board passed night on ship. | Weather fine and clear. Sea calm. |

2nd Cavalry Divisional Artillery.
-----------------------

Disembarked Havre 1.11.14.

WARWICKSHIRE BATTERY R. H. A.

NOVEMBER 1914.

# WAR DIARY or INTELLIGENCE SUMMARY.

(Erase heading not required.)

Army Form C. 2118.

| Hour, Date, Place | Summary of Events and Information | Remarks and references to Appendices |
|---|---|---|
| In Port at HAVRE. Nov. 1st 1914. | During morning unloading. It was found in process that a number of top-rails of gun & wagon limbers were badly bent. Several G.S. wagons also received injury. It must be noted that these injuries did not occur at LA HAVRE but doubtless occurred at SOUTHAMPTON during Embarkation. Later Battery proceeded to Camp at LA HÈVE. | Fine. |
| At LA HÈVE. Nov 2nd 1914. | Very wet night clearing about 9.15 am. Inspection of all stores. In afternoon Battery received orders to entrain at LA HAVRE with 3 days rations & did so the 1st train leaving at 4.59 am the next day. | Fine; frosty. |
| In train. Nov 3rd 1914. In train. Nov 4th 1914. | ST OMER was reached about 4.0 a.m. Later Battery proceeded to the village of ESQUERDES to billets. Very bad weather. Maj LEMIN RFA had arranged for billets. In afternoon a Staff Officer called with reference to Battery & Am [Ammunition] Column's arrangements & return. | Fine. Fog, wet. |

Army Form C. 2118.

# WAR DIARY
## or
## INTELLIGENCE SUMMARY.

(Erase heading not required.)

Instructions regarding War Diaries and Intelligence Summaries are contained in F. S. Regs., Part II. and the Staff Manual respectively. Title pages will be prepared in manuscript.

| Hour, Date, Place | Summary of Events and Information | Remarks and references to Appendices |
|---|---|---|
| At ESQUERDES Nov 5th 1914 | Battery billeted in Brit buildings. Two Transport officers called, also Col. Lord Brooke Br. V.O. | Fine, mild. |
| At ESQUERDES Nov 6th 1914 | Dr. Sir JOHN FRENCH called informally inspecting Battery and informing a few words as to his pleasure in seeing them out in France. Gr. CROFT was removed to No. 10 Stat. Vetry Hospital, SKOMER suffering from pneumonia. About 25 horses sick. | Fine, warm. |
| At ESQUERDES Nov 7th 1914 | One fresh case of pneumonia among horses. | Fine. |
| At ESQUERDES Nov 8th 1914 | Col. Lord Brooke called from HQ in motor. Stood by as apparent to firing line to observe fire. Battery carried out sabre cleaning practice. | Fog; fine later. |
| At ESQUERDES Nov 9th 1914 | Entrenching practice continued. Horse No. 73 died of double pneumonia. | Fog; fair later. |
| At ESQUERDES Nov 10th 1914 | Early in morning horse No. 9 died of enteritis. Capt. Seledon A.V.C. attributes the sickness to draft of horses sent from READING to THATCHAM just prior to departure. | Fog; damp. |

Army Form C. 2118.

# WAR DIARY
## or
## INTELLIGENCE SUMMARY.
*(Erase heading not required.)*

Instructions regarding War Diaries and Intelligence Summaries are contained in F. S. Regs., Part II. and the Staff Manual respectively. Title pages will be prepared in manuscript.

| Hour, Date, Place | Summary of Events and Information | Remarks and references to Appendices |
|---|---|---|
| At ESQUERDES. Nov. 11th 1914. | Maj. Genl. Chichester called about 5 p.m. | Dull, windy. |
| At ESQUERDES. Nov. 12th 1914. | Another call from Maj. Genl. Chichester but he did not see C.O. as we were out looking for alternative billets owing to continued sickness among horses. Sense of pistol in which Battery was parked called, complaining of injury to his permanent pasture. Capt. told him to place his complaint before Mayor of ESQUERDES. | Fine, cold. Very wet. |
| At ESQUERDES. Nov. 13th 1914. | | |
| At ESQUERDES. Nov. 14th 1914. | Battery moved to another field, the former one being become impossible to get from. In aft. a Staff A.V.O. called. | wet. |
| At ESQUERDES. Nov. 15th 1914. | About 10.15 a.m. an order was received from G.H.Q. to provide a gun-carriage for coffin of the late F.M. Earl Roberts. This was duly attended to as about 1.15 p.m. a gun with a detachment, under Lieut. R.C. Woodhouse proceeded to ST. OMER. Horse No. 203 died. Col. Lord Brooke M.V.O. called about 11.30 a.m. | Very wet. |

(Signed)

# WAR DIARY or INTELLIGENCE SUMMARY

Army Form C. 2118.

| Hour, Date, Place | Summary of Events and Information | Remarks and references to Appendices |
|---|---|---|
| At ESQUERDES. Nov. 16th 1914 | Sergt. Major Jones, with men, left for BOULOGNE to bring in Remounts. | Very wet. |
| At ESQUERDES. Nov. 17th 1914. | About 7.15 a.m. a detachment proceeded to ST OMER & acted as Guard of honour to the body of the late F.M. Earl Roberts. The gun carriage & detachment returned to billets about 11.45 a.m. During evening Sergt. Major Jones arrived from BOULOGNE with remounts having been much delayed by trains between stoppages. | Very wet. |
| At ESQUERDES. Nov. 18th 1914. | | Whole foot, slaughter. |
| At ESQUERDES. Nov. 19th 1914. | | Frost; snow; cold. |
| At ESQUERDES. Nov. 20th 1914. | Having opened in Standing Orders that the Battery had proceeded to HAZEBROUCK Battery remained in readiness to proceed, if orders came. Turn out 9.30 a.m. On road a Staff officer arrived with orders C.O. to proceed to VIEUX BERQUIN. Capt. + a Billeting party were sent on by motors + motor-bus. The Battery, owing to state of roads has forced to stop for night in billets at— EBLINGHEM. Two, (2) horses had to be left behind at— CONFOSSE MILL – (ESQUERDES) as unfit to travel. | Restrictions, roads, cold. Roads practically impassable. |

Ormsby

Army Form C. 2118.

# WAR DIARY
## or
## INTELLIGENCE SUMMARY.
*(Erase heading not required.)*

Instructions regarding War Diaries and Intelligence Summaries are contained in F. S. Regs., Part II. and the Staff Manual respectively. Title pages will be prepared in manuscript.

| Hour, Date, Place | Summary of Events and Information | Remarks and references to Appendices |
|---|---|---|
| At ESQUERDES - EBLINGHEM - | In morning Battery recommenced march arriving at VIEUX | Snow. Cold. |
| VIEUX-BERCQUIN. Nov 21st 1914. | BERCQUIN Billets about 4.30 p.m. | |
| at VIEUX BERCQUIN. Nov 22nd 1914. | Col. Lord Brooke. M.V.O. called. | Cold. Frost. |
| at VIEUX - BERCQUIN. Nov 23rd 1914. | 45 horses from ammunition column left to join Divisional Train continued. | |
| | Column. A mare jane birth prematurely to foal. | |
| at VIEUX - BERCQUIN. Nov 24th 1914. | Two officers from "D" Battery R.H.A called and gave | Slight thaw. |
| | most useful hints to both officers & men on their experience. | |
| at VIEUX - BERCQUIN. Nov 25th 1914. | Digging & more useful hints from officers referred to in | Cold a Thaw. |
| | date above. | |
| at VIEUX - BERCQUIN. Nov 26/1914. | | Cold; thaw after night-frost. |
| at VIEUX -BERCQUIN. Nov 27th 1914. | | Fine; very muddy. |
| at VIEUX. BERCQUIN. Nov 28th 1914. | Lieut Moore took over duty from Lieut Parker "D" Sub-section | heavier, and chilly |
| | Letter going to Ammunition Column - Another Battery mare | |
| | was prematurely confined of a foal. | |
| at VIEUX. BERCQUIN. Nov 29th 1914. | | Blustery, |
| at VIEUX - BERCQUIN. Nov 30th 1914. | | Very windy |

2nd Cavalry Divisional Artillery.
----------------

WARWICKSHIRE BATTERY R. H. A.

DECEMBER 1914.

# WAR DIARY
## or
## INTELLIGENCE SUMMARY.
*(Erase heading not required.)*

Army Form C. 2118.

| Hour, Date, Place | Summary of Events and Information | Remarks and references to Appendices |
|---|---|---|
| At VIEUX-BERCQUIN. Dec 1st 1914. | A hostile aeroplane was observed by N.O. while Battery was carrying out manoeuvres. | Windy, warmer. |
| At VIEUX-BERCQUIN. Dec 2 1914. | At 9.15 a.m. the Battery proceeded to a position about 2 miles N. of LATOUR BLUE on the road V.BERCQUIN-BAILLEUL and were inspected by H.M. the KING about 11.30 a.m. accompanied by H.R.H. the Prince of Wales. H.M. exchanged a few words of greeting with O.C. who afterwards called for 3 cheers for H.M. | Warm, colder later. |
| At VIEUX-BERCQUIN. Dec 3rd 1914. | Battery fine drill 9 a.m. Gen¹ GOUGH joining Battery at MERRIS. Sir John's horse-keepers arrived & sent on ead. | Cold, rainy. |
| At VIEUX-BERCQUIN. Dec 4th 1914. | Fatigue orders for inspection by F.M. Sir JOHN FRENCH. Order cancelled later. | Cold, wet; very windy. |
| At VIEUX-BERCQUIN. Dec 5th 1914. | A Staff Officer called about 1.30 with reference to Saddles. | Very wet. |
| At VIEUX-BERCQUIN. Dec 6th 1914. | | Frost at night; cold. |
| At VIEUX-BERCQUIN. Dec 7th 1914. | Dismounted parade at 10.45 a.m. Battery proceeded to VIEUX-BERCQUIN school, with other units of the 2nd DIV'N Div, were inspected by F.M. Sir JOHN FRENCH. | Milder, wet. |

Chomley

Army Form C. 2118.

# WAR DIARY
## or
## INTELLIGENCE SUMMARY.
(Erase heading not required.)

Instructions regarding War Diaries and Intelligence Summaries are contained in F. S. Regs., Part II. and the Staff Manual respectively. Title pages will be prepared in manuscript.

| Hour, Date, Place | Summary of Events and Information | Remarks and references to Appendices |
|---|---|---|
| At Vieux-BERCQUIN. Dec. 8th 1914. | — | Dull, warmer. |
| At Vieux-BERCQUIN. Dec. 9th 1914. | Visit from Army Paymaster 1.30 p.m. | Very wet. |
| At Vieux-BERCQUIN. Dec. 10th 1914. | — | Dull, drizzle. |
| At Vieux-BERCQUIN. Dec. 11th 1914. | An order arrived during morning for Battery to proceed to "F" Battery's trenches for firing. This order was subsequently cancelled until the morrow. The O.C. proceeded to reconnoitre position. | Cold, damp. |
| At Vieux-BERCQUIN. Dec. 12th 1914. | Battery paraded at 10 a.m. and reached billets at PONT MORTIER shortly. 1 p.m. Received orders to take up a position prepared by "J" Battery RHA ½ mile S. of FLEURBAIX to be in position before day-light. | |
| In "F" Battery's Trenches Dec 13 1914. | Shelling of farm-house believed to contain snipers, subsequently Right section only of Battery operating. Enemy's trenches. Two German Laying good if fuses burning regularly. Batteries replied but at first failed to find range. They however subsequently obtained range, shooting accurate | Cold, wet.  Clouded. |

Army Form C. 2118.

# WAR DIARY
or
## INTELLIGENCE SUMMARY.
(Erase heading not required.)

Instructions regarding War Diaries and Intelligence Summaries are contained in F. S. Regs., Part II. and the Staff Manual respectively. Title pages will be prepared in manuscript.

| Hour, Date, Place | Summary of Events and Information | Remarks and references to Appendices |
|---|---|---|
| Dec. 13th (continued) | Shooting. Detachments took cover in "dug-outs" and Section had to withdraw at Dusk. No casualties. | |
| R. TRENCHES near FLEURBAIX Dec. 14th 1914. | This day Battery did not go into action. G.O.C.R.A. III Div. (General Jackson) instructed one Section to prepare a position about ½ mile W. of that previously occupied. | Dull, cold. |
| Near FLEURBAIX. Dec 15th 1914 | Officers and gunners marched to new position and spent the day preparing it for guns. | Cold, raw. |
| Near FLEURBAIX. Dec 16th 1914. | At 4 a.m. L Section marched to take up position. Fire was opened at about 9 a.m. under the direction of O.C. XIV Brigade R.H.A (Col Robinson). Enemy replied with 5.9" guns. Explosive shrapnel then charging to high explosives. A Mare gave premature birth to foal while being harnessed up. No casualties. | Cold - drizzly. |
| At FLEURBAIX. Dec 17th 1914. | L Section & 1st Line Wagon returned to permanent billets at V. BERCQUIN. The R Section re-occupied position of previous day, Shelling Enemy's Trenches. Trees burnt differently | Cold, damp. |

Army Form C. 2118.

# WAR DIARY
## or
## INTELLIGENCE SUMMARY.
(Erase heading not required.)

Instructions regarding War Diaries and Intelligence Summaries are contained in F. S. Regs., Part II. and the Staff Manual respectively. Title pages will be prepared in manuscript.

| Hour, Date, Place | Summary of Events and Information | Remarks and references to Appendices |
|---|---|---|
| At Hurbain (cont.) | Horse on previous day being 12 over. A horse had to be destroyed being unfit to march. No casualties. | |
| At VIEUX-BERCQUIN. Dec 18th 1914. | Very bad weather. The Battery "stood to" by order. | Wet; windy. |
| At VIEUX-BERCQUIN. Dec 19th 1914. | | Wet; windy. |
| At VIEUX-BERCQUIN. Dec 20th 1914. | | Wet; very at intervals. |
| At VIEUX-BERCQUIN. Dec 21st 1914. | Genl Allenby was expected but by unforseen circum- Stances was unable to do so. | Wet. |
| At VIEUX-BERCQUIN. Dec 22nd 1914. | | Wet. |
| At VIEUX-BERCQUIN. Dec 23rd 1914. | | Snow; very cold. |
| At VIEUX-BERCQUIN. Dec 24th 1914. | A horse was drowned in a ditch during night. | Cold; fine. |
| At VIEUX-BERCQUIN. Dec 25th 1914. | Xmas Day. The Battery received the usual gifts from their Majesties & Princess Mary. | Sharp frost. |
| At VIEUX-BERCQUIN. Dec 27th 1914. | | Cold; wet. |
| At VIEUX-BERCQUIN. Dec 28th 1914. | | Cold; wet. |
| At VIEUX-BERCQUIN. Dec 29th 1914. | | Cold; wet. |
| At VIEUX-BERCQUIN. Dec 30th 1914. | Route march 9.30 am. | Rain, frosty later. |

(9 29 6) W 2794 100,000 8/14 HWV Forms/C. 2118/11.

Army Form C. 2118.

# WAR DIARY
## or
## INTELLIGENCE SUMMARY.
*(Erase heading not required.)*

Instructions regarding War Diaries and Intelligence Summaries are contained in F. S. Regs., Part II. and the Staff Manual respectively. Title pages will be prepared in manuscript.

| Hour, Date, Place | Summary of Events and Information | Remarks and references to Appendices |
|---|---|---|
| Athies BERCourt Dec 3, 1916 | In morning Army Paymaster called. In the afternoon Foot, rain later. General Gough also called. | |

Major General Commanding R.H.A.

A2 AG.6.

121/4257

b/ 2nd Cavalry Division

Warwickshire R.H.A.

Vol II. 1 — 31.1.15

Nil

CONFIDENTIAL

WAR DIARY.
of
WARWICKSHIRE. R.H.A.
from Jan 1st 1915. to Jan 31st 1915.

Army Form C. 2118.

# WAR DIARY
*or*
# INTELLIGENCE SUMMARY.
*(Erase heading not required.)*

Instructions regarding War Diaries and Intelligence Summaries are contained in F. S. Regs., Part II. and the Staff Manual respectively. Title pages will be prepared in manuscript.

| Hour, Date, Place | Summary of Events and Information | Remarks and references to Appendices |
|---|---|---|
| | | |

(73959) W4141—463. 400,000. 9/14. H.&J.,Ltd. Forms/C. 2118/10.

**Army Form C. 2118.**

# WAR DIARY
## or
## INTELLIGENCE SUMMARY.
*(Erase heading not required.)*

Instructions regarding War Diaries and Intelligence Summaries are contained in F.S. Regs., Part II. and the Staff Manual respectively. Title pages will be prepared in manuscript.

| Hour, Date, Place | Summary of Events and Information | Remarks and references to Appendices |
|---|---|---|
| Jan. 1st 1915. VIEUX BERQUIN. | | |
| Jan. 2nd " " | Lieut Earl Poulett & Capt Seldon returned from leave. batch left. | W.M. |
| Jan. 3rd " " | Church Parade - Lieut WOODHOUSE reported from leave. very cold | W.M. |
| Jan. 4th " " | 10 horses sent up to H.Q for cooking. 6 Cook & returned | W.M. |
| Jan. 5th " " | Maj. MURRAY returned from leave. | W.M. |
| Jan. 6th " " | Maj GEMMELL left for england on leave. | W.M. |
| Jan. 7 " " | very wet | |
| Jan. 8. " " | Orders received at 10.15 a.m. to proceed following day to 2nd IND. Division. 6th Lieutpunt attached in replacement of LOCON. | W.M. |
| Jan. 9. " VIEILLE CHAPELLE. | Marched with firing batty & 1st line wagon and ammunition Column to billets near VIEILLE CHAPELLE - 1 horse died on the march. Details left with sat VIEUX-BERQUIN. | W.M. |
| Jan. 10th " VIEILLE CHAPELLE | position reconnoitred - Lieut CLAYTON came. returned | W.M. |
| Jan. 11 " " | Battery marched at daybreak to a position about ½ mile E of LE TOURET and 1 mile S of LACOUTURE guns were brought into action near an orchard with steel work almost infront of positn wagon line at billets be VIEILLE CHAPELLE. (3 miles away) | W.M. |

# WAR DIARY
## or
## INTELLIGENCE SUMMARY.
*(Erase heading not required.)*

Army Form C. 2118.

| Hour, Date, Place | Summary of Events and Information | Remarks and references to Appendices |
|---|---|---|
| Jan 12th 1915. Nr LE TOURET. | Observing station chosen in RUE DE BOIS about 3000 x in front of batty. and 400 x behind British trenches. British & German trenches about 100 x apart. Everything nearly ready for opening fire next day. | |
| Jan 13th " | Opened fire and registered several points incl. light trin & intersection, was impossible to run up details to NEUVE CHAPELLE to VIEUX BERQUIN to bring up details to NEUVE CHAPELLE as visit. was too bad to see anything. Area in neighbourhood of THE RUE ANNE & WIZERNES - | |
| Jan 14th " | Opened fire on German guns (Howitzers in left). Observation was difficult & the fuzes went very much  in afterneon. Enjoyed another fine & very  little effect. Details fuzes went our line. I hope the troops of Nr VIEUX BERQUIN came clean. | |
| Jan 15th " | Generals DRAKE & PERCEVAL & coy came Re. to inform Stn. as to the condition of the trops. which were too far from our batty. afraid by shells to cart & rest on road. Shells at this corner my GEMMELL returns from leave. I have destroyed (broken leg). | |

Army Form C. 2118.

# WAR DIARY
or
# INTELLIGENCE SUMMARY.
(Erase heading not required.)

Instructions regarding War Diaries and Intelligence Summaries are contained in F.S. Regs., Part II. and the Staff Manual respectively. Title pages will be prepared in manuscript.

| Hour, Date, Place | Summary of Events and Information | Remarks and references to Appendices |
|---|---|---|
| Jan 16th 1915. Near LE TOURET | Very misty. Battery opened fire at un-observed objective but observation was very difficult. WM. | |
| Jan 17th 1915 " | Thick mist all day. No firing. WM. | |
| Jan 18th 1915 " | Batty stood fast all day awaiting orders. I have died (intend hereanap). WM. | |
| Jan 19. 1915 " | Strong mist all day. No firing. WM. | |
| Jan 20 " | Battery opened a German battery which was firing. Shelled the Rue de Bois. DE B.OIS. but did not silence it. Several other targets were engaged during the day. Much firing all day. German artillery much more active. WM. | |
| Jan 21. " | Batty silenced a German battery which was shelling a neighbouring aviary station and registered afresh on two influences. The enemy's war planes visits and barrage were evidently anxious to ... as it ceased firing after two rounds of gunfire. German artillery active. WM. | |
| Jan 22 " | Aeroplanes about. Old Hughes exchanged for brand new 18cwt French Watertruck. WM. | |

Army Form C. 2118.

# WAR DIARY
## or
## INTELLIGENCE SUMMARY.
*(Erase heading not required.)*

Instructions regarding War Diaries and Intelligence Summaries are contained in F.S. Regs., Part II. and the Staff Manual respectively. Title pages will be prepared in manuscript.

| Hour, Date, Place | Summary of Events and Information | Remarks and references to Appendices |
|---|---|---|
| Jan 23rd 1915. Nr LE TOURET. | Batty received orders from 2nd Division to march the following day. Guns much worn & recoil completely preventing advance. | |
| Jan 24. " | Batty marched to GUARBECQUE near AIRE and 15 miles - new billets for the night. 3 horses attached to Mobile Vet. Section on march. | |
| Jan 25. GUARBECQUE. | Batty marched to new billets at DOHEM in neighbourhood of WIZERNE. Ammunition Column rejoined Divisional Ammunition Column at PETIT BOIS. | |
| Jan 26. DOHEM. | 1 gun sent to AIRE (mardly workshop) for overhaul. billets much ∟ Coln provd for horses | |
| Jan 27. " | KAISER'S birthday. Batteries we are all put under own comm. | |
| Jan 28. " | | |
| Jan 29. " | | |
| Jan 30. " | Orders received to march into Brigade to new area | |
| Jan 31. " | near VIEUX BERQUIN Batt. marched with Brigade to billets in neighbourhood of LA MOTTE, in snowstorm, about 24 miles. 1 horse died on road. | |

A.2
Pkg 6

121/4504

2nd Cavalry Division

Warwickshire R.H.A.

Vol III 1 – 28.2.15

# WAR DIARY

## OF

# WARWICKSHIRE

## ROYAL HORSE ARTILLERY

FROM FEBRUARY. 1ST 1915.
TO FEBRUARY 28TH 1915.

Army Form C. 2118.

# WAR DIARY
## or
## INTELLIGENCE SUMMARY.

*(Erase heading not required.)*

Instructions regarding War Diaries and Intelligence Summaries are contained in F. S. Regs., Part II. and the Staff Manual respectively. Title pages will be prepared in manuscript.

| Hour, Date, Place | Summary of Events and Information | Remarks and references to Appendices |
|---|---|---|
| | | |

(73989) W4141—463. 400,000. 9/14. H.&J.Ltd. Forms/C. 2118/10.

Army Form C. 2118.

# WAR DIARY
## or
## INTELLIGENCE SUMMARY.
(Erase heading not required.)

Instructions regarding War Diaries and Intelligence Summaries are contained in F.S. Regs., Part II. and the Staff Manual respectively. Title pages will be prepared in manuscript.

| Hour, Date, Place | Summary of Events and Information | Remarks and references to Appendices |
|---|---|---|
| Monday Feb. 1. LA MOTTE | — Arrangements made for putting horses in divisional corn — | |
| Tuesday Feb 2.   " | All horses under cover. | |
| Wednesday Feb 3.  " | Bad weather, clear starlit | |
| Thursday Feb. 4.  " | One gun was sent to AIRE for repair in Travelling workshop, and one gun brought back. Completed. 3 horses evacuated to Mobile Vet. Sect. | |
| Friday Feb 5.  " | Route march | |
| Saturday Feb 6.  " | Church parade | |
| Sunday Feb 7.  " | Orders received from Brigade to concentrate | |
| Monday Feb 8.  " | at OULTERSTEEN — a short march in order | |
| Tuesday Feb 9.  " | Brigade in return. | |
| Wednesday Feb 10.  " | | |
| Thursday Feb 11.  " | Scheme for Officers carried out. | |

Army Form C. 2118.

# WAR DIARY
or
# INTELLIGENCE SUMMARY.
(Erase heading not required.)

Instructions regarding War Diaries and Intelligence Summaries are contained in F.S. Regs., Part II. and the Staff Manual respectively. Title pages will be prepared in manuscript.

| Hour, Date, Place | Summary of Events and Information | Remarks and references to Appendices |
|---|---|---|
| Friday Feb. 12. LA MOTTE | Marching order | |
| Saturday Feb. 13. " | Horses inspection | |
| Sunday Feb. 14. " | Adjutant went on leave 15 days' leave | |
| Monday Feb. 15 " | Staff ride for Officers | |
| Tuesday Feb. 16. " | Marching order – 4 horses found from 20 & two men killed White–Thompson. Billets & two horses. | |
| Wednesday Feb. 17 " | | |
| Thursday Feb. 18 " | | |
| Friday Feb. 19 " | Marching order | |
| Saturday Feb. 20 " | | |
| Sunday Feb. 21 " | Fine remounts joined from HAZEBROUCK by train | |
| Thursday Feb. 22 | General Allenby's orders | |
| Tuesday Feb. 23 | Adjutant returned from leave – Lord Portlett left on leave for England. Cold & snow. | |
| Wednesday Feb. 24 | Received orders to march with Brigade to BOHEM. | |

Army Form C. 2118.

# WAR DIARY
## or
## INTELLIGENCE SUMMARY.
*(Erase heading not required.)*

Instructions regarding War Diaries and Intelligence Summaries are contained in F. S. Regs., Part II. and the Staff Manual respectively. Title pages will be prepared in manuscript.

| Hour, Date, Place | Summary of Events and Information | Remarks and references to Appendices |
|---|---|---|
| Friday Feb. 26. LA MOTTE | Marched with Brigade to DOITEM and the horses put back into their former billets. | |
| Saturday Feb. 27. DOITEM | — | |
| Sunday Feb. 28. " | Church parade. | |

18/4893.

March 1915.

2nd Cavalry Division.

Warwickshire R.H.A.

Vol IV

A2
296

Army Form C. 2118.

# WAR DIARY
## or
## INTELLIGENCE SUMMARY.
*(Erase heading not required.)*

Instructions regarding War Diaries and Intelligence Summaries are contained in F. S. Regs., Part II. and the Staff Manual respectively. Title pages will be prepared in manuscript.

| Hour, Date, Place | Summary of Events and Information | Remarks and references to Appendices |
|---|---|---|
| Sunday March 1st DOHEM | Exercise in Gas drum. Lieut-Genl Pollett insp. it. | |
| Monday " 2nd " | In 11 Base Hospital BOULOGNE. Marching order. | |
| Tuesday " 3rd " | Lieut- Woodhouse went to POPERINGHE with his lorries to bring back guns from travelling workshop. | |
| Wednesday " 4th " | Brigade route march. | |
| Thursday " 5th " | Exercise. | |
| Friday " 6th " | Orders received for Co. to reconnoitre position near YPRES then occupied by Belgian battery with view to relieving it. | |
| Saturday " 7th " | C.O. went to YPRES with C.O's of D. E & J Batteries R.H.A. and reconnoitred position. Church parade. | |

# WAR DIARY
## or
## INTELLIGENCE SUMMARY.
*(Erase heading not required.)*

Army Form C. 2118.

| Hour, Date, Place | Summary of Events and Information | Remarks and references to Appendices |
|---|---|---|
| Monday March 8th DOHEM | | |
| Tuesday " 9th " | Marched at 6 a.m. with Brigade to old billets near LA MOTTE. | |
| Wednesday " 10 - LA MOTTE | Received orders at 10 a.m. from G.O.C. 2nd Cavalry Division as to the action of the division in event of attack at NEUVE CHAPPELLE opening a big enough gap in enemy's lines. 2nd division concentrated near NEUVE BERQUIN and remained there until evening. Returned to billets about 6 p.m. | |
| Thursday " 11 - " | Concentrated with the division at 7 a.m. at NEUF BERQUIN. Returned there all day. From billets near ESTAIRES in the evening. | |

Army Form C. 2118.

# WAR DIARY
## or
## INTELLIGENCE SUMMARY.
(Erase heading not required.)

Instructions regarding War Diaries and Intelligence Summaries are contained in F.S. Regs., Part II. and the Staff Manual respectively. Title pages will be prepared in manuscript.

| Hour, Date, Place | Summary of Events and Information | Remarks and references to Appendices |
|---|---|---|
| Friday March 12th ESTAIRE | Stood to all day, was limbered up about 5.30pm but did not move. | |
| Saturday " 13 " " | Stood to all day received orders to return to old billets near LA MOTTE about 5.30pm | |
| Sunday " 14 " LA MOTTE | | |
| Monday " 15 " " | | |
| Tuesday " 16 " " | | |
| Wednesday " 17 " " | | |
| Thursday " 18 " " | Lieut. Colonel Gilson the new C.R.A. 2nd Cavalry Division called & saw guns & horses. Course for junior officers started. | |
| Friday " 19 " " | | |
| Saturday " 20 " " | | |
| Sunday " 21 " " | Draft of 7 gunners + 13 drivers arrived. | |

Army Form C. 2118.

# WAR DIARY
## or
## INTELLIGENCE SUMMARY.
*(Erase heading not required.)*

Instructions regarding War Diaries and Intelligence Summaries are contained in F. S. Regs., Part II. and the Staff Manual respectively. Title pages will be prepared in manuscript.

| Hour, Date, Place | Summary of Events and Information | Remarks and references to Appendices |
|---|---|---|
| Monday March 22nd LA MOTTE | | |
| Tuesday " 23rd " | Served headquarters & a portion of billets | |
| Wednesday " 24th " | into area previously occupied by 5th Lancers. Horses during the asylum left to take command of 119th bakery R.F.A. Y th Division. | |
| Thursday " 25th " | | |
| Friday " 26th " | | |
| Saturday " 27th " | Church parade. | |
| Sunday " 28th " | | |
| Monday " 29th " | | |
| Tuesday " 30th " | Experimented with boiling to try & do away tea urns | |
| Wednesday " 31st " | & croning kitchen of Brigade field day. | |

W S Gerard (?) Major RHA
O.C. [signature]

Forms/C. 2118/10

121/5256.

2nd Cavalry Div

Warwickshire R.H.A.

Vol V 1 – 30.4.15

Army Form C. 2118.

# WAR DIARY
## or
## INTELLIGENCE SUMMARY.
*(Erase heading not required.)*

Instructions regarding War Diaries and Intelligence Summaries are contained in F. S. Regs., Part II. and the Staff Manual respectively. Title pages will be prepared in manuscript.

| Hour, Date, Place | Summary of Events and Information | Remarks and references to Appendices |
|---|---|---|
| April 1st 1915 LA MOTTE | Lieut Paul Poulets rejoined after being in hospital | |
| April 2nd " | at Boulogne since 28th Feb. | |
| April 3rd " | C.O. attended Brigade Staff Ride for C.Os | |
| April 4th " | However there visitation | |
| April 5th " | Palm Sunday Voluntary Church Parade | |
| April 6th " | Very wet. | |
| | Brigade Staff Ride 16 2nd continued. | |
| | Section went out under Section commanders | |
| | Captain Croxall and 2 subalt. Sieur joined | |
| | from Ripon | |
| April 7th " | Captain Croxall and Lieut Brown posted | |
| | to the ammunition columns, and Lieut Dunn | |
| | joined the battery from the column | |
| | Lt. Gibson called to discuss the position of | |
| | the officers over establishment | |
| | Instruction of section commanders in choosing | |
| April 8th " | position | |

Army Form C. 2118.

# WAR DIARY
## or
## INTELLIGENCE SUMMARY.
(Erase heading not required.)

Instructions regarding War Diaries and Intelligence Summaries are contained in F.S. Regs., Part II. and the Staff Manual respectively. Title pages will be prepared in manuscript.

| Hour, Date, Place | Summary of Events and Information | Remarks and references to Appendices |
|---|---|---|
| April 9th 1915 LA MOTTE | Section paraded under Section Commander. Col BUDWORTH C.R.H.A. 1st Cavalry Division called and took particulars of establishment and equipment, in view of the probable transfer of the Battery from 2nd to 1st Cavalry Division. | |
| April 10th " " | Battery gun drill and harness inspection. | |
| April 11th " " | Major Generals & Staff Woodhouse were found to be suffering from measles and removed to hospital at St. Omer. Church parade at 10.30. | |
| April 12th " " | Battery gun drill. One driver evacuated with measles. | |
| April 13th " " | Drill order. Several positions taken up. 2nd Lieut. Dixon joined the battery from the 2nd Cavalry Division by order of the C.R.H.A. In the afternoon the whole of the horses were inspected by Captain Adam of the veterinary officers. Five men sent to hospital with measles. | |

# WAR DIARY
## or
## INTELLIGENCE SUMMARY.

*(Erase heading not required.)*

Army Form C. 2118.

| Hour, Date, Place | Summary of Events and Information | Remarks and references to Appendices |
|---|---|---|
| April 14th 1915 LA MOTTE | Tactical instruction for officers and no.1 by Col. Gilson at Les Bois. A further case of measles reported. | |
| April 15th " " | Battery gun drill. Two more cases of measles | |
| April 16th " " | Still in same Route march to hunt for Cas Adjutant R.H.A. 2nd Cav. Div. called. | |
| April 17th " " | | |
| April 18th " " | Harness inspection. One case of measles. | |
| April 19th " " | Battery gun drill. General (Lieut) Thompson called and inspected the ammunition wagons Drill order and route march | |
| April 20th " " | Col. Barstow accompanied by Capt Barstow inspected horses and vehicles. He expressed his satisfaction with the condition of the battery. | |
| April 21st " " | | |
| April 22nd " " | Orders received from 1st Cavalry Division that the division was to stand ready to move at two hours notice to support the French north | |
| April 23rd | of YPRES. Orders received later that being | |

Army Form C. 2118.

# WAR DIARY
## or
## INTELLIGENCE SUMMARY.
(Erase heading not required.)

Instructions regarding War Diaries and Intelligence Summaries are contained in F.S. Regs., Part II. and the Staff Manual respectively. Title pages will be prepared in manuscript.

| Hour, Date, Place | Summary of Events and Information | Remarks and references to Appendices |
|---|---|---|
| April 24th 1915 LA MOTTE | In quarantine the battery was not to join in the concentration. | |
| April 25th " | Battery Gun drill. | |
| April 26th " | Sunday. Inspection at 11 a.m. Major Gammell and Lieut Woodhouse returned from hospital. | |
| April 27th " | Battery gun drill. Major Gammell wheeled to Hames in Capt Gamble A.D.V.S. 1st Cav Divison. | |
| April 28th " | Marching order 9 a.m. | |
| April 29th " | Battery gun drill. Lieut Lord Porlett sent to hospital with measles. | |
| April 30th " | Detachments practised in digging shell pits. Section went out under section commanders and practised coming into action in turn. | |

A.S. Gammell Major
O.C. Somewh? R.H.A.
1st R.H.A.

2nd Cavalry Division

Warwick. R.H.A.

War 1 — 31.5.15.

Army Form C. 2118.

# WAR DIARY
## or
## INTELLIGENCE SUMMARY.
(Erase heading not required.)

Instructions regarding War Diaries and Intelligence Summaries are contained in F.S. Regs., Part II. and the Staff Manual respectively. Title pages will be prepared in manuscript.

| Hour, Date, Place | Summary of Events and Information | Remarks and references to Appendices |
|---|---|---|
| 1915 May 1st LA MOTTE | Exercise and Battery gun drill. Horse & billet inspection by C.O. | |
| 2nd — | — | |
| 3rd " | Cleaning and Battery gun drill | |
| 4th " | Drill until 9 a.m. Route march, and parade in coming into action with the Battery commanders. Exercise and Battery gun drill. Brakes in repair. Switches satisfactory. | |
| 5th " | Exercise and battery gun drill. | |
| 6th " | Drill until 9 a.m. The Battery took up a position in the edge of the forest of Nieppe facing the big Bergues — Ghent Hazebrouck — Thurhem line present. | |
| 7th " | Exercise and Battery gun drill | |
| 8th " | Parade at 10 a.m. for C.O.'s inspection | |
| 9th " | Exercise. Gun drill under hut 1 | |
| 10th " | Drill until 9 a.m. | |
| 11th " | Exercise and Battery gun drill | |
| 12th " | Battery reported free of quarantine to H.Q. 9th Cavalry Brigade. Independent gun drill | |
| 13th " | — | |
| 14th " | Horses paraded for inspection by Col. Martin D.S.V.S. | |

Army Form C. 2118.

# WAR DIARY
## or
## INTELLIGENCE SUMMARY.
*(Erase heading not required.)*

Instructions regarding War Diaries and Intelligence Summaries are contained in F.S. Regs., Part II. and the Staff Manual respectively. Title pages will be prepared in manuscript.

| Hour, Date, Place | | Summary of Events and Information | Remarks and references to Appendices |
|---|---|---|---|
| 1915 | | | |
| 15 May | LA MOTTE | Exercise and inspection of billets by C.O. | |
| 16. " | " | Sunday Parade and inspection by C.O. | |
| 17. " | " | Orders received to move next day to new area | |
| 18. " | WORMHOUT | h.q. CASSEL. Battery marched at 9 a.m. with orders to proceed to LEDRINGHAM. While on the march orders received to go in to area between ESQUELBEC & WORMHOUT. | |
| 19. " | LEDRINGHAM | Permission received to take up billets at LEDRINGHAM and the battery moved there in the afternoon. | |
| 20. " | " | Reveille 7.30. | |
| 21. " | " | Reveille 7.30 Battery gun drill 10.30. | |
| 22. " | " | Still orders 9 a.m. Route march. Gen. de Lisle called. | |
| 23. " | " | Sunday Church Parade in field at H.Q. The C.O. received a telegram instructing him to report in person at Chateau between VLAMARTINGHE & YPRES. | |
| 24. " | VLAMARTINGHE | Battery marched at 7 a.m and billets in a field about 1½ mile E of Vlamertinghe. At 5 p.m. 3 guns relieved half of ? Battery in a position E. of the canal between Ypres & St Julien, the wagon line remaining in the field | |

(73989) W4141-463. 400,000. 9/14. H.&J.Ltd. Forms/C. 2118/10.

Army Form C. 2118.

# WAR DIARY
## or
## INTELLIGENCE SUMMARY.
*(Erase heading not required.)*

Instructions regarding War Diaries and Intelligence Summaries are contained in F.S. Regs., Part II. and the Staff Manual respectively. Title pages will be prepared in manuscript.

| Hour, Date, Place | Summary of Events and Information | Remarks and references to Appendices |
|---|---|---|
| 1915 May 25 YPRES | In the morning registered on various targets. In the afternoon shelled enemy working party constructing new trench S.E. of I. and warmth fire was reported as extremely effective. | |
| " 26 | Battery was given new Zone and registered on it. | |
| " 27 | Reached road with refill the In the evening two guns were withdrawn to wagon line, and relieved by 2 guns of Nottinghamshire Bryat. R.F.A. T. | |
| " 28 | Resisted from tranches to registr. In the evening the remaining gun was withdrawn and the battery returned cleaning the night to GELLS | |
| " 29 LEDRINGHEM | Sunday | |
| " 30 | Service 7.30 and nomen cleaning Col. Bulward (Staff) | |
| " 31 | Service 7.30. General Service Parade | |

[signatures]

2/6357

2nd Cavalry Division
Int
Aubin

Maurice R.H.A.
Vol VII
1 – 30-6-15

ar
926

June 1915 – Oct 1916

Army Form C. 2118.

# WAR DIARY
or
## INTELLIGENCE SUMMARY.
(Erase heading not required.)

| Hour, Date, Place | Summary of Events and Information | Remarks and references to Appendices |
|---|---|---|
| 1915<br>1 June<br>LEDRINGHEM | Gen Greenley inspected the Battery in marching order at 9 a.m. and expressed satisfaction with the turnout. In the afternoon the C.O. and the subalterns attended a demonstration by the A.D.M.S. of the use of respirators at Wormhoudt. Service and battery gun drill. | |
| 2 June | Service and inspection of billets and horses by C.O. | |
| 3 June | Service and inspection of gun drill. Church Parade in field at Herzeele. | |
| 4 June | Service and driving drill. Subsection gun drill. | |
| 5 June | Service and battery gun drill. | |
| 6 June | Service and mechanism gun drill. | |
| 7 June | Service and gun drill. The C.O. about working | |
| 8 June | reconnoitred the Cassel – Dunkirk Road and selected positions. | |
| 9 June | Service and battery gun drill. The horses were inspected by Capt. Gamble A.D.V.S. | |
| 10 June | | |
| 11 June | Early Service. Inspection of billets and horses by C.O. | |

Army Form C. 2118.

# WAR DIARY
## or
## INTELLIGENCE SUMMARY.
*(Erase heading not required.)*

Instructions regarding War Diaries and Intelligence Summaries are contained in F.S. Regs., Part II. and the Staff Manual respectively. Title pages will be prepared in manuscript.

| Hour, Date, Place | Summary of Events and Information | Remarks and references to Appendices |
|---|---|---|
| 1915 | | |
| 12 June LEDRINGHEM | Lieut. Lorn Powlett took the battery to church at the Field Ambulance, Ledringhem. | |
| 13 June | Services and interior gun drill. | |
| 14 June | The 9th Cavalry Brigade was inspected at 12 h headquarters by F.M. Sir John French at the Battery Southmore with the Officers. | |
| 15 June | Early service and cleaning drill - Lieut Powlett attended a staff ride with the brigadier of the Cavalry division. | |
| 16 June | Early driving drill. Battery gun drill | |
| 17 June | Early cleaning drill. Battery gun drill | |
| 18 June | Early Service. Col. Bosworth delivered a lecture to the officers on the duties of artillery in entrenched positions | |
| 19 June | Church parade 9 a.m. in headquarters field | |
| 20 June | Service, Interior gun drill | |
| 21 June | Early driving drill | |
| 22 June | Early Service. Battery gun drill | |
| 23 June | Brigade harassing over at 8.30 a.m. Route march in the early afternoon returning to billets at 12.30 | |

Army Form C. 2118.

# WAR DIARY
or
## INTELLIGENCE SUMMARY.
*(Erase heading not required.)*

Instructions regarding War Diaries and Intelligence Summaries are contained in F.S. Regs., Part II. and the Staff Manual respectively. Title pages will be prepared in manuscript.

| Hour, Date, Place | Summary of Events and Information | Remarks and references to Appendices |
|---|---|---|
| 1915 LEDRINGHEM. | | |
| 24 June | General Sundries by subsections. Col. Bird went to the officers. | |
| 25 June | Service inspection of horses and harness by C.O. | |
| 26 June | Battery marched to billets of B squadron 15th Hussars for church parade which was not held owing to rain. | |
| 27 June | Exercise and battery gun drill | |
| 28 June | Driving drill and subsection gun drill | |
| 29 June | General. Lieut. Potts and 20 men proceeded hastily furnished by the brigade to dig trenches between Poperinghe and Ypres. | |
| 30 June | Driving drill. | |

RPS Cameron Wright
DC Farnworth

121/6357

2nd Cavalry Division.
1st / 2 Cav Bde
a

Warwick R.H.A.
Vol VIII
1-31-4-15

ar
96

Army Form C. 2118.

Berwick R.H.A.

# WAR DIARY
## or
## INTELLIGENCE SUMMARY.
(Erase heading not required.)

Instructions regarding War Diaries and Intelligence Summaries are contained in F.S. Regs., Part II. and the Staff Manual respectively. Title pages will be prepared in manuscript.

| Hour, Date, Place | Summary of Events and Information | Remarks and references to Appendices |
|---|---|---|
| 1915. | | |
| 1st July LEDRINGHEM | Driving drill & gun drill. | |
| 2nd " | Exercise & Subsection gun drill | |
| 3rd " | Inspection of horses & kits by C.O. | |
| 4th " | Church parade in field of B. Squadron 16th Hussars. | |
| 5th " | Exercise & taking gun drill | |
| 6th " | " " | |
| 7th " | " " | |
| 8th " | The Officers took part in a scheme under the O.C. R.H.A. 7th Brigade R.H.A. | |
| 9th " | Exercise, riding drill & gun drill | |
| 10th " | Digging party under Lieut. Pelo relieved 5 2nd men under Lieut. The Earl Poulett | |
| 11th " | Church parade at 9th Cavalry Brigade Field Ambulance | |

Army Form C. 2118.

# WAR DIARY
or
## INTELLIGENCE SUMMARY.
(Erase heading not required.)

Instructions regarding War Diaries and Intelligence Summaries are contained in F.S. Regs., Part II. and the Staff Manual respectively. Title pages will be prepared in manuscript.

| Hour, Date, Place | Summary of Events and Information | Remarks and references to Appendices |
|---|---|---|
| 12th July LEDRINGHEM. | Officers Staff ride under scheme set by G.O.C. | |
| 13th " | 9th Cavalry Brigade. | |
| 14th " | Battery driving drill. | |
| 15th " | Exercise & gun drill. | |
| 16th " | Route march. | |
| 17th " | Exercise & billets for hull. | |
| | Lieut. Clayton R.A.M.C. was relieved by Lieut. Grant R.A.M.C. from 4th Cavalry Field Ambulance. Lieut. Clayton proceeding to No 20 General Hospital Boulogne being B. echelon attached to Wheels was | |
| 18th " | MORBECQUE to practise in moving across the line opinion under night section moved round with aid of mts. duck. This is an general entrained for the vehicles | |

# WAR DIARY
## or
## INTELLIGENCE SUMMARY.
*(Erase heading not required.)*

Army Form C. 2118.

Instructions regarding War Diaries and Intelligence Summaries are contained in F.S. Regs., Part II. and the Staff Manual respectively. Title pages will be prepared in manuscript.

| Hour, Date, Place | | Summary of Events and Information | Remarks and references to Appendices |
|---|---|---|---|
| 19th July | MORBECQUE | Practice in crossing Canal. | |
| 20 " | " | " " " " | |
| 21st " | " | " " " " | |
| 22nd " | " | " " " " | |
| 23rd " | LEDRINGHEM | Bn. marched back to permanent billets nr LEDRINGHEM. Digging party under Lieut. The Earl Poulett relieved by another party under Lieut. Hawkshawe. | |
| 24th " | " | Exercise & inspection. | |
| 25th " | " | Church parade. | |
| 26th " | " | Reconnoitring of position for defence of Trenches. | |
| 27th " | " | Scheme under G.O.C. 9th Cavalry Brigade. | |
| 28th " | " | Continuation of scheme. | |
| 29th " | " | Battalion came into "reserve". | |
| 30th " | " | Digging party under Lieut. Hawkshawe returned | |
| 31st " | " | Inspection. | |

Lt Col [signature]
Brig [signature] R.H.A.
O. [signature]

1080/121

1st Cavalry Division
9 Cav Bde

Warwick R H A
Vol IX
August 15

Army Form C. 2118.

# WAR DIARY or INTELLIGENCE SUMMARY.
(Erase heading not required.)

Instructions regarding War Diaries and Intelligence Summaries are contained in F.S. Regs., Part II and the Staff Manual respectively. Title pages will be prepared in manuscript.

| Hour, Date, Place | Summary of Events and Information | Remarks and references to Appendices |
|---|---|---|
| 1915 | | |
| 1st Aug. LEDRINGHEM | Sunday. Church parade at 9th Hussars billets. | |
| 2nd " MARDYCK | The 9th Cav. Brigade marched to MARDYCK nr DUNKIRK. A scheme of advanced guard action was worked out on the way. The battery marched without guns, arriving about midday. The men billeted in the afternoon. Bivouac in open field. Night very wet. Brigade drill on beach at 5 a.m. Brigade marched back to permanent billets in the afternoon. | |
| 3rd " MARDYCK | B. Echelon of Brigade inspected by G.O.C. | |
| 4th " LE DRINGHEM | Lieut. Woodhouse left to join 26th French Howitzer Battery VI Div. Lieut. Quinn & 31 men & 2 horses left to form digging party at ZUYDERINGHE. Driving drill. | |
| 5th " " | | |
| 6th " " | C.O.'s inspection of harness and horses. | |
| 7th " " | Sunday. Church parade at 15th Hussars billets. | |
| 8th " " | Driving & riding drill. Horses inspected by D.V.S. | |
| 9th " " | Cavalry Corps. One 13 pdr gun returned to "J" R.H.A. for instruction. | |
| 10th " " | Riding & driving drill. Gun drill. | |

R.P. Lewis Lieut i/c [?]
O.C. Warwick R.H.A.

Army Form C. 2118.

# WAR DIARY
## or
## INTELLIGENCE SUMMARY
(Erase heading not required.)

Instructions regarding War Diaries and Intelligence Summaries are contained in F.S. Regs., Part II. and the Staff Manual respectively. Title pages will be prepared in manuscript.

| Hour, Date, Place | Summary of Events and Information | Remarks and references to Appendices |
|---|---|---|
| 1915 LEDRINGHEM | | |
| 11 Aug | Exercise and gun drill. | |
| 12 " | Driving & riding drill | |
| 13 " | Digging party under Lieut. Ewen returned by first party under Lieut Ros. | |
| 14 " | Early service. C.O's inspection | |
| 15 " | Church parade at 9 in Hussars H.Q. Been received that Lieut. Worsheim had been killed the previous night while reconnoitring the 26th French hornifug battery. A shell fell in a communication trench near Hooge, & killed both him and the other officer of the battery. | |
| 16 " | Battery marched to bath at Wormhout. | |
| 17 " | Early driving & riding drill | |
| 18 " | Early exercise. | |
| 19 " | Driving & riding drill | |
| 20 " | Short route march in marching order | |
| 21st " | Early exercise - B.C. inspection | |

R. P. [signature] Lieut. for Major
D.C. Warwick Maj.

Army Form C. 2118.

# WAR DIARY
## or
## INTELLIGENCE SUMMARY.
(Erase heading not required.)

| Hour, Date, Place | Summary of Events and Information | Remarks and references to Appendices |
|---|---|---|
| 1915 | | |
| 22 Aug LEDRINGHEM | Church parade at 9 am. Cav. Field Ambulance | |
| 23 " | Four 18 pdr guns and light wagons arrived at ARNEKE. Exercise and fitting up new guns and wagons. | |
| 24 " | | |
| 25 " | 18 pdr ammunition less A.E. elements by Park and packed in wagons. | |
| 26 " | 15 pdr guns & wagons returned to ordnance, ammunition returned by Park. Battery at disposal of C.R.H.A. | |
| 27 " | Digging party under Lieut. Peto returned. | |
| 28 " | Exercise & inspection. Major Gemmell went into C.R.H.A. | |
| 29 " | to 1st Army area to reconnoitre positions. Church parade. | |
| 30 " | 7th Brigade R.H.A. attached to 1st Army. Lieut. Peto left in mot to prepare gun pits into digging party lent by R.F.A. 47th London Division. | |
| 31 " WARDECQUE | Battery marched with brigade and bivouacked at WARDECQUE. | |

R.B. Gemmell Lt Major
OC Warwick RHA

Army Form C. 2118.

# WAR DIARY
## or
## INTELLIGENCE SUMMARY
*(Erase heading not required.)*

Instructions regarding War Diaries and Intelligence Summaries are contained in F.S. Regs., Part II and the Staff Manual respectively. Title pages will be prepared in manuscript.

| Hour, Date, Place | Summary of Events and Information | Remarks and references to Appendices |
|---|---|---|
| 1915 11 Aug LE DRINGHEM | Exercise and gun drill. | |
| 12 " " | Driving & riding drill | |
| 13 " " | Digging party under Lieut. Roô. | |
| | Party under Lieut. Roô. | |
| 14 " " | Early exercise. C.O's inspection | |
| 15 " " | Church parade at 10 in Hussars A.Q. Have received that Lieut. Bronkhurst had been killed the previous night while commanding the 26th French howitzer battery. A shell fell in a communication trench near Hooge, & killed both him and the other officer of the battery. | |
| 16 " " | Battery marched to baths at Wormhout. | |
| 17 " " | Early driving & riding drill | |
| 18 " " | Early exercise. | |
| 19 " " | Driving & riding drill | |
| 20 " " | Short route march in marching order | |
| 21 " " | Early exercise. B.C's inspection | |

R.P.Pemburn(?) /pr Major
O.C. Warwick Bty

12/7050

1/st Cavalry Reserve

Warwick R H A.

Vol X

Sept 15.

**Army Form C. 21**

# WAR DIARY
## or
## INTELLIGENCE SUMMARY.
(Erase heading not required.)

Instructions regarding War Diaries and Intelligence Summaries are contained in F. S. Regs., Part II. and the Staff Manual respectively. Title pages will be prepared in manuscript.

| Place | Date | Hour | Summary of Events and Information | Remarks and references to Appendices |
|---|---|---|---|---|
| LEDRINGHEM | 1 Sep. | | Battery marched LAPUGNOY | |
| LAPUGNOY | 2 Sep. | | Remained at Lapugnoy for the day | |
| NOEUX-LES-MINES | 3 Sep. | | Marched 5 hrs 12 m. from wagon line at NOEUX-LES-MINES. Officers and NCOs reached in the evening a battery position at GRENAY | |
| GRENAY | 4 Sep | | Detachments continued digging gun pits which had been begun by a fatigue party of the 47th Div., and the guns were brought up to the position after dusk. | |
| " | 5 " | | Gun pits completed. | |
| " | 6 " | | Observing station & Telephone lines prepared | |
| " | 7 " | | Registered various targets. Cover & A gun pit struck by German shell. | |
| " | 8 " | | Fired a few rounds | |
| " | 9 " | | Fired on Loos | |
| " | 10 " | | Fired 12 rounds | |
| " | 11 " | | Fired 8 rounds | |
| " | 12 " | | Fired at German battery in conjunction with 3rd Heavy Brigade into aeroplane observation. | |
| " | 13 " | | Fired on several targets | |

**Army Form C. 2118**

# WAR DIARY
## or
## INTELLIGENCE SUMMARY
*(Erase heading not required.)*

Instructions regarding War Diaries and Intelligence Summaries are contained in F.S. Regs., Part II and the Staff Manual respectively. Title pages will be prepared in manuscript.

| Place | Date | Hour | Summary of Events and Information | Remarks and references to Appendices |
|---|---|---|---|---|
| GRENAY | 14 Sep | | Received 100 rounds H.E. | |
| " | 15 " | | Fired on mill at Loos with balloon observation. | |
| " | 16 " | | Received orders to be ready to move. Moved out about 10 pm & bivouaced at Nogre lines at Hoeuxles main. | |
| HOEUXLESMINES | 17 " | | | |
| STEENBECQUE | 18 " | | Marched at 10 am & bivouaced in fields at STEENBECQUE stn. | |
| LEDRINGHEM | 19 " | | Marched at 10 am & arrived at 3 pm at our billets at LEDRINGHEM | |
| " | 20 " | | General clean up | |
| " | 21 " | | Early reveille, clean up | |
| " | 22 " | | Brigade route march 8:45 am. Battery carried out Rheims winter Gen Trenchy. | |
| " | 23 " | | Practised crossing Steam with horses vehicles. Gen Greenley present. Brigade marched at 10 pm to billets in HEURINGHEM | |
| HEURINGHEM | 24 " | | Marched at 6 pm to ESTREES BLANCHES | |
| ESTREES BLANCHES | 25 " | | Marched to Vaudricourt & bivouaced in Chateau grounds. Lieut Shiner joined from 2/1 Battery. | |
| VAUDRICOURT | 26, 27 " | | Standing to at half an hours notice | |
| " | 28 " | | Marched to HESDIGNEUL & bivouaced in village street | |
| HESDIGNEUL | 29 " | | Marched to LAPUGNOY & bivouaced in goods yard of railway | |
| LAPUGNOY | 30 " | | | |

Warwickshire
R.H.A.
October 1915
Diary Missing

Mustafa Kemal Bey, in command of the 19th Division, despatched his only divisional reserve[1] to piquet the main ridge at

---
[1] Two companies of the 2/72nd Regiment.

---

Chunuk Bair. An hour later these troops began to arrive, and by 7 a.m. the crest of the ridge was at last held by a thin outpost line. About the same time Essad Pasha, assured at last that the attack on Lone Pine was merely a demonstration, ordered Colonel Kannengiesser to rush his two regiments northward to protect the main ridge, and this officer appears to have reached Chunuk Bair with his leading battalion a little after nine.[2]

---
[2] Kannengiesser gives the hour of his arrival as three hours earlier, but the weight of evidence is against him.

---

Meanwhile, soon after daylight, the crowd of shipping in Suvla Bay, the thousands of troops in the neighbourhood of Lala Baba, and the news of the advance of Birdwood's troops in the foothills north of Anzac persuaded Liman von Sanders that this was indeed the long-expected attack by the new British army, and that Hamilton was aiming at the capture of Sari Bair and the envelopment of his northern flank. At 6 a.m. he telegraphed to Feizi Bey to hurry south with the bulk of the 7th & 12th Divisions. At the same time he

1st Cav Bde

1st Cavalry Brigade
Warwickshire R.H.A.
Nov 1915.
Vol XII

124/7731

a/96

Army Form C. 2118.

# WAR DIARY of Warwickshire R.H.A.
## or
## INTELLIGENCE SUMMARY.
From 1.11.15
To 31.11.15

(Erase heading not required.)

Instructions regarding War Diaries and Intelligence Summaries are contained in F. S. Regs., Part II. and the Staff Manual respectively. Title pages will be prepared in manuscript.

| Hour, Date, Place | Summary of Events and Information | Remarks and references to Appendices |
|---|---|---|
| COHEM 1 nov to 10 nov. | Usual routine of exercise, gun drill & harness cleaning | |
| 10 nov " | Orders received that division will move to join 1st army | |
| 14 nov " | Billeting party marched to SEQUIÈRES near SAMER about 35 kilometres | |
| 15 nov " | Advance party marched to new billets | |
| 17 nov " | Battery marched with brigade arriving about 6 p.m. | |
| 18 nov to 24 nov SEQUIÈRES | Arranging new billets, exercise and stables | |
| 25 nov " | Drill order & route march | |
| 28 nov " | Church parade. Orders received that 7th Bugin R.H.A. is lent to 1st Army and to march next day | |
| 29 nov " | Battery marched to SCOTTE | |
| 30 " DELETTE | Battery marched to LA BUISSIÈRE | |

K.B. Greenwell
Capt R.H.A.
Commanding Warwickshire R.H.A.
5.12.15

Confidential.
-----------------

   D.A.G.,
      3rd Echelon,
         BASE.
   -----------------------

        Herewith War Diary for Warwick Battery R.H.A. from 21st to 29th February.

        During the other part of February, the battery was serving with 7th Brigade, R.H.A.


10-3-16.                    H Boyd Rochfort    Captain,
                         Brigade Major, 9th Cav. Bde.

Extract

D.A.G.,
    3rd Echelon,
        B A S E
- - - - - - - - - - - - - -

1. Reference your 140/452 dated 29th February, 1915.

(a) O.C. Warwickshire Battery states :-

    During the months of December and January this Battery was under the direction of Colonel Commanding 7th Brigade R.H.A. in action.

    Orders were received that in accordance with G.R.O. 1187 the necessary information would be incorporated in the 7th Brigade R.H.A. War Diary.

        .....

G.S.234
21/3/16.

        (sgd) R.H. Osborne Capt.
                General Staff,
                1st Cavalry Division.

**WAR DIARY** of Berwickshire Yeo. R.H.A.

or

**INTELLIGENCE SUMMARY.**

*(Erase heading not required.)*

Army Form C. 2118.

| Hour, Date, Place | Summary of Events and Information | Remarks and references to Appendices |
|---|---|---|
| QUESTRECQUES | | |
| April | | |
| 1st | Inspection of billets etc. | |
| 2 & 3 | Drill order, gun drill etc. | |
| 4 | | |
| 5 | | |
| 6 | Divisional parade on sands nr. HARDELOT. | |
| 7 | Drill order, riding, gun drill etc. | |
| 8, 9, 13 | | |
| 14 | Brigade field day | |
| 15, 16 | Usual routine | |
| 17 | Inspection of division by G.O.C. 1st Army | |
| | [ ] Riding & draining drills, gun drill etc. | |
| 18, 19, 20 | | |
| 21 | Good Friday | |
| 22, 23 | Usual routine | |
| 24 | Easter Monday. Holiday | |
| 25 | General Grenfell's Grand word drives & letting able to give a tactical scheme for | |
| 26, 27, 30 | drill purposes | |

Lt B. Greenwell
O.C. Berwick R.H.A.

Army Form C. 2118

WAR DIARY
or
INTELLIGENCE SUMMARY  Warwick Battery R.H.A.
*(Erase heading not required.)*

| Place | Date 1916 | Hour | Summary of Events and Information | Remarks and references to Appendices |
|---|---|---|---|---|
| SEQUIERES | Mar 1-4 | | Usual routine | |
| | 5 | | Battery moved to fresh billets at QUESTRECQUES N. of SAMER. Major Fanshawe Lt. Elam and 30 Gunners left for 1st Army area where they were attached to 157 Brigade R.F.A. for instructional purposes, relieving X Battery R.H.A. at RICHBOURG ST. VAAST. | |
| QUESTRECQUES | 6 | | Usual routine | |
| | 7-10 | | Battery took part in divisional route march via Sowreville, Samer | |
| | 11 | | Usual routine | |
| | 12,13 | | Drill order & route march | |
| | 14 | | | |
| | 16 | | Battery inspected by Brig. Genl Kirby. C.O. & Gunners retained 1st Army | |
| | 17-26 | | Usual routine | |
| | 27 | | Drill order, but country still too steep to do much | |
| | 28-31 | | Usual routine | |

Capt. R.H.A.
War...

MARY KEY'S
MISSING

these troops had recently suffered heavily at Helles, and the average strength of battalions was about 500 men.

---

Wehib Pasha, commanding the southern zone, was similarly ordered, despite his vehement protests, to despatch his sole reserve division[2] to Essad Pasha's

---

[2] the 4th Division at Serafim Farm. Linyan states that Wehib despatched this division northward of his own initiative, but other evidence shews that he reluctantly parted with it when ordered to do so.

---

assistance.

None of these movements, however, was of any immediate help to Essad Pasha. Throughout the night of the 6/7th August the Sari Bair ridge from Battleship Hill northwards remained undefended, and it is clear that had General Godley's columns succeeded in occupying it at dawn, many hours must have elapsed before the Turks could have mustered sufficient troops to dream of counter-attacking.

Unfortunately, the gallant but fruitless attacks carried out at dawn at the head of Monash Gully were of actual benefit to the Turks. The heavy casualties inflicted on the assaulting troops encouraged the Turkish soldiers, and relieved their divisional commander of all anxiety for the safety of that part of his line. About 5.30 a.m., hearing that a column of British troops was established on Rhodoendron Spur,

Army Form C. 2118

**WAR DIARY**
or
**INTELLIGENCE SUMMARY**

Woolwich R.H.A.

June 1916

| Place | Date | Hour | Summary of Events and Information | Remarks and references to Appendices |
|---|---|---|---|---|
| Scaull[?] | June 1st | | Drill as usual | |
| | 3 | | | |
| | 4 | | Front line trenches where Batt[al]t | |
| | 5 | | will [be?] put practice trenches [from?] 7[?]am | |
| | 6 | | with [ ] Divnm[?] [ ] line. | |
| | 7 | | Batty returned Divnm[?] at noon | |
| | 8 | | Practice as usual | |
| Quadrangue | 8 | | " | |
| | 9 | | Divin[?] [?] Shoot: A. sub from front line for 2nd Brige | |
| | 10 | | Capt. [?] Parker returned from [?] | |
| | 11 | | Practice as usual | |
| | 12 | | has been returned from [?] | |
| | 13 | | [?] to [?] for [?] Battry, [?] [?] were inspected by C.O. | |
| | 14 | | Sub turn & Lyon & [?] to train with [?] [?] | |
| | 15 | | (A section [?] one [?] | |
| | 16/17 | | Practice as [?]e | |
| | 18 | | Detach[ment] horses teams [?] [?] horses [?] arrived | |
| | 19 | | and Batty [?] at [?] [?] [?] at 5pm when | |
| | 20 | | [?] waffle[?] detrain at [?] Pontoon [?] POPERGHES ESTRUVAL. Batty | |
| | 21/22 | | under Col[on]el marched to POPERGHES ESTRUVAL L- | |
| | 23 | | [?] Battery [?] BERINGHAM 9.30 am arriving POPERGHES ESTRUVAL L- | |
| Pops-[?] | 24-25 | | B. Battery L.H. BERINGHAM 9.30 am | |
| | | | 4.30 a.m. | |

# WAR DIARY or INTELLIGENCE SUMMARY

Army Form C. 2118

Warwick R.H.A.

| Place | Date | Hour | Summary of Events and Information | Remarks and references to Appendices |
|---|---|---|---|---|
| Achiet le Grand | 25 | | Battery billets both moved to Chateau Brucan | |
| | 26 | 4.30 AM | Battery marched ...... | |
| | 27 | 4.15 AM | Billeting party under Captain moved to St Leger | |
| | | 8 PM | Remainder of Brigade arriving St Leger 1 AM on 28" | |
| St Leger | 28 | 11 AM | Battery marched when line knows moved to Querrieu | |
| | | 10 pm | Battery left St Leger arriving Querrieu 5.30 AM Kr 29 | |
| Querrieu | 29 | | | |
| | 30 | | Heavy ..... | |

CONFIDENTIAL

Army Form C. 2118

# WAR DIARY
## WARWICK R.H.A.
### INTELLIGENCE SUMMARY
JULY, 1916.

VOLUME No. 24

VOL 20

(Erase heading not required.)

Instructions regarding War Diaries and Intelligence Summaries are contained in F.S. Regs., Part II. and the Staff Manual respectively. Title Pages will be prepared in manuscript.

| Place | Date | Hour | Summary of Events and Information | Remarks and references to Appendices |
|---|---|---|---|---|
| QUERRIEU | July 1st | 5 A.M. | Battery marched to BRESLE, returning to QUERRIEU at 5 P.M. | |
| " | 2 | | | |
| " | 3 | | | |
| " | 4 | | | |
| LONGPRÉ | 5 | 7 A.M. | Battery marched to LONGPRÉ, arriving 2.30 P.M. | |
| " | 6 | 6.10 p.m. | | |
| " | 7 | | Horse lines & bivouacs flooded; men billeted in barns, horses moved on to the road | |
| " | 8 | | Routine as usual | |
| " | 9 | | | |
| " | 10 | | | |
| " | 11 | | | |
| QUERRIEU | 12 | 6.30 p.m. | Battery left LONGPRÉ | |
| " | 13 | 6.45 A.M. | arrived QUERRIEU | |
| BUIRE | 14 | 6.30 p.m. | left QUERRIEU, arriving 8.45 P.M. at BUIRE-SUR-ANCRE | |
| " | 15 | | Routine as usual | |
| " | 16 | | " | |
| " | 16-20 | | Battery firing daily | |
| " | 21 | | | |
| " | 22 | | Stood ReadFast | |
| " | 23 | | | |
| " | 24 | 9.30 A.M. | Battery left BUIRE, arriving 1 P.M. at QUERRIEU | |
| QUERRIEU | 25 6.30- | | Routine as usual | |
| " | 27-29 9.30 pm | | Battery firing daily | |
| " | 30 | | Church Parade | |
| " | 31st | | Routine as usual | |

Vol 21

CONFIDENTIAL.

WAR DIARY.

of

1/1st Warwickshire Battery Royal Horse Artillery.

AUGUST, 1916.

(VOLUME XXV.)

# WAR DIARY WARWICK R.H.A. Vol 25 August 1916

## INTELLIGENCE SUMMARY

Army Form C. 2118

(Erase heading not required.)

Instructions regarding War Diaries and Intelligence Summaries are contained in F.S. Regs., Part II. and the Staff Manual respectively. Title Pages will be prepared in manuscript.

| Place | Date 1916 | Hour | Summary of Events and Information | Remarks and references to Appendices |
|---|---|---|---|---|
| QUERRIEU | 1 Aug | 6 AM | Battery gun drill & exercise | |
| " | 2 | — | Route march. | |
| " | 3 | — | Stables under Brigade. Stables by left. 2nd Lieut Puckett start for R.E. Edn. | |
| " | 4 | — | Battery gun drill. | |
| " | 5 | — | Route to march. | |
| " | 6 | — | — begin hurray before leave for England. | |
| " | 7, 8 | — | | |
| " | 9 | 4:30 AM | Routine as usual. | |
| LONG | 10 | 5 AM | Battery left QUERRIEU, arriving 11 AM at LONG. | |
| GAMACHES | 11 | — | Battery left LONG arriving at GAMACHES 12:30 P.M. | |
| " | 12 | — | Routine as usual. | |
| " | 13–19 | — | This week as one, in accordance with G.O.C. 1st Cav Divs instructions, devoted to drill & riding & exercises & amusement. | |
| " | 20 | 11 AM | Church Parade. | |
| " | 21, 22 | — | Usual routine. Major in hurray returned from leave. | |
| " | 23 | 9 AM | Drill Order | |
| " | 24 | — | Inspection by Brig. Vaughan Montgomerie by G.O.C. 1st Cav. Div. | |
| " | 25 | 10 AM | Battery gun drill. | |
| " | 26 | — | Routine as usual | |
| " | 27 | 11 AM | Church Parade | Enfin |
| " | 28 | — | Usual Routine | |

Army Form C. 2118

# WAR DIARY
or
~~INTELLIGENCE SUMMARY~~

Warwick R.H.A.
Aug. Vol 2.

(Erase heading not required.)

Instructions regarding War Diaries and Intelligence Summaries are contained in F. S. Regs., Part II. and the Staff Manual respectively. Title Pages will be prepared in manuscript.

| Place | Date Aug | Hour | Summary of Events and Information | Remarks and references to Appendices |
|---|---|---|---|---|
| GAMACHES | 29" | 9AM. | Battery marched ETAUTE-BUT, & practice on the Belgian remoulis. 70 rounds were fired. Owing to the weather blocks in the turn obtained for her woman used nevetive. Aero-lines used. | |
| " | 30" | | | |
| " | 31" | | | |

E.R.Munro
Lieut
Warwick R.H.A.

1875 Wt. W593/826 1,000,000 4/15 J.B.C. & A. A.D.S.S./Forms/C. 2118.

Army Form C. 2118

# WAR DIARY WARWICKSHIRE R.H.A.
## or
## INTELLIGENCE SUMMARY

*(Erase heading not required.)*

Instructions regarding War Diaries and Intelligence Summaries are contained in F.S. Regs., Part II. and the Staff Manual respectively. Title Pages will be prepared in manuscript.

| Place | Date | Hour | Summary of Events and Information | Remarks and references to Appendices |
|---|---|---|---|---|
| Verginguend | 1916 Feb 21 | Evening. | Section of guns withdrawn from action. Night spent at Verginguend | |
| Amuzju | 22 | - | Section marched from Verginguend to Amuzju. Remaining section of guns withdrawn from action and marched to Amuzju where night spent. | |
| Theromenon | 23 | - | Marched from Amuzju to Theromenon. Weather extremely bad. Severe frost & snow | |
| Seaguinio | 24 | - | Marched from Amuzju to Seaguinio. Weather again bad. Owing to condition of roads guns & vehicles kept for the night at top of Seaves Hill | |
| Seaguinio | 25 | - | Guns & vehicles fetched from Seaves Hill. Weather very bad | |
| do | 26 | - | No event of importance. Routine as usual. | |
| do | 27 | - | No event of importance. Routine as usual | |
| do | 28 | - | Do Do | |
| do | 29 | - | Do Do | |

[signature] Capt. RHA

OFFICER COMMANDING
WARWICKSHIRE R.H.A.

Confidential

# WARWICK RHA WAR DIARY - VOL 20
## INTELLIGENCE SUMMARY September 1916

Army Form C. 2118.

Instructions regarding War Diaries and Intelligence Summaries are contained in F.S. Regs., Part II. and the Staff Manual respectively. Title pages will be prepared in manuscript.

(Erase heading not required.)

| Hour, Date, Place | Summary of Events and Information | Remarks and references to Appendices |
|---|---|---|
| 15/16 | | |
| GAMACHES September 1st | Usual Routine | |
| — 5th | | |
| BETTENCOURT 6. | Battery marched to BETTENCOURT | |
| DAOURS 7-11 | DAOURS arriving 7 pm | |
| — 12 | Usual routine | |
| — 13 | Drill order Battery inspected by C.R.H.A. | |
| — 14 | Usual routine | |
| CARNOY 15 | Battery marched to CARNOY valley | |
| — 16 | at CARNOY, C.R.H.A. arrived. | |
| DAOURS 17 | Col Newcome Arriving Lt Bri C.R.H.A. visited Battery. | |
| — 18-22 | Battery marched back to DAOURS | |
| — 23 | Usual routine | |
| CONDÉ 24 | Battery marched to CONDÉ | |
| AUXY-LE-CHATEAU 25 | — AUXY LE CHATEAU | |
| LINZEUX 26 | — LINZEUX | |
| | There being no adequate water supply at LINZEUX the | |
| FILLIEVRES 27-30 | Battery marched to FILLIEVRES | |
| | Usual routine. | |

Signed [signature]
Lieut R.H.A.
Commanding
Warwick R.H.A.

**WAR DIARY** Warwick R.H.A.

or

**INTELLIGENCE SUMMARY.** VOL. 27   October 1916

Army Form C. 2118.

| Hour, Date, Place | Summary of Events and Information | Remarks and references to Appendices |
|---|---|---|
| FILLIEVRES Oct. 1st 1916 6 P.M. | Church Parade | |
| " 2nd – 7th | Usual routine | |
| " 8th – 10 | C.O. left on leave to Paris | |
| " 11th | Usual routine | |
| " 12th | Divisional field day. C.O. returned from Paris. | |
| " 13th | Routine as usual | |
| " 14th | Divisional field day | |
| " 15th – 17 | " | |
| " 18 | Usual routine | |
| " 19 8.30 A.M. | Cav. Corps field day cancelled. Battery marched with 1st Cav. Bde to NEUVILLETTE arriving at noon. | |
| NEUVILLETTE 20th 9.30 A.M. | Battery marched to NAOURS arriving 11.30 A.M. | |
| NAOURS 21st | At Naours. Battery marched with 7th R.H.A. Bde. to be attached 522nd Inf. Div. | |
| " 22 8.45 A.M. 5 P.M. | Battery left own an occupied position near ST MESNIL. Battery left own an alt MARTINPART. | |
| MESNIL 23rd | waggon-line at MARTINPART. Mist prevented registration. The day was spent in clearing. | |
| " 24th | Registered a zero line in spite of bad light | |
| " 25th | Registered Sunk Trench etc. | |
| " 26th | Registered Mill Trench | |
| " 27th | Battery transferred to 79th Division, to obtain an enfilade on trenches in B.15. | |

R.W. [signature]
Lieut.  R.H.A.
Warwick  R.H.A.

Army Form C. 2118.

# WAR DIARY
## or
## INTELLIGENCE SUMMARY. (Vol 2)
*(Erase heading not required.)*

| Hour, Date, Place | Summary of Events and Information | Remarks and references to Appendices |
|---|---|---|
| MESNIL Oct. 28th | Light enemy bombardment. Threat of Bombardment reported. Arrangement made with 19th Div. that our 1/4th Lanc. batteries should reply to Beaucourt line if he did try from Regina trench, but low visibility prevented this. | |
| 29th | Very wet: shooting impossible. | |
| 30th | General Monkhouse, CRA 19th Div. resumed the Battery Subsidiary + line of our inhuse STANSA trench. An attempt to better this was made but the short was under effective fire from 18" Div. rifle & follow machine guns. A round of shrapnel fire at 3.55. This bring on forward wiring both forward wires being cut. | |
| 31st | | |

E.P. Lambert
Lieut-Col. R.A.

DD95/1116/3

1916-1918
1ST CAVALRY DIVISION
9TH CAVALRY BRIGADE

'Y' BATTERY R.H.A.

DEC 1916-DEC 1918 APR 1919.

"Confidential"

War Diary

of

Y Battery R.H.A.

December 1916

VOLUME No 1

Dec 1916 — Dec 1918

Vol I

# WAR DIARY or INTELLIGENCE SUMMARY.

Army Form C. 2118.

| Place | Date | Hour | Summary of Events and Information | Remarks and references to Appendices |
|---|---|---|---|---|
| BOURAINVILLE | 1/12/16 | 3pm | Battery arrived at BOURAINVILLE at 3pm & billeted there for the night. This battery came under administration of 1st Cav Div and 7th Bde RHA from the midnight Nov. 30/Dec 1st 1916. | |
| VERLINCTHUN | 2/12/16 | 3pm | Battery marched into billets at VERLINCTHUN arriving at 3 pm. | |
| " | 3/12/16 | | All personnel belonging to Warwickshire R.H.A. which had been handed over by Mon at MEAULT (1 Sgt, 1 Cpl, 1 Bmbr, 1 Smtr, 1 Saddler, 5 Gunners 11 Drivers) back to Warwickshire R.H.A. returning with the Mobile Section were sent | |
| " | 5/12/16 | | Inspection of horses by the A.D.V.S. 1st Cav Div. 76 horses cast for debility. 10 for injuries & 4 for laminitis. | |
| " | 6/12/16 | | 90 horses evacuated to Mobile Vet Sec at NEUFCHATEL | |
| VERLINCTHUN and CARLY | 7/12/16 | | Head Qrs. Right and Left Sections moved into billets at CARLY. Centre Section remaining at VERLINCTHUN. | |
| CARLY | 11-16 | | Section Training. | |
| CARLY | 14/12/16 | | 1 Sgt. 6 drivers 13 horses and 3 SAA carts joined battery for Mobile Section from 7th RHA. FSBc Ann Col. | |
| HESDIN - L'ABBÉ HESDIGDEUL | 16/12/16 | | Distribution of medals by G.O.C. 1st Cav Div at HESDIN - L'ABBÉ CHATEAU. a Sergt McGUIRE. P. Cpl TAYLOR F = Gun. GODFREY.RB received the Military Medal. Cpl. STROUD A. Cpl. TAYLOR F. received the Distinguished Conduct Medal. | |

Army Form C. 2118.

# WAR DIARY
## or
## INTELLIGENCE SUMMARY.
*(Erase heading not required.)*

| Place | Date | Hour | Summary of Events and Information | Remarks and references to Appendices |
|---|---|---|---|---|
| CARLY. | 19/12/16 | | Inspection of billets by G.O.C. 9th Cav. F.S.2. | |
| " | 10/12/16 | | Exchanged 6 18pr guns and 12 13pr Amun Wagons for 6 13pr Guns and 12 13pr Wagons at ETAPLES | |
| " | " | | Drew 41 L.D horses from HESDIGNEUL STATION | |
| " | 20/12/16 | | Drew 30 L.D horses and 15 riding horses from No 4 Remount Depot. ECHINGHEN. | |
| " | 22/12/16 | | 2/Lieut. G.H.A. TODD joined from R.M.C. WOOLWICH. | |
| " | 26/12/16 to 30/12/16 | | Section training | |
| " | 28/12/16 | | 2/Lieut G.H.A TODD attached to I Battery R.H.A for instruction in Gunning fire. | |
| " | 30/12/16 | | 22 L.D horses received | |

Confidential

Vol 2

— War Diary —

of

Y Battery R.H.A.

January 1917

Volume No 2

Army Form C. 2118.

# WAR DIARY
## or
## INTELLIGENCE SUMMARY.
(Erase heading not required.)

Instructions regarding War Diaries and Intelligence Summaries are contained in F. S. Regs., Part II. and the Staff Manual respectively. Title pages will be prepared in manuscript.

| Place | Date | Hour | Summary of Events and Information | Remarks and references to Appendices |
|---|---|---|---|---|
| CARLY | 1/1/17 | 9.30am | Inspection of horses & remounts in draught by g.o.c. 9th Cavalry Bde. | |
| " | 2/1/17 to 6/1/17 | | Section training. | |
| " | 8/1/17 to 13/1/17 | | Section training. | |
| " | 15/1/17 | | Section training | |
| " | 20/1/17 | | | |
| " | 16/1/17 | 11am | Inspection of billets & sanitary arrangements by A.D.M.S. 1st Cav. Div. | |
| " | 22/1/17 to | | Section training. | |
| " | 27/1/17 | | | |
| " | 29/1/17 to 31/1/17 | | Section training. | |

W Blakely Major RHA
"Y" Battery RHA

O.c. "Y"

"Confidential"

# War Diary

of

"Y" Battery

R.H.A

for February 1917.

Volume III

Vol 3

Army Form C. 2118.

# WAR DIARY
## or
## INTELLIGENCE SUMMARY.
(Erase heading not required.)

Instructions regarding War Diaries and Intelligence Summaries are contained in F. S. Regs., Part II. and the Staff Manual respectively. Title pages will be prepared in manuscript.

| Place | Date | Hour | Summary of Events and Information | Remarks and references to Appendices |
|---|---|---|---|---|
| CARLY | 1.2.17 to 3.2.17 | | Section Training | W.D.A. |
| | 5.2.17 to 10.2.17 | | do | W.D.A. |
| | 12.2.17 to 17.2.17 | | do | W.D.A. |
| | 19.2.17 to 24.2.17 | | do | W.D.A. |
| | 26.2.17 to 28.2.17 | | do | W.D.A. |

W.Elley Major
Comdg 1/8th Bn North'n Regt

2353 Wt. W2544/1454 700,000 5/15 D. D. & L. A.D.S.S.J/Forms/C. 2118.

Confidential

Vol 5

War Diary
of
"Y" Battery R.H.A.
for March 1917

Volume No IV

Army Form C. 2118.

# WAR DIARY
## or
## INTELLIGENCE SUMMARY.
(Erase heading not required.)

Instructions regarding War Diaries and Intelligence Summaries are contained in F. S. Regs., Part II. and the Staff Manual respectively. Title pages will be prepared in manuscript.

| Place | Date | Hour | Summary of Events and Information | Remarks and references to Appendices |
|---|---|---|---|---|
| CARLY | 1-3-17 to 3-3-17 | | Section training | |
| | 5-3-17 to 10-3-17 | | do | |
| | 12-3-17 to 17-3-17 | | do | |
| | 19-3-17 to 24-3-17 | | do | |
| | 26-3-17 to 31-3-17 | | do | |

W Afferly
Major, R.H.A
Commanding "Y" Battery, R.H.A

"Confidential"

1914

War Diary
of
"Y" Battery R.H.A.
April 1917
VOL No V

Army Form C. 2118.

# WAR DIARY
## or
## INTELLIGENCE SUMMARY.
(Erase heading not required.)

| Place | Date | Hour | Summary of Events and Information | Remarks and references to Appendices |
|---|---|---|---|---|
| | | | | |

Major, R.H.A.
Commanding "Y" Battery, R.H.A.

Confidential

Vol 6

War Diary
of
"Y" Battery R.H.A.
May 1917

Vol. No VI

Army Form C. 2118.

# WAR DIARY
## or
## INTELLIGENCE SUMMARY.
*(Erase heading not required.)*

Instructions regarding War Diaries and Intelligence Summaries are contained in F. S. Regs., Part II. and the Staff Manual respectively. Title pages will be prepared in manuscript.

| Place | Date | Hour | Summary of Events and Information | Remarks and references to Appendices |
|---|---|---|---|---|
| AUBROMETZ | 1/5/17 to 12/5/17 | | Battery Training | |
| Pressy les Pernes | 13/5/17 | | Marched from AUBROMETZ to PRESSY LEZ PERNES | |
| LABROUVIERE | 14/5/17 | | Marched to LABROUVIERE | |
| LABROUVIERE | 17/5/17 | | Left Section went into the line, took over from A/330 Bde at F11 b 3.1. | Maps BETHUNE 1/40,000 |
| " | 18/5/17 | | Right + Centre sections went into the line & took over six gun position from A/330 Bde at F11 b 3.1. | Map BETHUNE A in sheet 17/18.S |
| F11 b 3.1 Ry BETHUNE 1/20,000 | 19/5/17 to 31/5/17 | | In position covering 198th Infantry Bde. Zone. 1st Trench Maps LA BASSEE 36c N.W.1. from A9 b 4.3 to A10 c 3.1. Front quiet. Normal expenditure about 250 rds a day. | Ry BETHUNE 1/10,000 |

Wollerly Spren
Bolton RHA
Comdr.

Confidential

1917

War Diary
of
Y Battery RHA
June 1917
Vol VII

Army Form C. 2118.

# WAR DIARY
## or
## INTELLIGENCE SUMMARY.
*(Erase heading not required.)*

Instructions regarding War Diaries and Intelligence Summaries are contained in F. S. Regs., Part II. and the Staff Manual respectively. Title pages will be prepared in manuscript.

| Place | Date | Hour | Summary of Events and Information | Remarks and references to Appendices |
|---|---|---|---|---|
| | June. | | | |
| F11.B.31. Ryt. Bethune 20000. | 1-2. | | In position covering 198th Infantry Bde. | |
| Le Quesnoy | 3/6 | | Battery left gun position went back to Waggon Lines at LE QUESNOY | |
| Estaires | 4/6 | | Marched to ESTAIRES. Went into Bivouac just outside town | |
| " | 4-11 | | Remained at ESTAIRES. | |
| Le Quesnoy | 11 | | Marched back to Waggon Lines. Work the battery had previously occupied at LE QUESNOY. | |
| " | 11 | | In evening D 11th Battery went into position at X.22.d.5.8 (Bethune 20000) | |
| " | 12 | | Registered & found a raid shoot for 2/6 East Lancs Regt. Mad. night. | |
| X.24.a.11 Ryt.Bethune 20000 | 14 1 19 | | Changed position to X.24.a.11. Found for 2/6 East Lancs & 2/5 East Lancs. Normal expenditure about 100 rds a day. | |
| Le Quesnoy R.6.b. Ryt.Aire 36T.S. 40000 | 19 21. | | Battery left position & returned to Waggon Line. Battery marched to Waggon Line at R.6.b. Ref Sheet 36.S.E ¼ 40000. | |

Army Form C. 2118.

# WAR DIARY
## or
## INTELLIGENCE SUMMARY.
(Erase heading not required.)

Instructions regarding War Diaries and Intelligence Summaries are contained in F.S. Regs., Part II. and the Staff Manual respectively. Title pages will be prepared in manuscript.

| Place | Date | Hour | Summary of Events and Information | Remarks and references to Appendices |
|---|---|---|---|---|
| | June | | | |
| R66 | 22 | | A position was dug at M.21.d.1.6 (Ref Sheet 36.c.¹/₂₀₀₀₀) & ammunition for 500 rds/per gun taken up at night | |
| Ref Sheet 36 B ¹/₂₀₀₀₀ | 24 | | Night of 24th Guns were brought up | |
| | 25th | | Battery registered. This was the first time 9 shots till 28th | |
| | 26th | | 1 Gunner No. 102630 Gr HAYNES Wounded | |
| | 28. | 7.10 am | Battery fired a barrage supporting the attack of the 136th Inf Bde on Hill 60 | |
| | | | M.29.b (Ref sheet 36.c¹/₂₀₀₀₀) incl. 625 rds. | |
| | 29th | 10 pm | Fired barrage supporting the 137th Inf Bde in attack on hillocks W of LENS. | |
| | 30th | 2.15 am | Fired barrage supporting the 138th Inf Bde in attack on hillocks N of LENS. | |

W.S.Stonhynion(?) Lt Coll
Cmdg ¼ Batty RFA

Confidential

WAR DIARY
of
"Y" Battery R.H.A.
July 1917.
Vol. 8

Army Form C. 2118.

# WAR DIARY
## or
## INTELLIGENCE SUMMARY.
(Erase heading not required.)

Instructions regarding War Diaries and Intelligence Summaries are contained in F. S. Regs., Part II. and the Staff Manual respectively. Title pages will be prepared in manuscript.

| Place | Date | Hour | Summary of Events and Information | Remarks and references to Appendices |
|---|---|---|---|---|
| M2td 1-6 Ref Sheet 36C 20,000 | July 1st | 2.47 | Fixed barrage, supporting attack of the 46th Division on line ch W of LENS with a view to establishing a line approximately SOUCHEZ RIVER at N.25.6 & 6 to N.20.C | |
| | | 0.2. | ACONITE & ALOOF Trenches, thence to N.13a.9.5.6.5. (Ref French Map LENS 36° S.W. 1/10000) |  |
| | | | A slow rate of fire with occasional bursts was kept up all day as |  |
| | 2. | | Attack succeeded in centre but failed final objective on right & centre.<br>Left Guns No 99 36a Gunner SAWYER W wounded<br>Situation still obscure and slow rate of protective fire kept up till 3 p.m.<br>Withdrew from gun position at night marched back to waggon lines | |
| Estairs | 3rd | | | |
| S6B1.5 | 4th | | Marched at 9 a.m. to ESTAIRS. | |
| | 6th | | Four guns taken into action at S6B1.5 W of RICHBOURG St VAAST (Ry BETHUNE 20000. en-bwid Sketch). Covering the Portuguese. | |
| | 7th<br>8th<br>1st<br>14. | | Removing a two guns horse into action. Waggon line remained at ESTAIRS. Battery fired about 100 RDs a day. Artillery of both sides very quiet. | |
| ESTAIRS. | 15th | | Battery left gun position returned to waggon lines at ESTAIRS. | |
| | 16th | | Rejoined 9th Car Bgde, who arrived in the ESTAIRS area | |
| Estairs | 17th–21st | | Battery training. | |

Wotherly Jones, Major RHA.<br>Cmdr Y Batty.

Confidential

Vol 9

War Diary

of

7/ Battery R.H.A

for August 1917

VOL IX

Army Form C. 2118.

# WAR DIARY
## or
## INTELLIGENCE SUMMARY.
(Erase heading not required.)

| Place | Date | Hour | Summary of Events and Information | Remarks and references to Appendices |
|---|---|---|---|---|
| ESTAIRES. | Aug. 1 to 26. | | Battery Training. | |
| CUHEM. | 27th. | | Batty marched with 9th Cav. Bde. to CUHEM. | |
| RENTY. | 28th. | | Batty marched with 9th Cav. Bde. to RENTY. | |
| CARLY | 29th | | Battery Corps under Comd moved to 2RHA 1st Can. Div. & marched to CARLY. | Ref. HAZEBROUCK S.A. 1/100000 |
| " | 30st | | } Battery Training. | |
| " | 31st | | | |

W Burnley Major RHA
Battery
Canada

Confidential

Vol 10

War Diary
of
Y Battery RHA
Sep 1917

VOL X

Army Form C. 2118.

# WAR DIARY
## or
## INTELLIGENCE SUMMARY.
*(Erase heading not required.)*

Instructions regarding War Diaries and Intelligence Summaries are contained in F. S. Regs., Part II. and the Staff Manual respectively. Title pages will be prepared in manuscript.

| Place | Date | Hour | Summary of Events and Information | Remarks and references to Appendices |
|---|---|---|---|---|
| CARLY. | Sept 1st to 30. | | Battery training under C.R.H.A. 1st Cav. Div. | |
| | 26th | | 2/Lt H. Benson joined the battery. | |

W.M.Morby, Major.
Cmdg Y Batt. R.H.A.

Confidential

War Diary
of
"Y" Battery R.H.A.

— October 1917 —
Volume 11

Army Form C. 2118.

# WAR DIARY
## or
## INTELLIGENCE SUMMARY.
(Erase heading not required.)

"Y" Battery R.H.A. 1/10/14 to 31/10/14

Instructions regarding War Diaries and Intelligence Summaries are contained in F. S. Regs., Part II. and the Staff Manual respectively. Title pages will be prepared in manuscript.

| Place | Date | Hour | Summary of Events and Information | Remarks and references to Appendices |
|---|---|---|---|---|
| CARLY | 1st Oct | | Major W. B. Hayley RHA proceeded on three weeks leave of absence to England (recalled on the 9th) Battery Training under C.R.H.A. 1st Cav. Div. | |
| | 1st to 3rd Oct | | | |
| | 4th Oct | | Inspection by Major Gen Mullens Cdg 1st Cav Div. | |
| | 5th Oct | | Lieut C. Clark M.C. RHA transferred to 59th DAC and Lieut V.R.C.D. 1st RHA appointed to command. Additional Amm. Col attached Y Battery RHA. | |
| CARLY. | 7th Oct | | Battery marched to la BLEUE MAISON close to WATTEN. +Came under the orders of 9th Cav. Bde. | |
| BLEUE MAISON | 8th Oct | | Move to Mt WORMHOUDT area connected. Battery bivouacked at BLEUE MAISON for 3 days. | |
| CARLY. | 11th Oct | | Battery marched back to CARLY | |
| | 15th Oct | | Battery marched to ESTREE under the orders of 9th Cav. Bde. All the horses were got under cover. | |
| | 18th Oct | | Major W. B. Hayley proceeded on leave to England. | |
| | 19th Oct | | Two Corporals and three Bombardiers transferred to the R.F.A. on promotion. | |
| | 15th–31st | | Battery Training. | |
| | 29th | | Lieut R F Roston proceeded on leave to England. | |

M Stanley
Captain
RHA
Major Cdg Y Battery RHA

Confidential

War Diaries
of
Y Battery R.H.A.

for Nov 1917.

VOL NO 12.

CONFIDENTIAL

Army Form C. 2118.

# WAR DIARY
# or
# INTELLIGENCE SUMMARY.
(Erase heading not required.)

Y Battery R.H.A.
NOVEMBER 1917.
VOLUME 12.

| Place | Date | Hour | Summary of Events and Information | Remarks and references to Appendices |
|---|---|---|---|---|
| ESTRÉE | Nov. 1st | | Battery training. | |
| | 2nd | | Lieut. (Temp Capt) M. Sandry M.C. gazetted Captain. | |
| | 3rd | | Major W.B. Hayley & Lieut Rowley returned from leave. | |
| | 8th | | Battery marched to BOUIN. Good billets all horses under cover. | |
| | 10th | | " " Le MEILLARD " | |
| | 11th | | " " GUERRIEU " | |
| | 12th | | " " CHIPILLY " | |
| | 13th | | " " LE MESNIL-BRUNTEL, concentration area of Cavalry Corps | |
| | 14th | | " " " | |
| LE MESNIL-BRUNTEL | 15-20 | | No horse lines, men in huts | |
| | 20th | | Stood by awaiting orders to advance. | |
| | 21st | | Marched at 2 am for rendez-vous of 1st Cav. Div at FINS. Moved off about 12 noon with 9th Cav. Bde., which was in reserve. Marched to fm as METZ-EN-COUTURE where Brigade bivouaced for the night. Moved forward with 9 Cav. Bde. to MARSH TRESCAULT and halted at RIBECOURT. Rifle & M.G. firing said loud at RIBECOURT. Marched about 3.45 pm to MARCOING. Brought guns into action in the dark S.W. of MARCOING near railway embankment. | |

# WAR DIARY
## or
## INTELLIGENCE SUMMARY.

Army Form C. 2118.

| Place | Date | Hour | Summary of Events and Information | Remarks and references to Appendices |
|---|---|---|---|---|
| | Nov 21st | | Opening F.O. Count just E.Q. NOYELLES. Came under orders of O.C. 7th Bde R.H.A | |
| | 22nd | | Did not fire. Withdrew guns about 1 p.m. Marching back with 9th Cav. Bde to METZ-en-COUTURE when Brigade bivouaced for night | |
| | 23rd | | Marched with 9th Cav. Bde to FLESQUIERES + halted all day. Six guns brought up a comp. Bivouaced when we made for night. | |
| | 24th | | Stood by all day + at 3 p.m. received orders to march to BOURSIES + come into action under the orders of O.C. 9th Bde RHA with "H" + "I" Batteries R.H.A. Arr. position at J.4.b.4.1 (Ref. Manoeuvre map Special Sheet Parts of 57C N.W. N.E SH. 1/20,000) at 2.30 am after a very bad march over very bad roads via HAPPINCOURT - HERMIES - BERTINCOURT - BEAUMETZ-LEZ-CAMBRAI. Teams went back to waggon line at BEUGNY m man. CAMBRAI - BAPAUME road | |
| | 25 | | Registered. Quiet day | |
| | 26 | | Battery fired about 1444 rds on S.O.S. Lieut. H.L. HOPE MC RFA joined the battery | |
| | 27 ? 30 | | In action at same place. Chiefly used for barrage purposes. Vicinity of battery shelled a good deal at night. | |

# WAR DIARY or INTELLIGENCE SUMMARY

Y Battery, R.H.A.

VOLUME 13. December 1917.

| Place | Date | Hour | Summary of Events and Information | Remarks and references to Appendices |
|---|---|---|---|---|
| BOURSIES | 1 Dec | | Some gas shells fired into the Battery position. Gas masks worn to shield the incoming crew. | |
| | 2 Dec | | The Battery moved its position about 1½ miles owing to the British Withdrawal from BOURLON WOOD and MOEUVRES. the Battery dug all night in their gun pits camouflaged by Jason Bathes from DOIGNIES. | |
| | 3rd | | Registered – freezing hard | |
| | 7th | | The Battery came out of action and spent the night at the Wagon lines BEUGNY. | |
| | 8th | | The Battery marched to BOUCLY (TINCOURT) NR PERONNE | |
| | 9th | | The Right Section came into action relieving the section of 1 K Battery RHA at TEMPLEUX-LE GUERRARD on enrolled position – a battery wk made dug outs for each gun, and enrolled accommodation for all ranks. | |
| | 10th | | Remaining guns relieved the rest of 1 K Battery RHA at the same place. Shot 62 c NW F26O 25.50. Lieut R.F. Ronster RFA posted to 179 R.A.F.A. Bde. | |
| | 11th | | An advanced wagon line captured from horses and harness for No.1 gun established at K6 d S.3 (Refc 62 c NW) Gunner Collins slightly wounded by shrapnel at the O.P. | |

# WAR DIARY
## or
## INTELLIGENCE SUMMARY.

*(Erase heading not required.)*

Army Form C. 2118.

Vol. 14.

| Place | Date | Hour | Summary of Events and Information | Remarks and references to Appendices |
|---|---|---|---|---|
| TEMPLEUX- LE- GUERARD | January 1.1.18 | | Major R.B.P. CUST joined to command battery. | |
| | 1st to 8th | | No shooting owing to snow on ground. Very quiet. | |
| | 9th & 10th | | Occasional shelling of TEMPLEUX and neighbourhood of battery position, by day and night. | |
| | 12th | | B/2 Wright wounded - remaining at duty. | |
| | 16th | | Staff in officers coathouse - D/2 GELDER killed - B/2 BODDIE, D/2 COOK, and G/2 PARKER wounded - Major CUST and Lieut DILL slightly wounded at duty - | |
| | 17th | | B/2 Boddie and D/2 Cook died of wounds - buried at TINCOURT - | |
| | 22nd | | Right half battery moved to L.20.d. (N.E. of JEAN COURT) into open position. | |
| near JEANCOURT | 23rd | | Remaining three guns moved to same position. Registered. | |
| | 24th | | No firing and very quiet. | |
| | 25th-31st | | Battery ways lines at BOUCLY improved during the month by improvements to stabling, accommodation for men, and new horses rooms etc. All horses under cover, but stables too small and being extended. | |

31.1.18.

MWCust
Major R.H.A.
Cmdg "Y" R.H.A.

WAR DIARY
OF
"Y" Battery R.H.A.

MARCH 1915

VOLUME XV

APPENDIX 'C'

Army Form C. 2118.

# WAR DIARY
## or
## INTELLIGENCE SUMMARY.
(Erase heading not required.)

"Y" "B" Bty. March 1918

| Place | Date | Hour | Summary of Events and Information | Remarks and references to Appendices |
|---|---|---|---|---|
| | 1918 | | | |
| JEANCOURT | 1-13 Mch 13.v.14 | | In action N.W. of JEANCOURT. Busy building new positions & dug outs. Relieved by "Q" Battery R.H.A. | |
| VRAIGNES | 15ᵗʰ | | In Wagon Lines at VRAIGNES. | |
| Le Mesnil | 15ᵗʰ | | Moved to join 9ᵗʰ Bde Brigade at Le Mesnil. good billets, but horses all in open. | |
| " | 15ᵗʰ & 20ᵗʰ | | Cleaning up & individual training | |
| " | 20ᵗʰ | | Test "move to position of readiness Bernes" | |
| " | 21ˢᵗ | | At about 2.p.m. received orders to "move to position of readiness Bernes" moved with 9ᵗʰ Cav Bde to Bernes & on to the neighbourhood of Hervilly, returning after dark to bivouac at Bernes without coming into action. After assembling at rendezvous, Battery returned to billets. | |
| " | 22ⁿᵈ | | Came into action between Montigny Farm & Hervilly, shortly after daylight under orders of Lt Col Allardyce., comdg 3ˣ Bde. R.H.A. morning very foggy & did not fire. About 11 a.m. retired to new position at C.C.S. North of Bernes & fired on enemy advancing against Brown Line east of Hervilly & Hesbecourt. About 4 p.m. retired to take up fresh position near Beaumetz. On arrival there received orders to rejoin 9ᵗʰ Cav Bde at Bouvincourt & marched with them to Ennemain. About 11.45 p.m. marched off & take up position E of Brie. | |
| | 23ʳᵈ | 2.30 am | Came into action on high ground east of Brie, to cover front from Le Mesnil to Athies. | |

2353  Wt. W2544/1454  700,000  5/15  D. D. & L.  A.D.S.S./Forms/C. 2118.

Army Form C. 2118.

# WAR DIARY
## or
## INTELLIGENCE SUMMARY.
(Erase heading not required.)

Instructions regarding War Diaries and Intelligence Summaries are contained in F. S. Regs., Part II. and the Staff Manual respectively. Title pages will be prepared in manuscript.

(2)

| Place | Date 1916 | Hour | Summary of Events and Information | Remarks and references to Appendices |
|---|---|---|---|---|
| | 23rd | 4.30 AM | Received orders to march with 1st Cav Bde at Morchain about midday. Rejoined 9th Cav Bde at | |
| | | 2 PM | Came into action about 2 pm & fired till dark at enemy near Bois de Croix. Lt Todd acting F.O.O. with 19 Hussars east of Pargny down the slopes of the hill. Enfilading very good targets. Bridge & river. Enemy attacked in waves | |
| | 24th | | After dark returned with 9th Bde about 4 am to Barleux. Marched off with 9th Bde about 4 am to Barleux. Noted & felt there moved on in the afternoon via VAUX. To rendezvous east of Maricourt where orders were received to move to Montauban. Section came into action on the east of the village but could do no good as the situation was not cleared up till after dark, when the whole battery withdrew to bivouac at Plateau Siding near Carnoy. | |
| | 25th | | 6 guns came into action about 500 yds NE of Carnoy village to cover the cavalry front between Montauban & Bernafay Wood. Slight shelling of whole area during morning. About 11 a.m. moved 1 section into action at Northern end of Carnoy village behind the ridge. About midday received orders to withdraw the whole battery. East of Montauban S.E. of TRICOURT. 4 guns were withdrawn, the section remaining to cover the front. As the result of further information later, the four guns were brought back in the afternoon into action just west of the Carnoy-Montauban road and supported the front. Shell dropped forward with the Cavalry all day & kept communication with the guns by visual. Owing to the bad light however this was never satisfactory. | |
| | | | During the whole afternoon enemy 4.2 & 5.9 batteries shelled neighbourhood of battery position & wagon line without causing any casualties. About 6 pm hostile plane flew low over position & shortly afterwards both batteries started their shooting & shelling became heavy & the battery withdrew on receipt of orders at 6.15 p.m. Casualties 2/Lt Reader killed, Gnr. _____ Sgt Kelley, Sgt Wild, Gnr Francis, Dr. The Bennett, Dr. _____ left wounded. 5 horses killed, wounded. Moved back to Littehi at Busse for the night. Horses unfed. | |
| | 26th | 9.0 am | at 9.0 am marched to Meaulte ammunition dump to refill ammunition then on to Yzeux the Dorr at Bussy les Daours. Dr Barber wounded whilst accompanying Dr Riddle on a reconnaissance. | |
| | 27th | 10 am | Marched off at 10 am under 1st Cav Bde & advanced south of La Houssoye for the right at 4 am moved off & came into action with 4 guns South West of Morlancourt to cover the cavalry front. Merricourt to Sailly. Sec one section in action in reserve S.E. of Heilly all day without firing. Extended targets all day. Communications worked well. Hostile battery came into action on crest South of Morlancourt in morning & communications was at once engaged & prevented from firing all day. The detachments being driven from their guns & teams scattered on ground occasions when they attempted to approach the position. | |

Army Form C. 2118.

# WAR DIARY
## or
## INTELLIGENCE SUMMARY.
*(Erase heading not required.)*

(3)

Instructions regarding War Diaries and Intelligence Summaries are contained in F.S. Regs., Part II. and the Staff Manual respectively. Title pages will be prepared in manuscript.

| Place | Date | Hour | Summary of Events and Information | Remarks and references to Appendices |
|---|---|---|---|---|
| | 4/18 27/inst | | Infantry advancing over ridge west of Morlancourt were also driven back. Enemy seen to fall & those digging in on forward slopes were also engaged with visible effect throughout the day. In the afternoon a column of about 200 infantry followed by a long column detrampment attempted to move across from the valley running south from Morlancourt in a southerly direction after a few rounds this column broke into two parts which turned in opposite directions. Both were engaged & completely scattered over the country side in the greatest confusion the majority eventually making their way back into the Morlancourt valley from which they had come. Several messages were dropped from aeroplanes on the battery positions giving targets which were engaged. Shortly before dusk the battery moved back into billets at la Neuville for the night. | |
| | 28th inst | | Moved at 4.30 a.m. to rendezvous at Div. H.Q. at Fouilloy. Orders were there received to attack Right Section to 9 Bde/Centre Section to 2nd Bde/Left Section to 1st Bde, to support an attack on enemy's position between Warfusée. The runs to the north. Right Left Sects came into action in different parts of the Bois de VAIRE. The right section engaged the enemy at Warfusée to keep down hostile M.G fire. The left section came into action on the sunken covered position in front of the wood & was at once engaged by the enemy & had to withdraw after firing a few rounds, 1 long gun being put out of action. Casualties Gnr Burch Gnr HAZES Gnr HAZES & Cnr D'ARBY & Cnr D'ARBY wounded. The centre section remained in reserve and 5 Cav. Bde. Later on the afternoon the whole battery came into action just south the FOUILLOY - WARFUSÉE road fired along whole front held by cavalry. north of Warfusée where hostile attack was threatened. Battery withdrew to billets at vacquement about 10 p.m. | ...R.H.A. ...R.H.A Cmdg Y R.H.A |
| | 29e | | Stood to at 5.30 a.m. & reconnoitred position to cover retirement. No more lines at Vecquemont at 2.15 moved up into action on same position as previous afternoon, withdrawing to Fouilloy at dusk without firing. | |
| | 30e | | Moved into position with 2nd Bde. near Bois de L'Abbe. and Villers Bretton-meux remaining all day without coming into action - returned to Fouilloy at dusk. 1 horse killed, 1 horse wounded | 6.4.16 |
| | 31st & 3 April 5e | | In reserve at Fouilloy. | |
| | 4e | | Moved to Querrieu. to north end of AMIENS | |

APPENDIX III

Army Form C. 2118.

# WAR DIARY
## or
## INTELLIGENCE SUMMARY.

Vol 14.

(Erase heading not required.)

| Place | Date 1918 | Hour | Summary of Events and Information | Remarks and references to Appendices |
|---|---|---|---|---|
| Fontaine l'Etalon | June 1/30 | | Section Training | |
| | 2. | | Major R.B. Pewy-Cust D.S.O., M.C. R.H.A. appointed B.M.R.A. 2nd Div. | |
| | 2. | | Lieut. B.W. Diemer R.F.A. to 1st Army R.A. Reinforcement Camp. | |
| | 4. | | Capt. M. Staveley, M.C., R.H.A. to Command A/64 Bde. R.F.A. | |
| | 8. | | Major K.M. Bull D.S.O., R.H.A. assumed Command | |
| | 12 | | 2/Lt. J.E. Pridham R.F.A. Joined | |
| | 16 | | Lieut. N.L. Palmer R.F.A. Joined | |

[signature]
Major, R.H.A.
Commanding Y Battery, R.H.A.

APPENDIX 'C'

"I" R.H.A.

**WAR DIARY or INTELLIGENCE SUMMARY**

Army Form C. 2118.

Vol. 19. / I Cav / August 1918

| Place | Date | Hour | Summary of Events and Information | Remarks and references to Appendices |
|---|---|---|---|---|
| BEAUVOIRE-RIVIERE | August 1918 1st – 5th | | Section Training – Practically all horses in the Battery suffering from stomatitis | |
| | 5th | 10 p.m. | Battery marched to BERTEAUCOURT-LES-DAMES. | |
| | 6th | 7 p.m. | " " " billets near LONGPRÉ | |
| | 7th | 8.30 p.m. | " " " Rendezvous East of AMIENS | |
| | 8th | 3.30 a.m. | Arrived in concentration area. March very slow owing to congestion of traffic in AMIENS. | |
| | | 4.50 a.m. | Battery moved forward behind leading regiment of 9th Cav. Bde. along cavalry track to U.1.B.00 & thence to Monument in U.6.a. South of VILLERS BRETONNEUX arriving about 7.30 a.m. Movement very difficult owing to trenches & wire – Troops detailed to clear track were insufficient & gunners had to fall in several trenches & clear track. | |
| | | 8.15 a.m. | Moved to V.2.d.9.9. arriving about 8.45 a.m. | |
| | | 8.30 a.m. | " " V.3.c. East of MARCELCAVE. – from here onwards going was good. | |
| | | 10.10 a.m. | " " V.12.c. West of WIENCOURT. – Some machine gun fire wounding a few horses one of which had to be destroyed. | |
| | | 11.15 a.m. | Report received that enemy was on the run towards ROSIERES – 1st Life Guards & 19th Hussars ordered to gallop & strike. The Battery to come into action covering the attack & keep down machine gun fire coming from woods in W.22.c + d – Battery moved through L GUILLAUCOURT & |

# WAR DIARY
## or
## INTELLIGENCE SUMMARY.
*(Erase heading not required.)*

Army Form C. 2118.

| Place | Date | Hour | Summary of Events and Information | Remarks and references to Appendices |
|---|---|---|---|---|
| | 8th Sept (Con'd) | | Came into action at W.15.a. – Enemy machine guns wounded some horses slightly, & Gr. S. Brown was hit in the leg & had to be evacuated. Enemy artillery opened fire from M.G. fire from woods caused owing to our Tanks arriving at the Woods. – No good targets seen. – Battery shelled slopes S.E. of CAIX to cover advance of 19th Hussars. – Later enemy seen on slopes about E.6. – O.P. had to be changed & some delay caused by Battery Staff horses not coming up quickly. – When Battery opened fire GOC 9th A de retired them to stop as situation was obscure & it was thought that our cavalry was working up to the ridge. | |
| | | 7.10pm | Cavalry regiments returned to watering – Battery to remain in action & co-operate with Canadian Artillery. – A quiet night for the Battery but considerable enemy shelling in vicinity:- During these operations horses suffered from lack of water. – They did not get any water till the afternoon when they were watered from a drinking pond in GUILLAUCOURT. | |
| | 9th | 7.30 am | Battery withdrawn & moved to concentrate with rest of Brigade N. of farm LUCE about W.25+26 + water horses. | |
| | | 11 am | Battery advanced with Brigade Evally, in W.21 + 22. – Some shelling during advance one shell falling in rally, alongside Battery when Lieuten. Palmer was wounded & evacuated. | |
| | | 4.30pm | Brigade reached redoubt trench up behind POSIERES arriving about 6 p.m. | |
| | | 6.15pm | 8th Hussars retired to major MEHARICOURT & right section of Battery moved up & came into action about F.14.C. – A section of hostile guns opened fire from lines S. of LIHON & was taken on & silenced by right section. – No other targets seen. | |
| | | 9.15pm | Brigade was retired & took up outpost line for night – Right section Battery withdrawn & while |

# WAR DIARY
## or
## INTELLIGENCE SUMMARY.
*(Erase heading not required.)*

Army Form C. 2118.

(3)

| Place | Date | Hour | Summary of Events and Information | Remarks and references to Appendices |
|---|---|---|---|---|
| | August 1918 | | Battery came into action near road F.13.b.1 - F.14.c coming front from SUGAR FACTORY (F.9) to MEHARICOURT. | |
| | 10th | | A quiet night. Enemy aeroplanes active but no bombs dropped near Battery, or Wagon Lines which was in F.7.c. | |
| | | 4.15 am | Received orders that Brigade was to halt observe to area between CAIX & CAYEUX | |
| | | 7.50 am | Arrived in Bivouac area N.25.b. | |
| | | 5.10 pm | Marched with rest of 9th Div. Arty to a HARVILLERS & halted at E.9.6. | |
| | | 6.45 pm | Orders to return to Bivouac area recently vacated | |
| ↑ | 11th | 7.30 pm | Marched to billets at CAMON – Enemy bombing planes very active on route but no bombs dropped near 9 Can. Div. | |
| CAMON | 14th | | Inspected by FM Sir Douglas Haig, C-in-C - Lieut M.H. GIBSON to hospital - injured wrist | |
| | 16th | 9.30 pm | Marched & billets at - LE QUESNIL FARM | |
| LE QUESNIL Fm | 17th | | Lt. A.L. Hope to England on leave | |
| | 19th | | Battery marched with 9th Can. Div. to THIEVRES. | |
| | 20th | 11.30 pm | " " " via PAS - HENU - SOUASTRE & forward Concentration area. | |
| | 21st | 2.45 am | Arrived in Concentration area E.25. West of FONQUEVILLERS. | |
| | | 4.55 am | Zero hour – bombardment opened | |

# WAR DIARY
## or
## INTELLIGENCE SUMMARY.
(Erase heading not required.)

Army Form C. 2118.

(4.)

| Place | Date | Hour | Summary of Events and Information | Remarks and references to Appendices |
|---|---|---|---|---|
| | April 1918 | | | |
| | 21st | 7.30am | Moved forward with 9th Can. Bde via FONQUEVILLERS - ESSARTS Krallers in F.20 - 9.5rd Track all the way & an easy march - Battery remained here all day without coming into action - A | |
| AMPLIER | 21st | 5.15pm | for h/2 day, & no water for horses. Will share with remainder of 9th Can. Bde. to billets at AMPLIER | |
| AMPLIER | 26th | | Marched with 9th Can. Bde to billets at GRAND - RULLECOURT | |
| GRAND-RULLECOURT | 26th/31st | | Battery training when possible | |

Appendix C

Army Form C. 2118.

WAR DIARY
or
INTELLIGENCE SUMMARY.

"Y"

| Place | Date | Hour | Summary of Events and Information | Remarks and references to Appendices |
|---|---|---|---|---|
| GRAND ROLLECOURT | Sept. 1918 | | | |
| | 1st–6th | | Section Training | |
| | 7th | | Took part in Cavalry field exercise | |
| | 8th–12th | | Individual Training | |
| | 13th | 9 am | Major K.M. Ball. D.S.O. R.H.A. to England on leave | |
| | 13th | | Section Training | |
| | 16th | | March to billets at HAUTE-COTE | |
| | 17th | 6.30 pm | Left HAUTE-COTE and took part in Cavalry Corps Tactical Scheme in AUXI-LE-CHATEAU area, arriving at billets at LE-NERVILLE 5.15 pm | |
| | | | Lieut. C.A.N. TODD R.H.A. to England on leave | |
| | 18th | 10.40 pm | Marched to billets at HARDINVAL | |
| | 21st–22nd | | Cleaning up and Individual Training | |
| | 23rd | | Calibrated Guns | |
| | 24th | 1.50 pm | March to billets at ST. LEGER-LE-AUTHIE | |
| | 25th | 6.0 pm | Marched to MEAULTE and bivouacked | |
| | 26th | 7.30 pm | Marched to MANANCOURT arriving 2.30 am 27.9.18 and bivouacked | |
| | 28th | | Cleaning up A/C and individual training | |
| | 29th | 3.0 pm | Marched from MANANCOURT to HERVILLY arriving 6.50 pm and bivouacked | |
| | 30th | | HERVILLY | |

K. Stomach Capt.

Army Form C. 2118.

Instructions regarding War Diaries and Intelligence Summaries are contained in F. S. Regs., Part II. and the Staff Manual respectively. Title pages will be prepared in manuscript.

# WAR DIARY
## or
## INTELLIGENCE SUMMARY.
(Erase heading not required.)

| Place | Date | Hour | Summary of Events and Information | Remarks and references to Appendices |
|---|---|---|---|---|
| HERVILLY | October 1st | | Marched with 9th Cav. Bde. to rendez-vous near BELLICOURT – After standing to returned to bivouac at about 13.20 | |
| " | 2nd 4,5,6 | | Stood to awaiting orders | |
| " | 7th | 15.30 | Marched with 9th Cav. Bde. & bivouaced in valley S. of VILLERET. | |
| In the Field | 8th | 04.00 | Moved up to WIANCOURT area | |
| | | 08.30 | " " with Cav. Bde. to valley East of GENEVE | |
| | | 11.45 | Came into action between GENEVE and PREMONT w/orders to stop enemy digging in on high ground E. of SERAIN. Moving scattered parties seen & dispersed. Enemy shelling wagon lines wounded 3 O.R's & 3 horses | |
| | 18.10 | | Limbered up & marched back w/K Brigade to bivouac near BEAUREVOIR – Hostile aircraft active bombing roads at one point full alongside battery killing 1 driver & 3 horses & wounding three other horses. | |
| " | 9th | 08.00 | Commenced with w/K Bde. S. of BEAUREVOIR – 9th Cav. Bde. was now in reserve | |
| | | 10.20 | Moved up with Bde. to valley of RAU de la VILLE later moving up N. of PREMONT | |
| | | 18.00 | Ordered to bivouac near MARETZ | |
| " | 10th | 07.00 | Moved up with Brigade to valley between TROISVILLE & PREMONT – stayed there all day & returned to bivouac near MARETZ about 16.00. | |
| | 11th | | } In bivouac | |
| MARETZ | 12th | | | |
| | 13th | | Marched to TREFCON – Cleaning up & Training | |
| | 21st | | Preparation of Printed for Immediate Arrival by Cav Corps Commander at TREFCON | |
| | 22nd | | } Training – Sections out with regiments of Brigade for Tactical Exercises | |
| | 5th | | | |
| | 29th | | | |
| | 30th | | Battery out with 9th Cav Bde for Tactical Exercise | |

Y. B??
[signature] Major p.n.A

Y Batty RMA

Army Form C. 2118.

# WAR DIARY
## or
## INTELLIGENCE SUMMARY.
(Erase heading not required.)

**Nov. 1915**

| Place | Date | Hour | Summary of Events and Information | Remarks and references to Appendices |
|---|---|---|---|---|
| | Nov 1-6 | | Trefcon. Divisional training. 4ᵗʰ inst Major K. Ball DSO dep⁴ for 17ᵗʰ Div: R.A. | |
| | 7 | | Marches to BRUNECOURT | |
| | 8 | | " " PONT le MARCQ | |
| | 9 | | 2 (Ex TM) Sections marches to RUMES then to RAMECROIX | |
| | 10 | | 1 RX) detailed as batteries & attached to 8ᵗʰ Hussars marches to MONCHIN. LX att⁴ to 19ᵗʰ Hussars marches via TOURNAI, PERUWELZ — came into action on outskirts of Froewy-le-Bussual at 13:27. Retd to Willk Bussuat at sunset: Ex with HQ 9ᵗʰ DX & 15ᵗʰ Hols to E. of Villiers St Amand into action 12:30. Lt Hope & BSM Steedman 2 gunners wounded; Cx with Brew & Villiers St Amand 1700. | |
| | 11 | | Ex with HQ 9ᵗʰ Cav. DX & 15ᵗʰ Hols moved from VILLIERS ST AMAND 07.00 onwards to MAFFLES. Hostilities ceased 11.00: RX rejoins 12.15: LX marches to ISIERES returns to PAPOIGNIES (billets) 17.00: RX marches to MAFFLE RX + CX (billets). LX joins later. | |
| | 12 | | Cleaning up. 14ᵗʰ Maj. C.H. Peaseworth DSO joins battery assumes command | |
| | 13/16 | | marches to CALINELLE (billets). | |
| | 15. | | Mobile X under 2 Lt. JENNINGS dep⁴ to 7ᵗʰ Bde A.C. | |
| | 17. | | Marches to NEUVILLERS. | |
| | 18. | | " ECAUSSINES D'ENGHIEN. | |
| | 19/21 | | Halt & clean up. | |

# WAR DIARY
## or
## INTELLIGENCE SUMMARY.

*(Erase heading not required.)*

Army Form C. 2118.

Y Battery RHA
Nov. 1918.

| Place | Date | Hour | Summary of Events and Information | Remarks and references to Appendices |
|---|---|---|---|---|
| | 21st | | Marched to St GERY. | |
| | 22nd | | " " TILLIER | |
| | 23rd | | Halted | |
| | 24th | | Marched to MARNEFFE | |
| | 25/26 | | Halted | |
| | 27 | | March to ESNEUX | |
| | 28 | | Halted | |
| | 29th | | Marched to GOE | |
| | 30th | | Halted. | |

E Heavensworth Maj RHA

# WAR DIARY
## or
## INTELLIGENCE SUMMARY.

*(Erase heading not required.)*

Army Form C. 2118.

| Place | Date | Hour | Summary of Events and Information | Remarks and references to Appendices |
|---|---|---|---|---|
| | 18th 17=30 | | Z/1 M.R. Bty RHA transferred to I Battery RHA. Freezing hard, ground covered in snow, no firing and new WPL went forward to the battery position. | |
| | | | Volume 13 2nd Wed. | |

M. Stanley
Capt RHA
Commanding Y Battery RHA

# War Diary or Intelligence Summary

APPENDIX 2

Summary of Events and Information

| Place | Date/Hour | | Remarks |
|---|---|---|---|
| GERMANY | 1 | March to LAMMERSDORF in Germany (16 miles) | |
| | 2 + 3 | Halt | |
| | 4 | March to BERIGASWEILER (17½ miles) | |
| | 5 | March to ESCH (16 miles) | |
| | 6 | Halt | |
| | 7 | March to ANSTEL (15 miles) | |
| | 8 | Halt | |
| | 9 | March to the Artillery Barracks COLOGNE (16 miles) | |
| | 10 + 11 | Halt | |
| | 12th | March to SCHELEBUSCH (13 miles) Inspected by G.O.C. II Army on the HOHENZOLLERN BRIDGE. | |
| | 13 | March to OHLIGS (12 miles) | |
| | 14 | Halt | |
| | 15 | March to Artillery Barracks COLOGNE (18 miles) | |
| | 16 | " " MILLENDORF (18 miles) | |
| | 17 to 31 | Winter quarters. | |

Krauwroth
Major. R.H.A.
Commanding "F" Battery R.H.A.

War Diary and Intelligence Summary
1st January 1919.

| Place | Date, hour | Summary of Events and Information | Remarks |
|---|---|---|---|
| MILLENDORF | JAN 1st to 31st | This month was spent in costuming horses, instructing junior NCO's to a certain amount of drills & barrack w.k as far as the abnormal allotment of leave added to demobilization difficulties allows me. The paper strength of the battery varied from 6 Officers 185 Marianka 222 horses 54 Officers 175 OR 212 horses but at times the actual Other rank strength was as low as 108. All T.o.2 horses were malleined no reacts. Horses were posted for P.B army, Sale report during the month 70 sales, 4 T. many 78 X, 74 Y, 70 Z. No horses joined during the month but 11 were evacuated. 15 Men joined during the month & 14 were evacuated or demobilized. The weather from Jan 20th was 1st reinforcements chiefly snow & last frost. Previous to 20th cold but fine. Health of Horses excellent |  |

EPrasswater

# WAR DIARY or INTELLIGENCE SUMMARY

Army Form C. 2118.

Y Battery R.H.A.

February 1919

| Place | Date | Hour | Summary of Events and Information | Remarks and references to Appendices |
|---|---|---|---|---|
| MULLENDORF | FEB 1-28 | | The amount has been agents conditions gradually regained - no only of 6 carriages etc. I am too busy and saw but put advantage has been being a lead those spaces in Cologne the troops | |
| | 2 | | Snow fell on 4, 5, 6 Gds D + horses LH to be change to get 10, 20, 21 to go Lieut. TODD Palm came from a general and now the conscripts who finished Re-carrying sched course closed down. Two classes arrive with team | |
| | 12 | | Had over all our BP's OF ammunition 5/7/R.H.A at Calogre All am X horsed aid medinat Z horses are returning and appears all rifles are unavailable things being returns ammunition for 13, 22 & 24 7 & 20 R.H.A in exchange for 12J and XA | |
| | 14 | | Lieut. TODD & PALMER 6th laws for 2 mths leave-pay no 78 for 7 years service M.J. Fr. MULLENS & party of us. | |
| | 15 | | Sent 13P OF ammunition from Cologne | |
| | 16 | | The X at half permanent was totally gift stable was immovable to scald half various. The new fallen plans a very heavy rain and will put of cellet. Horses have been generally in the water and may have been gutted still a leave. 3 horses struck off during the 9 month | |
| | 26 | | | |

C. Bean My R.H.A
Maj Y RHA
28/7

Army Form C. 2118.

# WAR DIARY
## or
## INTELLIGENCE SUMMARY.
(Erase heading not required.)

CENTRAL REGISTRY
HEADQUARTERS
WIMEREUX.

| Place | Date | Hour | Summary of Events and Information | Remarks and references to Appendices |
|---|---|---|---|---|
| MILLENDORF | April | | The month has been spent disposing of horses for demobilization & those horses have been polished & men have taken | |
| | 7.5 | | full advantage of | |
| | April 8. 10 to 15.85 | | Marched from MILLENDORF to ICHENDORF to meet need for Officers College there | |
| ICHENDORF | 12th | | All Horses & men were sent away for demobilization, Army &c | |
| | | | Battery at bare strength with | |
| | | | 2 Lieut R.H.A period to "Y" Battery R.H.A. | |
| | 14/15 | | Capt K.T.G. Stewart Mc. R.H.A proceeded to England for demobilization | |
| | 25 | | 16th B.E. R.H.A held recent to General Meeting. Men were anxious... | |
| | 29th | | Battery entrained at Grevens for ANTWERP in a very slow... | |
| | 30 | 7.00 | arrived ANTWERP & delivered at Embarkation Camp and had most excellent | |
| | | | Weather condition very bad | |

"Y" BATTERY
R.H.A

No.............
Date..........

Commanding "Y" Battery R.H.A.

00 05/1116/4

## 1916-1918
## 1ST CAVALRY DIVISION
## 9TH CAVALRY BRIGADE.

9TH MACHINE GUN SQUADRON
MAY 1916 - DEC 1918
MAR 1919

To HUSSARS WE
BOX 1166

# WAR DIARY
## or
## INTELLIGENCE SUMMARY

Army Form C. 2118

| Place | Date | Hour | Summary of Events and Information | Remarks and references to Appendices |
|---|---|---|---|---|
| | 1 | | Billets | |
| | 2 | | " | |
| | 3 | | " | |
| | 4 | | " | |
| | 5 | | " | |
| | 6 | | " | |
| | 7 | | " | |
| | 8 | | " | |
| | 9 | | " | |
| | 10 | | " | |
| | 11 | 11 A.M. | Divisional Route March | |
| | 12 | | Billets | |
| | 13 | 12 Noon | Court of Enquiry re T. Young No. 5429 (19 L. Hussars Detachment) Lieut Jones President | |
| | 14 | | In Billets | |
| | 15 | | " | |
| | 16 | | " | |
| | 17 | | " | |
| | 18 | | " | |
| THEROUANNE | 19 | 3.30 pm | Arrived THEROUANNE en route for BETHUNE area to join XI Corps mounted Billets hired for night | |
| L'ECLÈNE | 20 | 4 pm | Arrived L'ECLÈNE 4pm – Billeted | |
| | 21 | | In Billets – Country very low & marshy – subject to floods. | |
| | 22 | | " | |
| | 23 | | " | |
| | 24 | | " | |
| | 25 | | " | |
| | 26 | | " | |
| | 27 | | " | |
| | 28 | | " | |
| | 29 | | " | |
| | 30 | | " | |

# WAR DIARY
## or
## INTELLIGENCE SUMMARY

(Erase heading not required.)

Army Form C. 2118

9th Machine Gun Coy

| Place | Date 1916 | Hour | Summary of Events and Information | Remarks and references to Appendices |
|---|---|---|---|---|
| L'ECLEME | 1 April | — | In billets. | |
| | 2 | | | |
| | 3 | | | |
| | 4 | | | |
| | 5 | | | |
| | 6 | | | |
| | 7 | | | |
| | 8 | | | |
| | 9 | | | |
| | 10 | | | |
| | 11 | | | |
| | 12 | | | |
| | 13 | | | |
| | 14 | 2.30pm | Secret Orders received from 106 Brigade (No 14) that the 106th BRIGADE will relieve the 56th BRIGADE in the NEUVE CHAPELLE Section on the 16th instant. | M 27 a.7.3 Combles Sheet BETHUNE |
| | 15 | 5.30pm | Lieut M.A.C Halliday + 6 men sent on to spend the night in the gun positions | |
| EUSTON CORNER | | 7 am | Tour Trench Park embussed for ZELLOBES | |
| | | 9 am | Marched from ZELLOBES to EUSTON CORNER | |
| | | 10.30am | With Guides + tent Gun Equipment + Gun Teams sub-sectors to relieve 56th Brigade | M 27 d.7.3. |
| | | | Established H. Qrs at EUSTON CORNER. | |
| | | | Gun Positions + Posts taken over No 1.3.4 + 6 posts in front line | |
| | | | PORT-ARTHUR. | S.14.D. 9½.1½. |
| | | | ST. VAAST | M 33. C.0.0 |
| | | | EUSTON | M 34. a. 1.8 |
| | | | LORETTO | M 33. b.3.5 |
| | | | PONT LOGY. S | S 4.C. 9½.1. |
| | | | OXFORD | |
| | | | PONT LOGY N | |
| | | | PONT LOGY. N | |

# WAR DIARY or INTELLIGENCE SUMMARY

Army Form C. 2118

| Place | Date | Hour | Summary of Events and Information | Remarks and references to Appendices |
|---|---|---|---|---|
| EUSTON CORNER | 17 | — | Two Guns searched the BOIS DE BIEZ with indirect fire between 7.30 pm & 8.15 pm. Night sit. | |
| | 18 | | Relieved men in Nos 1, 3 & 4, 5 positions by men from rear posts. | |
| | 19 | | Quiet day – traile M.G's very active during the night on FORT ARTHUR – along front line parapets. | |
| | 20 | | Men in 1, 3, 4, & 6 positions relieved by men from rear posts. Weather wet – transports in bad state. | |
| | 21 | 11.30 am | No. 11371 Pte Amos G. killed at No 4 position by Enemy sniper on Artillery & Trench Mortar. Shelled Enemys front line a.13 the R. of the LA BASSEE RD. Three Machine Guns co-operating with the artillery searching BOIS DE BIEZ "LA TOURELLE" & tracks indirect fire. Enemy retaliated with trench Mortars on front line trenches. Very still day. S.O.S. 35th Division new recalls – M.G. Defence of Keeps – Posts | |
| | 22 | | Squadron Relief from BACK BILLETS. Two men of 106th BRIGADE 2 hrs later to each Gun in KEEPS & POSTS. Very wet. | |
| | 23 | | Two new indirect fire positions "drilled" by PONT LOGY CORNER & EUSTON KEEP. Men in Nos 1, 3, 4 & 6 positions relieved by men from rear posts. | |
| | 24 | | Quiet day – Trench Mortar & Machine Gun fire during night. | |
| | 25 | | Very quiet – Three Machine Guns search tracks & roads along which Enemy reliefs are known to come to Battalions opposite our front – were relieved to be carrying on a relief. | |
| | 26 | | New defence scheme for M. Guns along NEUVE CHAPELLE sector made out & approved by G.O.C. | |
| | 27 | | 104th BRIGADE relieves 106th BRIGADE in NEUVE CHAPELLE sector. | |
| | 28 | | Quiet day. Pte Jennings Shrapnel Wound in hand. | |
| | 29 | | 104 Machine Gun Company attached to Squadron for instruction. Take Officers & M.C.O's round BRIGADE line. | |
| | 30 | | | |

# WAR DIARY or INTELLIGENCE SUMMARY

Army Form C. 2118

9 Can Bde M.G. Sqn

May 1916 – Dec 1918

| Place | Date | Hour | Summary of Events and Information | Remarks and references to Appendices |
|---|---|---|---|---|
| L'ECLEME | 1 May | | 104 Brigade M.G. Cy. we attached to Squadron for instruction. Three men on each gun team. Single BOIS DE BIEZ with instruction, relief from 7.30 to 9.30. Enemy neighbourhood quiet. Sited new emplacement for night-gun in Brigade Sector. Battalion in front-line relieved. | |
| | 2. | | | |
| | 3. | | Quiet day – Intervel fire 8.30 pm & 9.15 pm on BOIS DE BIEZ + tracks | |
| | 4. | | Quiet day. Enemy Machine Guns very active during the night | |
| | 5. | | All Squadron Guns in posts + NCO's relieved by 104th Brigade M.G. Cy | |
| | 6. | | Cold & windy. Completed 2 new M gun emplacements for the 4 Squadron Guns. Battalion in front-line relieved | |
| | 7. | | Enemy shelled PORT ARTHUR with shrapnel | |
| | 8. | 9.30 pm | Attempted Raid on Enemy Trenches by Party of Battalion Bombers in cooperation with Artillery + Trench Mortars. Enemy retaliation on front-line between + CROIX BARBEE | |
| | 9. | | Quiet day – Indr: Squadron relief | |
| | 10. | | Machine Guns + Teams Guns in front-line fired on hostile working parties. much enemy wire. working. Forgh.pt in 1 | |
| | 11. | 12 noon | Squadron Guns Relieved by Guns + Teams of 104 Brigade M. Gun Cy - handed over to O.C. Th. Cy Squadron back in BILLETS L'ECLEME | |
| | 12 | | BILLETS | |
| | 13 | | Squadron marched via ST HILAIRE, ESTREE BLANCHE to COYECQUES + billeted there | |
| | 14. | | Squadron marched via FAUQUENBERGHES, BENCOURT & DESVRES + billeted there | |
| | 15 | | BILLETS | |
| | 16 | | " | |
| | 17 | | " | |
| | 18 | | " | |
| | 19 | | Squadron move into Bivouac in COURSE | |
| | 20 | | BIVOUACS | |
| | 21 | | " | |
| | 22 | | " | |
| | 23 | | " | |
| | 24 | | " | |
| | 25 | | Squadron moved into CAMP at ECHAULT marching via SAMER, CONDETTE/route | |
| | 26 | | | |
| | 27 | | | |
| | 28 | | | |
| | 29 | | | |
| | 30 | | | |
| | 31 | | | |

# WAR DIARY
## or
## INTELLIGENCE SUMMARY
*(Erase heading not required.)*

Army Form C. 2118

9 Cav Bde In Sqdn
June 1916

| Place | Date | Hour | Summary of Events and Information | Remarks and references to Appendices |
|---|---|---|---|---|
| ECAULT | 1 June | | Camp. | |
| | 2 | | " | |
| | 3 | | " | |
| | 4 | | " | |
| | 5 | | " | |
| | 6 | | " | |
| | 7 | | Returned to billets at COURSE marching via CONDETTE, SAMER route. | |
| | 8 | | Divisional Scheme | |
| | 9 | | Divisional Scheme | |
| | 10 | | Billets. | |
| | 11 | | " | |
| | 12 | | " | |
| | 13 | | " | |
| | 14 | | " | |
| | 15 | | " | |
| | 16 | | " | |
| | 17 | | " | |
| | 18 | | " | |
| | 19 | | " | |
| | 20 | | " | |
| | 21 | | " | |
| | 22 | | " | |
| | 23 | | " | |
| | 24 | | Brigade moved via PAPENTY — RECQUES — MONTREUIL STN — BRIMEUX — Nd CAMPAGNE-LEZ-HESDIN — ST-REMY-AUX-BOIS to DOURIEZ area. Left billets 8 p.m. Arrived new area 4.30 A.M. | Reference Map Calais Abbeville Arras Amiens |
| | 25 | | Brigade marched via YOISIN — St.RIVAR L'AUTHE — LE BOISLE — BOUFFLIERS — WILLENCOURT to BEAUVOIR-RIVIERE an artist however having YOISIN at 12.30 A.M. Arrived new area 6 A.M. Wet day. | |
| | 26 | | Brigade continued to march via HEZECOURT — MT. RENAULT FM — BERNAVILLE — BERNEUIL A ST. LEGER LES DOMARTS area public however. Departure started arriving area at 7.15 p.m. arrived new area 2 A.M. Very wet march. | |
| | 27 | | March continued via FLESSELLES — BERTANGLES — COISY — ALLONVILLE to QUERRIEU area, also however. Departure | |
| | 28 | | Brigade arrived at 10 p.m. reached new bivouacs at 5.30 A.M. In bivouac QUERRIEU. | |
| | 29 | | In bivouac QUERRIEU. | |
| | 30 | | In bivouac QUERRIEU | |

CONFIDENTIAL

War Diary
of
9th. Machine Gun Squadron

July 1916

Volume No 6.

Confidential

**Army Form C. 2118**

# WAR DIARY
## or
## INTELLIGENCE SUMMARY
*(Erase heading not required.)*

9th Machine Gun Squadron  July 1916   Volume No 6

Instructions regarding War Diaries and Intelligence Summaries are contained in F.S. Regs., Part II. and the Staff Manual respectively. Title Pages will be prepared in manuscript.

| Place | Date | Hour | Summary of Events and Information | Remarks and references to Appendices |
|---|---|---|---|---|
| QUERRIEU | 1st | 3 a.m. | The Brigade moves early VIA QUERRIEU-PONT NOYELLES RD junction ½ mile SSW of B of BRESLE to BRESLE area. Arrived 6.30 a.m. Returned to QUERRIEU AREA at 5 p.m. Remained in Bivouac at QUERRIEU | Rd Map AMIENS |
| " | 2nd | | | |
| " | 3rd | | | |
| " | 4th | | | |
| LONGPRÉ | 5th | 6.30 a.m. | Brigade march early VIA AMIENS – PICQUIGNY to LONGPRÉ area. Arrived at 2 p.m. Very wet day. In Bivouac at LONGPRÉ. Weather good. | Rd Map ABBEVILLE |
| " | 6th | | | |
| " | 7th | | | |
| " | 8th | | | |
| " | 9th | | | |
| " | 10th | | | |
| QUERRIEU | 11th | 8.20 p.m. | Brigade moved late in evening VIA PICQUIGNY – AMIENS to N QUERRIEU area arrived 6 a.m. of 12th. In Bivouac at QUERRIEU | |
| BUIRE | 13th | 6.30 p.m. | Brigade moves with 2nd Cavalry Brigade to BUIRE SUR L'ANCRE moving by track N of QUERRIEU – ALBERT RD running through FRANVILLERS – BRESLE – LAVIEVILLE returns crossing ALBERT RD at D17A9 & moving through D17C & D29B arrived 9.30 p.m. In Bivouac at BUIRE. Brigade ready to move at 3 hours notice from 4 a.m. Brigade ready to move at 2 hours notice from 3 a.m. | Rd Map Same |
| " | 14th | | | |
| " | 15th | | | |
| " | 16th | | | |
| " | 17th | | | |
| " | 18th | | | |
| " | 19th | | | |
| " | 20th | | | |
| " | 21st | | | |
| " | 22nd | | | |
| " | 23rd | | | |
| QUERRIEU | 24th | 9.30 a.m. | Brigade moves by R of crossing in ALBERT – QUERRIEU RD at D16 track running N & parallel to ALBERT QUERRIEU RD in rear of 2nd Cavalry Brigade to QUERRIEU area. Arriving about 2 p.m. In Bivouac at QUERRIEU. Weather fine & very hot. | |
| " | 25th | | | |
| " | 26th | | | |
| " | 27th | | | |
| " | 28th | | | |
| " | 29th | | | |
| " | 30th | | | |
| " | 31st | | | |

R.H. Sellett, Captain
Commanding 9th Machine Gun Squadron

# War Diary
## of
## 9th Machine Gun Squadron.
### August 1916.

Volume No 9

Confidential.

Army Form C. 2118

9th Machine Gun Squadron
August 1916

# WAR DIARY
## or
## INTELLIGENCE SUMMARY
*(Erase heading not required.)*

Instructions regarding War Diaries and Intelligence Summaries are contained in F.S. Regs., Part II. and the Staff Manual respectively. Title Pages will be prepared in manuscript.

| Place | Date | Hour | Summary of Events and Information | Remarks and references to Appendices |
|---|---|---|---|---|
| QUERRIEU | August 1st | | In Bivouac at QUERRIEU. | |
| " | 2nd | | " " " " | |
| " | 3rd | | " " " " | |
| " | 4th | | " " " " | |
| " | 5th | | " " " " | |
| " | 6th | | " " " " | |
| " | 7th | | " " " " | |
| " | 8th | | " " " " | |
| LONGUET | 9th | | Brigade moved at 5 a.m via VILLERS-BOCAGE - VIGNACOURT - ST OUEN - SURCAMPS to the COCQUEREL area. Squadron bivouac at LONGUET arriving at 1 p.m. | Ref. Sheets Amiens 12 Abbeville 11 |
| GAMACHES | 10th | | Brigade continued its march at 8.30 a.m. via PONT REMY - LIMEAUX - HUPPY - GREBAULT MESNIL - VISMES AU VAL - FLORIVILLE to GAMACHES arriving at 2 p.m. | Ref. Sheets Amiens 12 Abbeville 11 |
| " | 11th | | In Bivouac at GAMACHES | |
| " | 12th | | " " " " | |
| " | 13th | | " " " " | |
| " | 14th | | " " " " | |
| " | 15th | | " " " " | |
| " | 16th | | " " " " | |
| " | 17th | | " " " " | |
| " | 18th | | " " " " | |
| " | 19th | | " " " " | |
| " | 20th | | " " " " | |
| " | 21st | | " " " " | |
| " | 22nd | | " " " " | |
| " | 23rd | | " " " " | |
| " | 24th | | " " " " | |
| " | 25th | | " " " " | |
| " | 26th | | " " " " | |
| " | 27th | | " " " " | |
| " | 28th | | " " " " | |
| " | 29th | | " " " " | |
| " | 30th | | " " " " | |
| " | 31st | | " " " " | |

Captain
Commdg. 9th Machine Gun Squadron

Vol 8

# War Diary
## of 9th Machine Gun Squadron
### September 1916
### Volume No 8

Confidential

# WAR DIARY or INTELLIGENCE SUMMARY

Army Form C. 2118

| Place | Date | Hour | Summary of Events and Information | Remarks and references to Appendices |
|---|---|---|---|---|
| GAMACHES | 1st Septr | | In bivouac at GAMACHES | |
| " | 2nd " | | " | |
| " | 3rd " | | " | |
| " | 4th " | | " | |
| " | 5th " | | " | R/Sectn Abbeville 14/1 Dieppe 16/100000 Dieppe 16 R. Amiens 17/20000 |
| " | 6th " | 9.30 am | Brigade moved via TRANSLAY and OISEMONT to BETTENCOURT. Squadron left at 9am, arrived 3.30pm | |
| BETTENCOURT | 7th " | 1.15 pm | Brigade moved via RIVIERRE – HANGEST sur SOMME – AILLY sur SOMME – AMIENS to a bivouac area East of the river HALLUE between DAOURS and QUERRIEU. Squadron bivouaced at DAOURS. Left Bettencourt at 1pm arrived at 9pm. | |
| DAOURS | 8th " | | In bivouac at DAOURS | |
| " | 9th " | | " | |
| " | 10th " | | " | |
| " | 11th " | | " | |
| " | 12th " | | " | |
| " | 13th " | | " | Peronne Sheets 57cSW 62d |
| " | 14th " | 7.30 am | Division moved to the CARNOY VALLEY on "Lotz" organization. Brigade moved on J.22 – BONNAY BRIDGE – track on J.14,15,16,11 – track to FILIFORME TREE – (1 mile West of) BRONFAY FARM. Halted, off saddled, watered, and rested for 3 hours at MORLANCOURT. Crossed the MARICOURT–FRICOURT road in a squadron at 5.30pm arrived at 6.30pm. In bivouac in the CARNOY VALLEY. Squadron to be ready to move at 20 minutes notice from 10 a.m. Hours 7.30 to 6.30 a.m. 9 a.m. 20 | |
| CARNOY VALLEY | 15th " | | In bivouac in the CARNOY VALLEY | |
| " | 16th " | | " | |
| " | 17th " | 3 pm | Division returned to DAOURS – LANEUVILLE bivouac Area. Brigade moved by squadrons between 1 and 3pm via track W/o BRONFAY FARM – track to FILIFORM TREE – tracks in J.11,16,15,14 to BONNAY BRIDGE – track in I.27a. Squadron crossed the MARICOURT–FRICOURT road at 2pm arriving at DAOURS at 7pm. In bivouac at DAOURS | |
| " | 18th " | | Haute Raid on Amiens | |
| " | 19th " | | " | |
| " | 20th " | | " | |
| " | 21st " | | " | |
| " | 22nd " | | Anti-aircraft action with Aeroplane. No 18 Squadron R.F.C. | Very wet weather |

Army Form C. 2118

# WAR DIARY
## or
## INTELLIGENCE SUMMARY
(Erase heading not required.)

Instructions regarding War Diaries and Intelligence Summaries are contained in F. S. Regs., Part II. and the Staff Manual respectively. Title Pages will be prepared in manuscript.

| Place | Date | Hour | Summary of Events and Information | Remarks and references to Appendices |
|---|---|---|---|---|
| DAOURS | Aug 23rd | 7.30 am | Brigade march via N.4.c - crossroads - M.2.a.1.1. - AMIENS station - South of SOMME to old CONDE line. Squadron watered West of PICQUIGNY arriving at CONDE FOLIE at 3 p.m. | Reference Maps 1/20,000 AMIENS 1/100,000 Reference Maps 1/20,000 FRENS 1/100,000 |
| CONDE FOLIE | 24th | 7.30 am | Brigade continued its march via L'ETOILE - VAUCHELLES LES DOMARTS - BRUCAMPS - DOMQUEUR - PROUVILLE to BEALCOURT - WAVANS - NOEUX etc. Squadron bivouaced at BEALCOURT arriving at 2 p.m. | |
| BEALCOURT | 25th | 9 am | Brigade continued its march via NOEUX - BOURG au BOIS - HAUT MESNIL - BOIS du WAIL - GALAMETZ - VILLERIM and Squadron bivouaced at GALAMETZ arriving at 12 noon. | |
| GALAMETZ | 26th | | In bivouac at GALAMETZ | |
| " | 27th | | " | |
| " | 28th | | " | |
| " | 29th | | " | |
| " | 30th | | " | |

[signature]
Major,
Comdg 9th Machine Gun Squadron.

WAR DIARY.
of
9th MACHINE GUN SQUADRON.

OCTOBER 1916.
VOLUME No. 8

CONFIDENTIAL

# WAR DIARY / INTELLIGENCE SUMMARY

Army Form C. 2118

9th Machine Gun Sqdn.
OCTOBER 1916
VOLUME No 8.

| Place | Date | Hour | Summary of Events and Information | Remarks and references to Appendices |
|---|---|---|---|---|
| GALAMETZ | OCTOBER 1st | - | In bivouac at GALAMETZ | |
| " | 2nd | - | " " " | |
| " | 3rd | 9am | No 1657 Pte E.A. Hackett admitted hospital and struck off the strength. Tactical scheme with 1st Cavalry Division (cancelled owing to rain). No 817 Pte B. Reynolds admitted hospital and struck off the strength. | |
| " | 4th | | In bivouac at GALAMETZ. A.D.V.S. 1st Cavalry Division inspection of horses. No 50677 Pte E Ferns and No 18845 Pte E Rohman evacuated to Base Hospital and struck off the strength. | |
| " | 5th | | In bivouac at GALAMETZ | |
| " | 6th | 9.30am | Firing on range. No 769 Pte E.O. Boardman evacuated to Base Hospital & struck off the strength. | |
| " | 7th | | No 50658 Pte S.J. Brown evacuated to Base Hospital and struck off the strength. | |
| " | 8th | | No 47057 Corpl. A. Green taken on strength. No 141 Pte S. Newby to Base Hospital & struck off the strength. | |
| " | 9th | | No 1159 Rc G/P O. Duffield admitted hospital and struck off the strength. | |
| " | 10th | | " " " " | |
| " | 11th | 9am | Tactical scheme with 1st Cavalry Division. No 51111 Rc Cpl Boorer awarded Military Medal. | |
| " | 12th | | Signalling Divisional Test ROLLENCOURT. 2pm O.C. ASC 1st Car Div inspection. No 43574 Pte W.B. Mocks and No 43767 Pte L. Walpo (RAMC) returned to duty to 9th Car Field Ambulance. | |
| " | 13th | 9am | No 43710 Pte H North and No 40195 Pte J Kilcoun (RAMC) attached. In bivouac at GALAMETZ. Tactical scheme with 1st Cavalry Division (cancelled owing to rain). No 1606 Pte H Lundy " " " " | |
| " | 14th | | admitted hospital and struck off the strength. | |
| " | 15th | | In bivouac at GALAMETZ. No 583 Pte L/Cpl Atkins admitted hospital and struck off the strength. | |
| " | 16th | | | |
| " | 17th | | | |
| " | 18th | | No 50783 Pte H Clarke admitted hospital and struck off the strength. Divisional Tactical Scheme. 1st Car Div V 3rd Car Div (Cancelled owing to rain). | |
| " | 19th | 7.30am | Squadron moved via FREVENT and ARBRES to NEUVILLETTE. Left 7.30am. Arrived 11am. Very wet. No 1401 Pte W. Mattinson admitted hospital and struck off the strength. Rwr Pt Jones M.S.T.C. UCKFIELD U.K. struck off the strength. | Ref sheets 6&7 1/40000 |
| NEUVILLETTE | 20th | 8.40am | Squadron moved via DOULENS and BEAUVAL to WARGNIES. Left 8.40am. Arrived 12 noon. Lieut B Boyton Davies MRCVS Home arrival. | |
| WARGNIES | 21st | | In bivouac at WARGNIES. No 691 Pte F. Shott admitted hospital & struck off the strength. | |

Army Form C. 2118

# WAR DIARY
## or
## INTELLIGENCE SUMMARY

*(Erase heading not required.)*

Instructions regarding War Diaries and Intelligence Summaries are contained in F.S. Regs., Part II. and the Staff Manual respectively. Title Pages will be prepared in manuscript.

| Place | Date | Hour | Summary of Events and Information | Remarks and references to Appendices |
|---|---|---|---|---|
| | OCTOBER | | | |
| MARGNIES | 22nd | | In billets at MARGNIES | |
| " | 23rd | | Squadron packed up ready to move at an early hour the following morning towards the line | |
| " | 24th | | (Cancelled for 24 hours owing to rain) In billets at MARGNIES (Move cancelled for further 48 hours owing to continuous rain) | |
| " | 25th | | No.117411 Pte H Shepherd (194) evacuated to Base Hospital and struck off the strength | |
| " | 26th | | (Move cancelled till 29th October) No 7443 Pte H Hewitt admitted hospital and struck off the strength | |
| " | 27th | | | |
| " | 28th | | | |
| HAVERNAS | 29th | 8 a.m. | Squadron moved to HAVERNAS | |
| " | 30th | | In billets at HAVERNAS (move cancelled till 31st October) Tactical scheme with squadron 15th Hussars | |
| " | 31st | 10.15 a.m. | Squadron moved to HALLOY LES PERNOIS. Move cancelled till 1st November. | |

R. J. ld.
Major.
Commdg. 9th Machine Gun Squadron.

Vol 10

War Diary
of
9th Machine Gun Squadron

November 1916.
Volume No 9

Confidential.

# WAR DIARY or INTELLIGENCE SUMMARY

Army Form C. 2118

J. Maclin Ess Syn

VIII M2 Q

| Place | Date | Hour | Summary of Events and Information | Remarks and references to Appendices |
|---|---|---|---|---|
| HAILOY LES PERNOIS | NOVEMBER 1st | | In billets at HAILOY | |
| " | 2nd | | No 50672 Pte J. Moakes admitted hospital. No 50763 Pte W.J. Eakin admitted Hospital | |
| " | 3rd | | | |
| " | 4th | | Horse cancelled till 6th November | |
| " | 5th | | | |
| " | 6th | | | |
| " | 7th | | Horse again cancelled | |
| " | 8th | | Squadron moved to Western end of town to make room for the 19th Hussars | |
| L'HEURE (CROUX) SAUCHOY | 9th | 10am | Squadron moved to L'HEURE (CROUX). left at 10am arrive 4pm | |
| | 10th | 9am | Squadron continued march to SAUCHOY. Left at 9am arrived 3pm. No 50740 Pte G. Pole admitted Hospital | |
| | 11th | | Squadron continued march to WIRWIGNES (OESVRES) Left at 8.30am arrived 4.30pm Squadron now billeted in made from billets | |
| WIRWIGNES | 12th | | In billets at WIRWIGNES | |
| | 13th | | " | |
| | 14th | | " | |
| | 15th | | " | |
| | 16th | | " | |
| | 17th | | No 1657 Pte W.J. Haskin admitted Hospital. No 50728 " A. Hall " | |
| | 18th | | No 1658 Pte E. Clarke to Base (on the way) and struck off the strength of the Squadron | |
| | 19th | | | |
| | 20th | | No 1510 L/Cpl A. Butcher taken on strength of the Squadron Inspection of billets by G.O.C. 9th Cav. Bgde. No 1559 Pte W.E. Clarke admitted Hospital | |
| | 21st | | | |
| | 22nd | | Lieut R. Seeth Davies admitted Hospital | |
| | 23rd | | | |
| | 24th | | | |

Army Form C. 2118

# WAR DIARY
## or
## INTELLIGENCE SUMMARY
(Erase heading not required.)

Instructions regarding War Diaries and Intelligence Summaries are contained in F.S. Regs., Part II. and the Staff Manual respectively. Title Pages will be prepared in manuscript.

| Place | Date | Hour | Summary of Events and Information | Remarks and references to Appendices |
|---|---|---|---|---|
| WIRWIGNES | November 25th | | In billets at WIRWIGNES. | |
| | 26th | | No 1599 Pte L. J. Newbury admitted hospital. | |
| | 27th | | " | |
| | 28th | | No 799 Pte G. A. Gaunt & No 1215 L. Cpl. W. H. Bremner admitted hospital. Lieut B. A. Hayter to England as instructor. M.G. Training Centre UCKFIELD. | |
| | 29th | | No 27037 Corpl. H. Brown admitted hospital. | |
| | 30th | | " | |

M K Mason Major.
Commdg. 9th Machine Gun Squadron.

"CONFIDENTIAL"

WAR DIARY.

of
9th MACHINE GUN SQUADRON.
December 1916.

Volume No 10.

Army Form C. 2118

# WAR DIARY
## or
## INTELLIGENCE SUMMARY
(Erase heading not required.)

9th Machine Gun Coys
December 1916 Volume 1

Instructions regarding War Diaries and Intelligence Summaries are contained in F. S. Regs., Part II. and the Staff Manual respectively. Title Pages will be prepared in manuscript.

| Place | Date | Hour | Summary of Events and Information | Remarks and references to Appendices |
|---|---|---|---|---|
| MIRVILLERS | 1 | | 9. Billets at MIRVILLERS. Individual training under Section Arrangements commenced. Each Section to have 3 days per week | |
| | 2 | 9.30am | Inspection of horses by A.D.V.S. not bending Divis in - following remarks | |
| | | | No 1. Section - small stamp of small horses | |
| | | | Good. Condition. | |
| | | | 2 " " A larger stamp - good Condition. | |
| | | | 3 " " Good stamp " | |
| | | | 4 " " Small useful stamp | |
| | | | 5 " " | |
| | | | 6 " " Good Condition | |
| | 3 | | | |
| | 4 | | | |
| | 5 | | | |
| | 6 | | | |
| | 7 | | Practise for tactical exercise with Divisional school. No 51632 Copl E Sunderland admitted hospital. | |
| | 8 | 8.30am | | |
| | 9 | | | |
| | 10 | | Tactical Exercise with Divisional school round LE BOIS JULIEN | Calain 13. |
| | 11 | | | |
| | 12 | | | |
| | 13 | | | |
| | 14 | | | |
| | 15 | 9.30 | Inspection of Transport by Brigade Transport Officer | |
| | 16 | | Inspection by G.O.C. 9th Cavalry Brigade of Nos 1,5 & 6 Section training. | |
| | 17 | | | |
| | 18 | | No 50719 Cpl J. Littlewood arrived from Base & taken on strength | |
| | 19 | | No 50742 Sergt J. L. Denton returned from England & taken on strength. | |
| | 20 | | | |
| | 21 | | | |
| | 22 | | | |
| | 23 | | | |
| | 24 | | | |

# WAR DIARY
## or
## INTELLIGENCE SUMMARY
*(Erase heading not required.)*

Army Form C. 2118

| Place | Date | Hour | Summary of Events and Information | Remarks and references to Appendices |
|---|---|---|---|---|
| MIRMIGNES | 25th Decr | | In billets at MIRMIGNES. Prospective Move of McDermans cancelled | |
| " | 26 | | " | |
| " | 27 | | " | |
| " | 28 | 9.30 am | Inspection of Squadron and billets by G.O.C. 1st Cavalry Division and 9th Cavalry Bde. following remarks: Horses and Turnout satisfactory. Canteen & steps good. Lecture on feathers on making of billets, and uniform economy of leatherware. | |
| " | 29 | | " | |
| " | 30 | | " | |
| " | 31 | | Captain A.H. Mitchell, 2nd i/c taken ou strength. | |

R.K. Jutt
Major,
Commdg. 9th Machine Gun Squadron.

CONFIDENTIAL.

War Diary
of
9th Machine Gun Squadron
January 1917.
Volume 11

Army Form C. 2118

# WAR DIARY
## or
## INTELLIGENCE SUMMARY
*(Erase heading not required.)*

Instructions regarding War Diaries and Intelligence Summaries are contained in F. S. Regs., Part II. and the Staff Manual respectively. Title Pages will be prepared in manuscript.

| Place | Date | Hour | Summary of Events and Information | Remarks and references to Appendices |
|---|---|---|---|---|
| WIRWIGNES | JANUARY 1st | 2 p. | In billets. Inspection of Squadron Transport by G.O.C. 9th Cavalry Brigade and O.C., A.S.C., 1st Cav. Division. Ordnance party proceeded to BOURTHES to prepare new billets. | CALAIS 13/1/17 |
| " | 2nd | | In billets. | |
| " | 3rd | | Projected move of Squadron to BOURTHES cancelled owing to suspected outbreak of cerebro spinal meningitis reported. | |
| " | 4th | 10 am | Squadron moved via LA BELLE ETOILE — LECOURTEAU — FAUCHELLES to BOURTHES | |
| BOURTHES | 5th | | In billets. No 50695 Pte J. Hurst having arrived is taken on strength of Squadron. | |
| " | 6th | | " " | |
| " | 7th | | " " | |
| " | 8th | | " " | |
| " | 9th | | Practice of new drill for Cavalry M.G. Squadrons as suggested by M.G.T.C. UCKFIELD. Question of Lt Jones and Serjeant A.J. Aylwin mentioned despatches, see London Gazette, Gazette 4/1/17. | |
| " | 10th | | | |
| " | 11th | | | |
| " | 12th | | | |
| " | 13th | 10:30 am | G.O.C. 9th Cavalry Brigade inspects Squadron in billets. | |
| " | 14th | | | |
| " | 15th | 9 am | Inspection of horses by Veterinary Officer. | |
| " | 16th | | | |
| " | 17th | | | |
| " | 18th | | | |
| " | 19th | | | |
| " | 20th | | | |
| " | 21st | | | |
| " | 22nd | | Inspection of horses by Veterinary Officer. Geo Beilies H.Squadron | |

# WAR DIARY or INTELLIGENCE SUMMARY

Army Form C. 2118

| Place | Date | Hour | Summary of Events and Information | Remarks and references to Appendices |
|---|---|---|---|---|
| BOURECQ | JANUARY 2nd | | Transport convoy consisting of 1 G.S. Wagon, 1 water cart and 44 horses, marched to NOEUX LES MINES. Officers, 2 S.O.R., 7 L.G.S. Wagons & 91 O.R. entrained at THEROUANNE, proceeding near THEROUANNE en route to NOEUX LES MINES. Billeted for night 2/3rd at THEROUANNE, proceeding next morning to NOEUX LES MINES. | Ref Feels HAZEBROUCK LE113 1000.0 |
| NOEUX LES MINES | 2nd | | Dismounted trench party consisting of 3 officers, 1 N.C.O. and 91 O.R. attached to the Squadron for instruction. 10 officers and 9 O.R. of 8th L.A.B. | |
| " | 25th 26th | | Dismounted trench party continued DESVRES 6.20 am arrived NOEUX LES MINES 3pm - party attached 73rd Inf. Brigade of 24th Division for instruction. | |
| " | 27th | | Advance patrol consisting of two 14H from each gun proceeded to positions to be occupied by these teams. Returns following day owing the alteration in Divisional relief Order. | |
| LES BREBIS | 28th 29th 30th | | Trench party moved to LES BREBIS. 2 huts at LESBREBIS. Advance patrol consisting of two 14H from each gun proceeded to positions to be occupied by Lieut Kemp Squadron relieves 73rd M.G. Coy in the LOOS - MAROC sector taking over the following positions - F1, S11, S12, S13A, S14, S15, UR24, R27, R28, R29, R30, R31. Line allotted 14th division with 3 Batteries. | |
| | 31st | | Rifles, drinks and left. Lieut G.A. Hudgson joined trench party. Fine day, hard frost. Squadron Headquarters established at R.23 | |

R.R. Webb. Major.
Comdg 9th Machine Gun Squadron.

SECRET.

Vol XI
Army Form C. 2118.

# WAR DIARY
## or
## INTELLIGENCE SUMMARY.
*(Erase heading not required.)*

9th Machine Gun Squadron
VOLUME No XII

Instructions regarding War Diaries and Intelligence Summaries are contained in F.S. Regs., Part II. and the Staff Manual respectively. Title pages will be prepared in manuscript.

| Hour, Date, Place | Summary of Events and Information | Remarks and references to Appendices |
|---|---|---|
| February 1st. M. M. Section LOOS-MAROC Sub. | Gtld. posts. Good observation. T.M. activity about noon on Northern and Southern Seps. | LENS 36c NW1. LOOS 36c SW. |
| 2nd. | Frost continues. Quiet day. Approx position of enemy M.G. firing across Southern side of LENS-BETHUNE road located | |
| 3rd. | Frost. Undue trenching of open in Nieuwelets at J15 And J14 a very apparent matter. Quiet day. | |
| 4th. | Gun at H. on information from Patrol Officers. Large enemy working party lying on ridge 5th of TRIANGLE. 4 dead bodies observed on line next morning. No. of M.P. moved to Dug Out by St JAMES ST moved back to Dug Out at R23. | |
| 5th. | | |
| 6th. | Quiet day. Saw smoke shelling chiefly W33 very at morning stand - to. | |
| 7th. | Heavy T.M. should new TRAVERS KEEP for first time. TARGETS TRIANGLE. TRAVERS. | |

SECRET.

Army Form C. 2118.

# WAR DIARY
## or
## INTELLIGENCE SUMMARY.
(Erase heading not required.)

| Hour, Date, Place | Summary of Events and Information | Remarks and references to Appendices |
|---|---|---|
| February 8th 16th Service Bn K R Rifles<br>LOOS-MAROC-<br>SECTOR | N° 47180 Pte C. HUTCHINSON M.G.C. killed by an<br>aerial dart at P.1 position — QUIET DAY. | |
| " 9th | AERIAL DARTS active at morning and evening stand-to. | |
| " 10th | along KING ST and QUEEN'S ST.<br>Extra tack front. Guard difficulty to keep gas<br>fires going during very low temperature. | |
| " 11th | Successful raid on MENGES trench near HOLLOCH. | |
| " 12th | 24th Division relieved by 37th Division — 70th Bde relieved by 110th Bde<br>Heavy trench warfare mortar on KING ST, QUEEN'S ST,<br>GERMAN ST with S.G.I. T.M. H.E. N° 50781 Pte<br>C. Montague wounded. Appears enemy retaliated<br>for 18 pr Test. | |
| " 13th | S.O.S Bombarding to raid on Eastern side of LOOS<br>COALFIELD. Raid was to be made by 3rd Bn R.B.<br>Raid cancelled at zero — 4 as 4 H STOKES<br>received orders not to fire off smoke barrage,<br>owing to failure of this barrage earlier<br>to belonging to a raid near QUARRIES HULLOCH. | |

**SECRET.**

Army Form C. 2118.

# WAR DIARY
## or
## INTELLIGENCE SUMMARY.
*(Erase heading not required.)*

Instructions regarding War Diaries and Intelligence Summaries are contained in F.S. Regs., Part II. and the Staff Manual respectively. Title pages will be prepared in manuscript.

| Hour, Date, Place | Summary of Events and Information | Remarks and references to Appendices |
|---|---|---|
| Feb. 13th Continued. | ARTILLERY. Enemy Battery reported in line following guns bombarded. 1 Gun a LOOS CRASSIER R.31. R.30 R.29. R.27. R.26. 10th Bn East Lancs have heavy retaliation on this front. Cast. 20 Casualties. | |
| " 14th | Heavy trench bombardment of our tres. between 4am 10th Bn East Lancs. Unit duly relieved - to 517749 Light Bowen to 51738 Pte J. Kelin and No 50709 Pte C.J. Puckett wounded. Visit of G.O.C. 1st Cdn. Div. CAPT. I. MITCHELL joins TRENCH PARTY. RELIEF ARRIVED. Quiet day. Relief in line normal. 14.0.R.J. | |
| " 15th | | |
| " 16th | Thin obs in Trenches very Cct and Muddy. | |
| " 17th | 71 Gun moved to Res. by order of G.O.C. 112nd Bde. No. 50695 Pte J.Grier accidentally wounded by Revolver shot. | |
| " 18th | Relief of 14 OR's from BHR. PARTY. | |
| " 19th | Heavy Jh. Gun successfully - Heavy artillery on Left Sub sector. aims HARBOURS CARTER. | |
| " 20th | 112nd Bde. Carry and DUMMY reid on enemy's trenches 1100 A POINT just N. of of BETHUNE - LENS road. | |

Army Form C. 2118.

# WAR DIARY
or
INTELLIGENCE SUMMARY.

(Erase heading not required.)

JENET

Instructions regarding War Diaries and Intelligence Summaries are contained in F. S. Regs., Part II. and the Staff Manual respectively. Title pages will be prepared in manuscript.

| Hour, Date, Place | Summary of Events and Information | Remarks and references to Appendices |
|---|---|---|
| February 28th. to the trenches. LOOS-MAROC SECTON. | Very much to early morning. 2nd Canadian Bar raid postponed for further 24 hrs on account of large mud by Canadian ourour Smoother path with guns. | White Major Comdg. of 6. L. G. L. R. |

Confidential.

War Diary.
of
9th Machine Gun Squadron.
March 1917.

Volume No 13.

Army Form C. 2118.

# WAR DIARY
## or
## INTELLIGENCE SUMMARY.
*(Erase heading not required.)*

Instructions regarding War Diaries and Intelligence Summaries are contained in F.S. Regs., Part II. and the Staff Manual respectively. Title pages will be prepared in manuscript.

| Place | Date | Hour | Summary of Events and Information | Remarks and references to Appendices |
|---|---|---|---|---|
| LOOS-MAROC | March 1st | | Projected raid by 3rd Canadian Infantry Batt'n with guns of Squadron co-operating, cancelled. | |
| " | 2nd | 2 A.m. | Following guns co-operated in raid by 3rd Canadian Inf. Bde. on front M10C 22.75 to M15.13. | LENS 36.S.VI.1. |
| | | | 90.81 – R23, R24, R25, R29, R24, R31. | |
| " | 3rd | | Parties from 16th Machine Gun Coy visited the position preparatory to taking over on the following day. | |
| " | 3rd | | 12 guns of the Squadron occupying the following positions – S11, S13A, R23, R24, R25, R24, R28, S14, S15, R29, R30, R31, relieved by 12 guns of the 16th Machine Gun Coy, via the LOOS-MAROC sector. Relief complete by 2 p.m. French party returned to LES BREBIS for the night. | |
| LES BREBIS | 4th | | Dismounted truck party left LES BREBIS in motor lorries at 11 a.m. to rejoin the Squadron at BOURTHES, arriving 6 p.m. Transport left NOEUX LES MINES and billeted for the night at THEROUANNE. | |
| BOURTHES. | 5th | | In billets at BOURTHES. French Transport arrived from THEROUANNE at 4 p.m. | CALAIS. 13. |
| " | 6th | | Inspection of horses by Veterinary Officer at 9.30 a.m. | |
| " | 7th | | Inspection of horses by C.O.C. 9th Cav. Bde. 2.30 p.m. No.5200 L/Cpl Seagar and No.5066 Pte Perrin taken on the strength. | |

Army Form C. 2118.

# WAR DIARY
## or
## INTELLIGENCE SUMMARY.
*(Erase heading not required.)*

Instructions regarding War Diaries and Intelligence Summaries are contained in F. S. Regs., Part II. and the Staff Manual respectively. Title pages will be prepared in manuscript.

| Place | Date | Hour | Summary of Events and Information | Remarks and references to Appendices |
|---|---|---|---|---|
| | March | | | CALAIS 13. |
| BOURTHES | 8th | | In billets at BOURTHES. Party of reinforcements arrived (9 O.R.) | |
| | 9th | | " " " " S.Q.M.S. Towers accidentally shot in the hand. - Struck off the strength. | |
| | 10th | | " " " " | |
| | 11th | | " " " " | |
| | 12th | | " " " " Lieut. L. Eade admitted hospital with Rose measles. | |
| | 13th | | " " " " | |
| | 14th | | " " " " | |
| | 15th | | " " " " | |
| | 16th | | " " " " No 418224 A/S.Q.M.S. McLure arrived and taken on the strength. | |
| | 17th | | " " " " No 57706 Pte S. Bates admitted hospital with German measles. Men sleeping in NISSEN HUT placed in quarantine. | |
| | 18th | | In billets at BOURTHES. | |
| | 19th | | " " " " Squadron Signallers proceeded to QUESTRECQUES for examination. No 52023 Pte Hopley, No 52093 Pte E.Hogg, & No 52240 Pte S.Jamieson (Signallers) taken on strength of Squadron. | |
| | 20th | | In billets at BOURTHES. | |

# WAR DIARY
## or
## INTELLIGENCE SUMMARY.
*(Erase heading not required.)*

Army Form C. 2118.

| Place | Date | Hour | Summary of Events and Information | Remarks and references to Appendices |
|---|---|---|---|---|
| BOURTHES | March 21st | | In billets at BOURTHES | CALAIS 1.3. |
| | 22nd | | " " " | |
| | 23rd | | " " " | |
| | 24th | | " " " Squadron Transport moved to new billets at ZOTEUX. Lieut. B. Gordon Davis appointed Transport Officer. Examination of Squadron Signallers by 1st Signal Squadron. Result - 8 1st Class | |
| | 25th | | In billets at BOURTHES. | |
| | 26th | | " " " Box Respirators of the Squadron fitted by Divnl Gas Officer at 9.30 a.m. D.D.V.S. inspection of horses proposed for casting, for others then Veterinary Exams at DESVRES 11.30 a.m. | |
| | 27th | | In billets at BOURTHES. Inspection of horses by P.O.C. 9th Cav. Bde. & A.D.V.S. 1st Cav. Div. at 9.45 a.m. | |
| | 28th | | " " " | |
| | 29th | | " " " Party consisting of 1 Officer, 1 Sergt, S.S. Cpl and 10 O.Rs. proceeded to ECHINGHEN to join 13 R. and 10 L.D. remounts. | |
| | 30th | | In billets at BOURTHES. Captain A.J. Critchell proceeded to M.G.T.C. UCKFIELD. | |
| | 31st | | " " " | |

R.J. Wills / Major
Commdg 9th Machine Gun Squadron.

CONFIDENTIAL

# War Diary
## of
## 9th Machine Gun Squadron.
## April 1917.
### Volume No 14.

SECRET.

Army Form C. 2118.

# WAR DIARY
or
# INTELLIGENCE SUMMARY.
(Erase heading not required.)

9th Machine Gun Squadron.

Instructions regarding War Diaries and Intelligence Summaries are contained in F.S. Regs, Part II. and the Staff Manual respectively. Title pages will be prepared in manuscript.

| Hour, Date, Place | Summary of Events and Information | Remarks and references to Appendices |
|---|---|---|
| APRIL. | | |
| 1st In Billets at BOURTHES. | 11 O.Rs. sent to Base for transfer to Infantry. | |
| 2nd " | Dismounted party of Squadron moved to ST NEZT to be Divisionalised. | |
| 3rd " | 50,168 Sgt. R. Booker taken on strength. | |
| 4th " | 50,665 Pte. Milano and 52,585 Pte. Jones taken on strength. | |
| 5th " | | |
| 6th " | | |
| 7th " | Brigade moved at 9 a.m. via HENNEVILLE – FRUGES – RUSSEAUVILLE – BIMBY to PIERREMONT arriving at 4 p.m. | CALAIS 13. HAZEBROUCK 5A LENS 11. |
| 8th " | Brigade continued march at 12 noon and moved via ST. POL to a bivouac area S. of AUBIGNY near the MOULIN ROUGE INN. | LENS 11. 51C. Fine, warm day. |
| 9th. Bivouac at CAPELLE-FERMONT. | Squadron at two hours notice. Two Sections (Nos 3 & 4) attached to 19th Hussars. Squadron attached to 1stC of D. Captain Mac Gregor. 1st Airshire Yeomanry attached M.G.C. Car. joined Squadron as 2nd in Command, vice Captain R.H.V. Bell. | Very bad weather |
| 10th " | Squadron still at two hours notice. 5 O.Rs. reinforcements. | Snow and sleet |
| 11th " | " | each day. |
| 12th " | Squadron attached to Canadian Corps. "C" & "E" were notified. Two Sections Nos 1 & 8 attached to 19th Hussars, at two hours notice. | |
| 13th " | | |
| 14th " | | |
| 15th " | | |

SECRET

WAR DIARY
or
INTELLIGENCE SUMMARY.
(Erase heading not required.)

Army Form C. 2118.

| Hour, Date, Place APRIL. | Summary of Events and Information | Remarks and references to Appendices |
|---|---|---|
| 16th In billets at VACQUERIE-LE BOUCQ. | Squadron moved via TILLOY LES MERNAVILLE - IZELLES HAMEAU - AMBRINES - MOUVIN HOUVIGNEUL - FREVENT to VACQUERIE LE BOUCQ. Half the horses of the Squadron under cover. | Good weather. Only water available near Village from wells 35 to 50 metres deep & from very dirty ponds in yards. |
| 17th " " " | | |
| 18th " " " | | |
| 19th " " " | Squadron moved billets to ROUGEFAY. All horses under cover. | |
| 20th In billets at ROUGEFAY. | | |
| 21st " " " | | |
| 22nd " " " | Inspection of Small Box Respirators by Divisional Gas Officer. | |
| 23rd " " " | Inspection of Horses by G.O.C. 9th Car. Bde. and A.D.V.S. 1st Cav. Div. | |
| 24th " " " | | |
| 25th " " " | | |
| 26th " " " | | |
| 27th " " " | | |
| 28th " " " | Inspection of Squadron Transport by G.O.C. 9th Cav. Bde., and O.C. A.S.C. | |
| 29th " " " | | |
| 30th " " " | Strength of the Squadron, 11 Officers, 2 300 O.Rs; 266 horses. 1 Sgt. from 13th Army School attached as Physical Drill Instructor. 1 Sgt. from "Y" Battery R.H.A. attached as Driving Instructor. 1 Corpl. from Sanitary Section attached for Sanitary duties. | |

R.W.W...
Major.
Comndg. 9th Machine Gun Squadron.

CONFIDENTIAL

# WAR DIARY
## OF
## 9TH MACHINE GUN SQUADRON.
## MAY 1917.
### VOLUME - XV.

SECRET.

Army Form C. 2118

# WAR DIARY
## or
## INTELLIGENCE SUMMARY
(Erase heading not required.)

Instructions regarding War Diaries and Intelligence Summaries are contained in F. S. Regs., Part II. and the Staff Manual respectively. Title Pages will be prepared in manuscript.

| Place | Date 1917 MAY | Hour | Summary of Events and Information | Remarks and references to Appendices |
|---|---|---|---|---|
| ROUGEFAY | 1st | | In Billets. N.C.Os. Class of Instructions in Physical Drill under Sergt Instructor 3rd Army Commenced. | L.N5 11 |
| " | 2nd | | " Inspection of Squadron at work by G.O.C. 9th Cav. Bde. Party of 40 O.Rs. reinforcements arrived. | " |
| " | 3rd | | " Squadron moved to new billets at LIGNY-SUR-CANCHE owing to area being required by Infantry of 3rd Army. | " |
| LIGNY-SUR-CANCHE | 4th | | In Billets. Brigade Scheme for O.C. 2nd in Command and 2nd Battalions. | |
| " | 5th | | " | |
| " | 6th | | " Inter-Brigade Competition. 9th Cavalry Brigade v 89th Infantry Brigade. The following men of the Squadron were selected to represent the Brigade:- Football - Pte. Cuthbert. Tug of War. Pte. Belben. Boxing - Ptes. Inns & Churchill. | |
| " | 7th | | In billets. | |
| " | 8th | | " Inspection of Shooting arrangs. by G.O.C. 9th Cav. Bde. | |
| " | 9th | | " Squadron Judicial Scheme for Officers and Sergeants. Rendezvous BRIQUETERIE 3¾mile Nth FREVENT on NUNCQ - FREVENT road. | |
| " | 10th | | In billets. Inspection of billets by G.O.C. 9th Cav. Bde. | |
| " | 11th | | " Inspection of Horses by Veterinary Officers. | |
| " | 12th | | " | |
| " | 13th | | " The Squadron moved independently via NUNCQ - ST. POL - VALHUON to PERNES. Left 7.50 a.m. arrived 4 p.m. | |
| " | 14th | | The Squadron moved via CABONNE - RIGOVART - MARLES-LES-MINES - to LABEUVRIERE. In bivouac. | |
| LABEUVRIERE | 15th | | In bivouac. | |
| " | 16th | | " | |
| " | 17th | | " The Squadron French party marched via GOSNAY - NOEUX-LES-MINES to PHILOSOPHE. This party now attached to 71st Inf. Bde. 6th Division. | |

1875  Wt. W593/826  1,000,000  4/15  J.B.C. & A.  A.D.S.S./Forms/C. 2118.

Army Form C. 2118

# WAR DIARY
## or
## INTELLIGENCE SUMMARY
(Erase heading not required.)

Instructions regarding War Diaries and Intelligence Summaries are contained in F. S. Regs., Part II. and the Staff Manual respectively. Title Pages will be prepared in manuscript.

| Place | Date MAY | Hour | Summary of Events and Information | Remarks and references to Appendices |
|---|---|---|---|---|
| PHILOSOPHE | 18th | | Squadron relieved 118th M.G. Coy. in the CITE ST ELIE Sector, taking over the following positions: R56, R55, R54, FARMERS LANE, V32, V35, R51, R52 DUDLEY DUMP (two guns) R50 and ST GEORGES POST. There were driven into Groups of H.Q., 2 Right, Centre and Left Sections. | HAZEBROUCK |
| LABEUVRIERE | 19th | | The Squadron moved to ANNEZIN — In Bivouac. | |
| VERMELLES | 20th | | In the trenches. Very quiet. | |
| " | 21st | | The Squadron co-operated with the Infantry in a Dummy Raid in front of CITE ST ELIE, guns at the following positions being used – R52. R51 and 013 H. | |
| " | 22nd | | In the trenches. 6th Division practiced concentration of machine gun fire in which the following guns of the Squadron took part. R52. R51. 013 H. Left Group. 013 H. Central Group. V33. At 12 noon a Daylight Raid on the front and second enemy lines was made by one company of the 1st Leicesters. The Squadron guns putting up a barrage on the enemy reserve lines. Very little retaliation was made by the enemy, who sent over a few rounds from his artillery and trench mortars. 4/7069 Pte Stripping slightly wounded. Much rain in night 21/22nd, also this morning. | |
| " | 23rd | | In the trenches. Fairly quiet. Fine warm day. | |
| " | 24th | | " " " " " " | |
| " | 25th | | Enemy's artillery very active. Anti-aircraft position at ST GEORGES POST badly knocked about. | |
| " | 26th | | More hostile Artillery activity than usual against gun position in Right Group. A bombing party of this Squadron (together with two Pr. Pa. (one in no mans land and one in unoccupied front line) waited for an enemy working party, | |

# WAR DIARY
## or
## INTELLIGENCE SUMMARY
*(Erase heading not required.)*

Army Form C. 2118

| Place | Date | Hour | Summary of Events and Information | Remarks and references to Appendices |
|---|---|---|---|---|
| VERMELLES | 27th | | in order to obtain a prisoner of identification, but no wiring party appeared. | |
| " | 28th | | The Squadron again waited for an enemy wiring party, but were rewarded with gas shells and had to retire. Major R.H.Settle, 39872 Pte Deeks and 44711 Pte Lewis being gassed. At 5 a.m. 4 Companies of the Sherwood Foresters made a Daylight Raid on the enemy's trenches, dugouts etc. – Artillery and guns of the Squadron putting up a heavy barrage. The enemy retaliated very thickly with Heavies, "Minnies" and "Whiz-bangs". At 4 p.m. guns of the Squadron, in conjunction with other machine guns of the Division, practised a swedish barrage from its enemy's support to reserve lines. | |
| " | 29th | | The 12 guns of the Squadron were relieved by 12 guns of the 71st Machine Gun Company, relief being complete by 10 a.m. when the Squadron marched to billets at MAZINGARBE and attached to 16th Infantry Brigade | |
| MAZINGARBE | 30th | | " | |
| " | 31st | | in billets. | |

Chas Macnair  Captain.
Comdg. 9th Machine Gun Squadron.

SECRET

Vol 17

War Diary
of
9th Machine Gun Squadron.
June 1917.

SECRET.

Army Form C. 2118

# WAR DIARY
## or
## INTELLIGENCE SUMMARY
*(Erase heading not required.)*

Instructions regarding War Diaries and Intelligence Summaries are contained in F.S. Regs., Part II. and the Staff Manual respectively. Title Pages will be prepared in manuscript.

| Place | Date | Hour | Summary of Events and Information | Remarks and references to Appendices |
|---|---|---|---|---|
| MAZINGARBE | June 1st 1914 | | In billets. | |
| | 2nd | | The French party marched to ANNEZIN to rejoin back party. In billets. | |
| ANNEZIN | 3rd | | In billets. The following reinforcements arrived :- 47414 Pte L.W. Beard. 52698 Pte Barratt. 51875 Pte Bradley. 39165 Pte W. Fowler. 50587 Pte W. Walker. 52421 Pte W. Moon. 50659 Pte Hughes. | |
| LA GORGUE | 4th | | The Squadron moved with the Brigade to LA GORGUE via LOCON – ZELOBES – LESTREM. In bivouac, HAZEBROUCK. | SA |
| | 5th | | In bivouac. | |
| | 6th | | " Inspection of Remounts by the A.D.V.S. 1st Cav. Div. | |
| | 7th | | " The following reinforcements arrived :- 39950 Pte J. Jones. 39955 Pte F. J. Pettifer. 39951 Pte R. Pirie. | |
| | 8th | | In bivouac. | |
| | 9th | | " | |
| | 10th | | " | |
| | 11th | | The Brigade moved via LESTREM – ZELOBES – LOCON to the LABEUVRIERE area, the Squadron moving to billets at ANNEZIN. | |
| ANNEZIN | 12th | | In billets. | |
| | 13th | | The French party consisting of 6 officers 112 O.R.s and 10 horses marched to SAILLY LABOURSE, en route for trenches. In billets for the night. | |

**Army Form C. 2118**

# WAR DIARY
## or
## INTELLIGENCE SUMMARY

*(Erase heading not required.)*

Instructions regarding War Diaries and Intelligence Summaries are contained in F.S. Regs., Part II. and the Staff Manual respectively. Title Pages will be prepared in manuscript.

| Place | Date | Hour | Summary of Events and Information | Remarks and references to Appendices |
|---|---|---|---|---|
| In the trenches | 14th | | Two guns of 1st Squadron relieved guns and teams of the 10th M.G. Coy in the Hulluch sector. A gun of 18th M.G. Coy attached to Sqdn. in reserve Mazingarbe. 2 guns of 10th M.G. Coy also attached to Sqdn. for duty in line. Sqdn. HQrs. move to Mazingarbe. | Loos 36c. NW3 |
| | 15th | | Sqdn. HQrs move to ADVANCED BN. HQrs in HULLUCH TUNNEL. I picked team under LIEUT. EADE attached to 11th Buffs for special training in connection with coming operations empera training at H1100 A&NE. Raid by the 18th Inf. Bn. on enemy trenches at N1a 5888 and 43.d 00 40 05 30 ANE and first roughly 2000 R.A's divided into three groups. Right centre left. Raid accommodated over no-mans-land Hulluch craters at 2.30pm found no signs of enemy hostility either [illegible] of trept mc. trophies found. No front trenches held by night. Sub-battalion relief on night 16/17. | 1/10,000 and 36 B NE and SE |
| | 17th | | H.Q. Infinbmato all open air except in Northern Shaft G.E. or Moulin or Folly morning at Hay Alley. Good Dugouts everywhere. | |
| | 18th | | 10.14 Bd. extends its front 1000's to south taking over line to Railway Alley exclusive from 18th Inf. Bn. Sqdn. 10th over from Fosse pm. - 1 sec. a 14 Fn M.G. By. attached to Sqdn. for 18 pm Isley. No Gmp Relieving - Cellars "X" group. | |
| | 19th | | Relieves teams in Northern Shaft and Fork Hay Alley positions by teams from anothe position R46.49.49. Very hot trenches. | |
| | 20th | | Sqdn. HQrs. move up Tunnel to the Dugoot in Green curve shaft. A further section of 1st Fr. 14 M.G. By. attached to Sqdn. & relieve 1 detachment of Sqdn. & a detachment of 10th M.G. Coy in X group. And a detach of 10th M.G. Coy in X group. | OKJ |

# WAR DIARY or INTELLIGENCE SUMMARY

*(Erase heading not required.)*

Army Form C. 2118

Instructions regarding War Diaries and Intelligence Summaries are contained in F. S. Regs., Part II. and the Staff Manual respectively. Title Pages will be prepared in manuscript.

| Place | Date | Hour | Summary of Events and Information | Remarks and references to Appendices |
|---|---|---|---|---|
| S.H. Marches | 21st 22nd | | Preparations and reconnaissance of HULLUCH CRATERS for coming raid. Two gun numbers - Commanders of bombing groups taken over CRATER in charge by Lt. Fourth Lt. CRATER Clayre. Bomber by LIEUT EADES Rocks, in which MAZINGARBE and No 10 SIEGE Bty N. HACKETT assisted. Benjamin, Hughes. Final arrangements made if weather fine. | LOOS 36c NW3 & SW Sheet) MAZINGARBE SHEET J 36b NE 36b SE |
| HULLUCH | 23rd | | full party now up of under also Myers, Slater, Mitchell arrived there about 2 pm. |  |
|  |  |  | NORTHERN SHAFT B.d CRATER PARTY - Here also about 2 pm. |  |
|  | 24th | 9 pm | Raid by 12 officers and about 300 men on the area H13a 38.35 – H13a 60.40 – H13a 70.58 – H13a 60.85 – H13a 20.82. A.G. barrage of 39 guns on flank especially on J E & D & flank. (Only 19 mm shooting own heads of Raiders) from zero – zero +50 minutes. Rifle that time at Bugo hed in barrage. Slow time to zero of J.O.5. Lt. Eade and 80 on gun top accompanied by 12 bombers take up position in first Crater from NORTH. Enemy rifle pickets & Lewis Guns rifled. Lt Eades M.C. & Md. operation very successful – many enemy shot in this needed by reading party looting structures, kit daily unarmed in CRATER for 2 hrs till the whistlement of Police needing party had seen effected – R.G. barrage good |  |
|  | 25th | 3 am | 9 guns of the 14th & 3 and 4 guns of the 14th H.A.G. Battery relieved by 13 guns of the 18 H.A.G. Bty. The 14th section of 12 1907a H.A. Cor unlimbering 9.30 am. Rebel complete 6am. Bullet over 13 00 10th H.Q. Boy & J |  |
|  |  |  | S.G. moves to 46 Division area. to CITÉ DES BUREAUX LIÉVIN, advanced HQ 3 officers according. pro position arrived 6 pm. Remainder at 2.30 pm. 26/vm. |  |

Army Form C. 2118

# WAR DIARY
## or
## INTELLIGENCE SUMMARY
(Erase heading not required.)

Instructions regarding War Diaries and Intelligence Summaries are contained in F.S. Regs., Part II. and the Staff Manual respectively. Title Pages will be prepared in manuscript.

| Place | Date | Hour | Summary of Events and Information | Remarks and references to Appendices |
|---|---|---|---|---|
| IN ACTION CITÉ DES BUREAUX | 26th | | Further reconnaissance of gun positions. Further harassing and searching fire. Positions begun during night. SQDN. bivouaced at LES BREBIS. | LENS B6 & S.W.I. ED. 8a 1/10,000. |
| | 27th | | Further preparation of gun positions during the night. | |
| | 28th | | Supplies were laid between groups. Two Brigade attack on ADVINCOURT ad ABODE TRENCHWORK 7.10 pm. Guns of 17th fire inboard fire Zero-Zero +15 mins. and this harassing and searching fire through night. CITÉ DES BUREAUX bombarded with gun shells No 39951 Pte J. LINEN wounded. | |
| | 29th | | Harassing fire throughout day on outskirts of LENS. Reconnoitred Avc 65. Opened rapid on withdrawal from gun positions. Gnr Killen from 5 pm - 4 am. ECM 10pm. | |
| IN ACTION CITÉ DE RIAUMONT | 30th | | Reconnoitred harassing fire positions in M30a CITÉ DE RIAUMONT. Began digging 2 pm. Sgt. Horn ad. an advi of S. to move down to new positions about 8 pm. Sgt. Horn in column. | |

1875  Wt. W593/826  1,000,000  4/15  J.B.C. & A.  A.D.S.S./Forms/C. 2118.

CONFIDENTIAL.

Vol 18

War Diary
of
7th Machine Gun Squadron
July 1917.

**SECRET**

Army Form C. 2118

Instructions regarding War Diaries and Intelligence Summaries are contained in F.S. Regs., Part II. and the Staff Manual respectively. Title Pages will be prepared in manuscript.

# WAR DIARY or INTELLIGENCE SUMMARY
*(Erase heading not required.)*

| Place | Date July | Hour | Summary of Events and Information | Remarks and references to Appendices |
|---|---|---|---|---|
| In the trenches | 1st | — | Trench Party at LENS. Machine Guns firing in small bursts all day. Nothing else to report. Struck off Strength. No 39994. Pte. Warren H.S. wounded 1/7/17. 52065. Pte. Jarvis. H.E. wounded gassed 1/7/17. 50662. Pte. Lawrence. G. do. do. 47414. Pte. Beard. S. evacuated to No 1. C.C.S. (Sick) 1/7/17. | |
| " | 2nd | | Trench Party at LENS. Hadley any firing at all. Squadron commenced relaying 10.30pm moved LES BREBIS in small parties. Germans very toxey sending over gas shells during the evening. | |
| LES BREBIS | 3rd | | Trench Party resting at LES BREBIS. Back Party at ANNEZIN. | |
| " | 4th | | " " Inspection of arms, P.H. helmets, Box Respirators & billets at 11.30 a.m. | |
| ANNEZIN | 5th | | Moved to ANNEZIN by bus 4 p/c p.m. In billets. Inspection of all Guns and Spare part boxes. Taken on strength No 97468. Arm. Staff Sgt. Glover. | |
| " | 6th | | In billets. | |
| " | 7th | | In billets. Advance Party consisting of 10 guides moved off to trenches, to take over the part of the line left by the 18th M.G. Coy at 2.15 pm. Major R.N. Settle and Officers departed en route for trenches at 7 a.m. French Party left ANNEZIN 2.15 pm by motor bus en route to LES BREBIS, moved to and came evening. Lieut E.E. Millard arrived from Base and taken on the strength of the Squadron. | |
| In the Trenches. | 9th | | Both sides very quiet during the day. 12.15 a.m. an enemy party of about 50 attempted a raid on our trenches. The Squadrons gun fire were brought to bear on enemys raid. The enemy released gas at 1.2 a.m. 57734. Pte M.Onslow evacuated to No 18 C.C.S estimated approx strength of the Squadron. | |
| " | 10th | | 14.750 rounds S.A.A fired during the night 9/10th. Two guns ranging on junction NOVEL NETLEY. | |
| " | 11th | | 10/11th. 1.45 a.m. enemy attempted raid at junction NOVEL NETLEY. | |
| | | | 9.500 " " " | |

1875   Wt. W593/826   1,000,000   4/15   J.B.C. & A.   A.D.S.S./Forms/C. 2118.

Army Form C. 2118

# WAR DIARY
## or
## INTELLIGENCE SUMMARY
(Erase heading not required.)

Instructions regarding War Diaries and Intelligence Summaries are contained in F.S. Regs., Part II. and the Staff Manual respectively. Title Pages will be prepared in manuscript.

| Place | Date | Hour | Summary of Events and Information | Remarks and references to Appendices |
|---|---|---|---|---|
| In the trenches | 1917 July 12th | | 11,500 rounds S.A.A. fired during the night 11/12th. Raid was made by us on enemy lines at 10 p.m. between H.13.c.62.00 and H.13.c.60.80. 50127 Pte. H. Cooke wounded. | LENS 1/20,000 Trench Map. |
| " | 13th | | Both sides very quiet during day. Two left Groups relieved by 2 Canadian Machine Gun Coy. and returned to LES BREBIS to await arrival of the Right Groups. Captain A.S. Dunham arrived from N.G. (Cav.) T.C. Mortiers. | |
| " | 14th | | Two Right Groups and HQrs. commenced relieving at 10.30 p.m. and on completion returned to LES BREBIS. Trench party returned to ANNEZIN arriving 4.45 a.m. 15th inst. | |
| ANNEZIN | 15th | | In billets. | HAZEBROUCK 5A 1/100,000 |
| " | 16th | | The Brigade moved to new area about NEUF BERQUIN and march via first NOR VENDIN - A. T. LES - CHOCQAUX - LOCON - LESTREM - A of ESTAIRES, the Squadron being billeted on the ESTAIRES - NEUF BERQUIN road, about 1 mile W. of ESTAIRES. | |
| ESTAIRES | 17th | | In billets. The following reinforcements arrived:- 42411 Pte. E. Lewis, 57864 Pte. J. Roberts, 57727 Pte. A.T. Hackett, 105310 Pte. T. Foader, 105309 Pte. J.E. Lewis, 105313 Pte. R.S. Smith, 105311 Pte. W. Bridand, 105308 Pte. R. Jarvis, 39057 Pte. A. Shatford. 50404 Pte. W. Prickett concentrated to No.1 General Hospital Patrick to this strength of the Squadron. | |
| " | 18th | | In billets. Horse Inspection by G.O.C. 9th Cav. Bde. & A.D.V.S. 1st Cav. Div. | |
| " | 19th | | " | |
| " | 20th | | 1st Cav. Div. ordered to find a dismounted Brigade to act as reserve behind the Centre Division of the XI Corps (1st Portuguese Division) 9th Brigade to find our Battalion under Major Bartlett, 15th Hussars, with the 12 guns of the 9th M.G. Squadron. Ready to move. | |
| " | 21st | | In billets. Training. | |
| " | 22nd | | " " | |
| " | 23rd | | " " The following reinforcements arrived. 105316 Pte. H. Topley, 105315 Pte. | |
| " | 24th | | | |

F.S. Tuffu.

Army Form C. 2118

# WAR DIARY
## or
## INTELLIGENCE SUMMARY
*(Erase heading not required.)*

Instructions regarding War Diaries and Intelligence Summaries are contained in F.S. Regs., Part II. and the Staff Manual respectively. Title Pages will be prepared in manuscript.

| Place | Date | Hour | Summary of Events and Information | Remarks and references to Appendices |
|---|---|---|---|---|
| ESTAIRES | 1915 July 25th | | In billets. Training | |
| " | 26th | | " " | |
| " | 27/15 | | " " Lieuts Eade, Henderson & Millard proceeded to trenches to get work Company Commander to show him guns were detailed to view positions. | |
| " | 28th | | In billets. Training. Lieut J. Bridges and squadron signallers took part in a Divisional Signalling Scheme. Horse inspection by A.D.V.S. 1st Cav Div. | |
| " | 29th | | In billets. Training. | |
| " | 30th | | Lieut J. Bridges attached Divisional Signalling Scheme. | |
| " | 31st | | In billets. Training. | |
| | | | Strength of Squadron | |
| | | | | Officers | O. Ranks | Horses | R.D. | Pack |
| | | | | 10 | 274 | 181 | 18 | 42 |
| | | | attached | 2 | 3 | | | |
| | | | | | 12 | | | |
| | | | Attached from 1st M.G.S. gdn. | | | | | |

1st Battalion 2nd for Captain
Commanding Machine Gun Squadron

26/1/1

Vb 19

WAR DIARY

of

9th Machine Gun Squadron.

August 1917.

Volume XXVIII.

Confidential

SECRET.

Army Form C. 2118.

Instructions regarding War Diaries and Intelligence Summaries are contained in F. S. Regs., Part II. and the Staff Manual respectively. Title Pages will be prepared in manuscript.

# WAR DIARY
## or
## INTELLIGENCE SUMMARY
(Erase heading not required.)

| Place | Date | Hour | Summary of Events and Information | Remarks and references to Appendices |
|---|---|---|---|---|
| ESTAIRES. | August 1st | | In billets. | HAZEBROUCK |
| | 2nd | | 1 Rider evacuated to B.V.H. and is struck off the strength of the Squadron | " |
| | 3rd | | 1 Rider " " " " " " " " " " | " |
| | 4th | | " " " " " " " " " " " | " |
| | 5th | | In billets. Lieut J.B.A. Hayter left for the 2nd Machine Gun Squadron as 2nd in Command and struck off the strength of the Squadron. No 50605 Pte Baker J. transferred to 2nd Machine Gun Squadron and is struck off the strength of the Squadron. 1 Rider evacuated to B.V.H. and is struck off the strength of the Squadron. No 50865 Pte G.J. Milam transferred to 2nd Machine Gun Squadron | " |
| | 6th | | and is struck off the strength of the Squadron. 3 Riders having been transferred to the 2nd Machine Gun Squadron are struck off the strength of the Squadron | " |
| | 7th | | In billets | " |
| | 8th | | In billets. No 50704 Pte W. Prickett discharged from hospital and taken on the strength of the Squadron. | " |
| | 9th | | In billets. | " |
| | 10th | | " " | " |
| | 11th | | " " | " |
| | 12th | | " " Firing on the long range at MORBECQUE. No 39871 Pte A. Scott evacuated to No 51. C.C.S. and is struck off the strength of the Squadron | " |
| | 13th | | In billets. Firing on the long range at MORBECQUE. | " |

# WAR DIARY
## or
## INTELLIGENCE SUMMARY

Army Form C. 2118

| Place | Date | Hour | Summary of Events and Information | Remarks and references to Appendices |
|---|---|---|---|---|
| ESTAIRES | August 14th | | In billets. The following men having been despatched to the No 2 I.B. Base Depot are struck off the strength of the Squadron. No 50686 Pte Baldwin. 53163 Pte Fowler S. 50712 Pte Mickleen A. 105276 Pte Hudson A. 50689 Pte Hughes R. 50757 Pte James A. 51430 Moores A. 39980 Lawrence J. 47480 Jackson W.R.H. 50119 Roberts H. 105261 Yeston A. 38884 Newton H. 39856 Carpenter F.R. 39876 Irving G. 39985 Shelton A. 105310 Foster J. 50727 Larkin G. 50654 Day A. 50700 Merritt F. 50707 Spencer A. 105266 France W. 50024 Seymour G.S. 50774 Burcher A.R.A. 50778 Kelly R.Y. 50178 Osborne S. 50702 Osborne A. 50762 Gent J.W. 80696 Vaughan G.P. 39950 Jones J. 39861. Squire S. 51720 Marshall J. 51843 7157. Linton H. 105289. Graham H. In billets. 2.R. and I.H.D surrendered to D.V.H. and is struck off the strength of the Squadron. | are HAZEBROUCK'S |
| | 15th | | In billets. The following men were despatched to M.G.C. Base Depot and are struck off the strength of the Squadron. No 50128. Pte Hall H. 50784. Pte Hague S. No 40779. Pte Knight L. No 50674 Pte Holmes H. No 52211 Pte Wall A.H. No 47069 Pte Kipping. No 50663 Pte Maynard to 51412 Pte Bowser. The Squadron took part in a Brigade Tactical Exercise above LA GORGUE | " |
| | 16th | | NEUF BERQUIN and MERVILLE. In billets. No 50752 Pte J. Barlow evacuated to No 51. C.C.S. and is struck off the strength of the squadron. No 5uu13 Pte Barlow No 51739 | " |
| | 17th | | Pte Kitchen J.B. No 51895 Pte Yardley H.S. No 50701 Pte Penfold H. No 47028 Pte Barwell Id. were transferred to M.G.C. Base Depot and are struck off the strength of the Squadron. | " |

Army Form C. 2118

# WAR DIARY
## or
## INTELLIGENCE SUMMARY

(Erase heading not required.)

| Place | Date | Hour | Summary of Events and Information | Remarks and references to Appendices |
|---|---|---|---|---|
| ESTAIRES | August 18th | | In billets. | HAZEBROUCK 5A |
| " | 19th | | " | " |
| " | 20th | | The A.D.M.S. inspected the Squadron Billets | " |
| " | 21st | | Inspection of the Squadron in mounted marching order by the C.M.G.O and G.O.C. 9th Cavalry Brigade. | " |
| " | 22nd | | In billets | " |
| " | 23rd | | " | " |
| " | 24th | | The team chosen to represent the Squadron competed in the Divisional Shoot at PACAUT and chosen to represent 1st Cavalry Division at Corps Horse Show. 2.I.D proceeded to 15th Hussars, 2nd to 19th Hussars, 2 to Reds. Yeomanry and one struck off the strength of the Squadron. | " |
| " | 25th | | " | |
| " | 26th | | " | |
| " | 27th | | The Squadron moved with the Brigade to an area about ESTRÉE-BLANCHE. HAZEBROUCK 7A the Squadron bivouacing at PIPPEMONT. Three show party under Capt MacAndrew, move to SIRACOURT. | |
| PIPPEMONT | 28th | | The Squadron moved with the Brigade to an area about VERCHOCQ. CALAIS 13. The Squadron bivouacing at AIX-en-EIGNY. | |
| AIX en EIGNY | 29th | | The Squadron moved with the Brigade to an area about FRENCQ. LEFAUX. BREXENT. via HUCQUELIERS - ENQUIN - POUT DE HAUT the Squadron marching to Billets at LEFAUX. 2.R. and 1.H.D. evacuated to B.V.H. and struck off the strength of the Squadron. | |

1875  Wt: W593/826  1,000,000  4/15  J.B.C. & A.  A.D.S.S./Forms/C. 2118.

Army Form C. 2118

# WAR DIARY
## or
## INTELLIGENCE SUMMARY
*(Erase heading not required.)*

| Place | Date | Hour | Summary of Events and Information | Remarks and references to Appendices |
|---|---|---|---|---|
| LE FAUX | August 30th | | Sgt. J. Ellis. 2 Riders and 1 A.D. having arrived are taken on the strength of the Squadron | 30.8.17. G.R.A.18. 13 |
| " | 31st | " | Sent A. S. Turnham and No 52135 Sgt Humphries S. proceeded to Squadron. 31.8.17. The following men proceeded to the M.G.K. Base Depôt and are struck off the strength of the Squadron 31.8.17 No 105813. Pte Smith R.G. No 50158. Pte Whelan J. Sgt Kengh of the Squadron. Officers 8 Others 222 2 3 Horses R.D. Packs. R. M. 71. 42 | " |

R.K.[signature]
Commanding 9th Machine Gun Squadron

WAR DIARY

of

9th MACHINE GUN SQUADRON,

SEPTEMBER, 1917.

VOLUME No. XIX.

CONFIDENTIAL.

**SECRET**

**Army Form C. 2118**

**WAR DIARY**
or
**INTELLIGENCE SUMMARY**
(Erase heading not required.)

Instructions regarding War Diaries and Intelligence Summaries are contained in F.S. Regs., Part II. and the Staff Manual respectively. Title Pages will be prepared in manuscript.

| Place | Date | Hour | Summary of Events and Information | Remarks and references to Appendices |
|---|---|---|---|---|
| LEFAUX | 1st 2/9/17 | — | Settling in. Major B. MOJ. (i.e. LEFAUX AREA) | CA 2A15.13 |
| " | 3/9/17 | — | No 037055 S/sgt NAYLOR. H. (A.S.C.) attached for duty to agricultural war. Arranging teams + Competitions for personnel. Whilst the Meeting etc. Box Respirator drill were worn throughout 3/9 in to 3:30 p.m. continuously. Corpl Sweetman R.A.M.C attached to Sistr 2/9/17 | |
| " | 4/9/17 | 8.30 | Schooling & Training of Pack horses by the Commanding Officer & 2/c/Command. No 50741 S.S.M. Hall admitted temporary Hospital 3/9/17 | No 51428 Pte Norman T discharged |
| " | 5/9/17 | | Capt. SWEETMAN R.A.M.C. transferred to Birds Yeomanry. Capt. G. KIRKHOPE R.A.M.C attached to Sqdn as M.O. 4/9/17. Lecture by Divisional Gas Officer + N.C.Os attended. Lieut H.D.BELFORD taken on strength. 4/9/17 | |
| " | 6/9/17 | 11.15am | Inspection of horses by A.D.V.S. & Training for Sports | |
| " | 7/9/17 | | Training in Sports & Ordinary Routine. Pte James H. No 50791 admitted Temporary H.P. No 50744 S.S.M. Hall discharged temp H.P. 6/9/17 | |
| " | 8/9/17 | 5.40pm | No 105263 Pte ASHMAN.T. struck off strength. Horses Rs.6. L.D. 4 Cas.L. by A.D.V.S. struck off strength. 6/9/17 | |
| " | | | Serum inoc. Horses at BEACH. No 51735 L/Cpl JEEVES.J admitted Temporary Hospital 7.9.17. No 105275 Pte MAXTED F.J has been granted Restoration of CLASS II P.P. from 2.5.17. | |
| " | 9/9/17 | | The turnout of the L.G.S. wagons on the strength of a Machine Gun Squadron to reduced from 18 to 15th No 598 M.G.G. 17 July 1917 | |
| " | 10/9/17 | | Medical Scheme. Held in Local Area. Gun Armament still on Pack. No 50731. Pte JAMES.H discharged Temporary hospital 8-9-17. Regt. The claim of 215. under A. Order 269. of 1916 as of No 51704 Pte ALLWOOD.W.H. has been passed. 9/9/17. | |
| " | 11/9/17 | | Machine Scheme. Continuation of Scheme. Horse No 58 destroyed. Struck off Strength 10-9-17. | |
| " | 12/9/17 | 10.30AM | Inspection of Billets. No 51735 L/Cpl JEEVES.J discharged temporary Hospital. 11-9-17 | |
| " | 13/9/17 | 2.45pm | Ordinary Routine & Inspection of Clothing at 2.45pm. HORSES. R.2. L.B.V.H + struck off strength 12/9/17 | |
| " | 14/9/17 | 10 am | Divine Service. Parade. B.Q. Woodward transferred to B.V.H. + struck off Strength 13-9-17. | |
| " | 15/9/17 | | Continuation of Clothing Inspection. Ordinary Routine. Inspection of Horses by D.D.R. for casting | |
| " | 16/9/17 | | Claim of "15" remedies Army Order 269 on account of 51695 Sgt Tomlinson H.J. has been passed E20. 51423 Pte Rushworth W.T. | |
| " | 17/9/17 | 6.30 | Parade to Water for practice M.C. Refreshment Competition in Brigade Rifle Competition 3 L.D. HORSES Taken on Strength. 14-9-17. | |
| " | 18/9/17 | 5.30 | Parade in Firing Practice. G.O.C. grand Polo Tournt. No 44100 Pte IRWIN.W + No 50676 Pte UNDERHILL.E admitted Temporary Hospital. 17-9-17. | |
| " | 19/9/17 | | Ordinary Routine. No 2465 Staff Armourer S/L CLOVER.H.H. + No 51702 S/S PRATT.F. admitted Temporary Hospital 18-9-17. No 50676 Pte UNDERHILL.E discharged Temporary Hospital 18-9-17. | No 51710 Pte BROWNE appointed Unpaid Lance Cpl |
| " | 20/9/17 | 8.30 2.45 | Parade Mounted with Packs for Practice in M.G. Detachment Competition. No 41120 evacuated to B.V.H. struck off Strength 20-9-17. | |
| " | | | G.R. + 3 L.D Cast. by D.D.R on 15-9-17 Evacuated to Base struck off 20-9-17 | |

**SECRET.**

Army Form C. 2118

# WAR DIARY
## or
## INTELLIGENCE SUMMARY
*(Erase heading not required.)*

Instructions regarding War Diaries and Intelligence Summaries are contained in F.S. Regs., Part II. and the Staff Manual respectively. Title Pages will be prepared in manuscript.

| Place | Date | Hour | Summary of Events and Information | Remarks and references to Appendices |
|---|---|---|---|---|
| LEFAUX | 21/9/17 | — | 1st CAVALRY DIVISION ATHLETIC SPORTS. Shooting on Range (Voluntary) + Ordinary Routine. | CXLV/3/13 |
|  | 22/9/17 | 2 p.m. | Divine Service for Non Conformists. Ordinary Routine |  |
|  | 23/9/17 | 11.45 |  |  |
|  | 24/9/17 | 3 p.m. | Squadron proceeded to SANER to go through Gas Test. |  |
|  | 25/9/17 | 9 a.m. | Parade for Divisional Scheme in the LEFAUX area. No 41100 Pte IRWIN.W discharged to Imp. Hospital |  |
|  | 26/9/17 | 9.30 | Eliminating Trials of Shooting off for Rifle Meeting |  |
|  | 27/9/17 | — | BRIGADE RIFLE MEETING. |  |
|  | 28/9/17 | — | Lieut Earle C. J. Lieut Halliday M.A.C. detailed to act as Umpires in Divisional Scheme. Sergt C Hadley No 50504 left for Div Gas School to undergo a course of instruction |  |
|  | 29/9/17 |  | No 50442 Sergt Sexton G. discharged to Temporary Hospital 28-9-17. N.R. 45750 taken on Strength of Squadron 29-9-17 |  |
|  | 30/9/17 | 9.30 | Divine Service + Ordinary Routine |  |

[signature] Major
Commanding 9th Machine Gun Squadron

"Confidential"

## WAR DIARY

9th Machine Gun Squadron

October 1917.

VOLUME 20

# WAR DIARY
## INTELLIGENCE SUMMARY.
*(Erase heading not required.)*

9th Machine Gun Sqdn. Army Form C. 2118. 1/10/17 to 31/10/17

| Place | Date October | Hour | Summary of Events and Information | Remarks and references to Appendices |
|---|---|---|---|---|
| LE FAUX | 1st | | In billets. Inspection of horses by O.C. 30th Mobile Veterinary Section. 2nd Lieut. Bailey arrived from BASE DEPOT and taken on the strength of the Squadron from 1.10.17 | |
| Do. | 2nd | | In billets. Inspection of the Squadron by L.O.C. 9th Cavalry Brigade. | |
| Do. | 3rd | | In billets. Nos. 3 and 4 sub-sections take part in a Regimental Exercise with the 19th Hussars. Nos. 5 and 6 sub-sections take part in a Regimental Exercise with the Beds. Yeomanry. | |
| Do. | 4th | | In billets. Firing on Brigade Rifle Range. Kent & London Babies having been transferred to the 1/1st M.A.C. is struck off the strength of the Squadron from H.10.M. (Authority Brigade L.L.Q.1110.) | |
| Do | 5th | | In billets. Preparing for move. | |
| Do | 6th | | The Squadron marches with Brigade to the SAMER area. The Squadron billeted for the night 6/7th October at LONG FOSSE. | |
| LONG FOSSE | 7th | | The Squadron marches with Brigade via HENNEVEUX — REBERGUES — LE POIRIER — BONNINGUES — LES ARDRES — TOURNEHEM — MORDACQUES — ZUDROVE. No 24168 Armourer Staff Sergeant Giner A.H. No 3A879 Pte Ward. & No 51718 Pte Clarke is to and 10 SHORT Pte Marchant to evacuated and struck off the strength of the Squadron from 7. 10. 17 | |

Army Form C. 2118.

# WAR DIARY
## or
## INTELLIGENCE SUMMARY.
(Erase heading not required.)

Instructions regarding War Diaries and Intelligence Summaries are contained in F. S. Regs., Part II. and the Staff Manual respectively. Title pages will be prepared in manuscript.

| Place | Date October | Hour | Summary of Events and Information | Remarks and references to Appendices |
|---|---|---|---|---|
| LUDROVE | 8th. | | In billets. | |
| Do. | 9th. | | 6 Riders arrived and taken on the strength of the Squadron from 9.10.17. 1 Rider evacuated to Base Veterinary Hospital and struck off the strength of the Squadron from 9.10.17. | |
| Do. | 10th. | | In billets. | |
| Do. | 11th. | | The Squadron moved to a rest area about SAMER, and billeted for the night 11/12th October at LONG FOSSE. | |
| LONGFOSSE | 12th. | | The Squadron entrained at CHURCH WIERRE - AU - BOIS at 10.45am and marched to LEFAUX under own arrangements. | |
| LEFAUX. | 13th. | | In billets. Improvements of billets etc. | |
| Do | 14th. | | Major R.H. Sadler President of a F.G.C.M. assembling 15th. Answers H. Brs. No 50734 Pte Owen. M. No 50112 Pte Whitehead. A. 50102 Pte Osborne. C. and No 50654 Pte Day H.J. having arrived from BASE DEPOT are taken on the strength of the Squadron from 14.10.17. 4 Riders having arrived are taken on the strength of the Squadron from 14.10.17. 1 Rider having died is struck off the strength of the Squadron from 14.10.17. The Squadron move to a rest area about RECQUES, and billeted for the night 15/16th October at RECQUES. | |
| Do | 15th. | | | |

Army Form C. 2118.

# WAR DIARY
## or
## INTELLIGENCE SUMMARY.

(Erase heading not required.)

Instructions regarding War Diaries and Intelligence Summaries are contained in F. S. Regs., Part II. and the Staff Manual respectively. Title pages will be prepared in manuscript.

| Place | Date October | Hour | Summary of Events and Information | Remarks and references to Appendices |
|---|---|---|---|---|
| RECQUES. | 16th | | In billets. Nos. 3, 4, and 5 Sub-sections, H.Qrs. and Transport moved to billets at MONTCAVREL. Nos. 1, 2, and 6 Sub-sections remained at billets in RECQUES. | |
| MONTCAVREL | 17th | | In billets. Improvement of billets and horse-standings. No. A 2889 Armourer Staff Sergeant Wheat T. having arrived from BASE is taken on the strength of the Squadron from 17.10.17 | |
| Do. | 18th | | Improvement of billets and horse standings. | |
| Do. | 19th | | In billets. Health Inspection by O/C. Officer in charge Q.R. Machine Gun Intelligence and Lieutenant Henderson H.R. evacuated to ENGLAND and struck off the strength of the Squadron from 19.10.17. (Authority A.A. and Q.M.G. 1st Cav. Div. 10956 dated 26/10/17. Lieut. Q.V.O. Radcliffe having arrived from BASE DEPOT is taken on the strength of the Squadron from 19.10.17. | |
| Do. | 20th | | In billets. No 6811 Rfm. Geoghegan 4th Royal Irish Rifles 27025 Pte. Kerr R. 8th Inniskilling Fusiliers 27747 Pte Qacy Q.S. 13th Northumberland Fusiliers } having arrived from 1st Corps Labour Coy are attached to this Unit for duty from 20.10.17. 6 Riders and 1 L.D. arrived and taken on the strength of the Squadron from 20.10.17. | |

**Army Form C. 2118.**

# WAR DIARY
## or
## INTELLIGENCE SUMMARY.
*(Erase heading not required.)*

Instructions regarding War Diaries and Intelligence Summaries are contained in F. S. Regs., Part II. and the Staff Manual respectively. Title pages will be prepared in manuscript.

| Place | Date OCTOBER | Hour | Summary of Events and Information | Remarks and references to Appendices |
|---|---|---|---|---|
| MONTCAVREL | 21st | | In billets. No 7031655 Driver Naylor J detached to Q.M. Marley Field Ambulance from 21.10.17. | |
| | | | 1 Rider detached to 9th battery Field Ambulance from 21.10.17. | |
| | | | The following promotions and appointment took place:- | |
| | | | No 50716. 1/Sergt Shreeve. W. promoted Acg Sergeant from 17.7.17 | |
| | | | 50715. Corpl. Hardwell. H. " " " " | |
| | | | 50719 Corpl. Lubbock. F. " " " " | |
| | | | 51098. A/Corpl. Keech. S.P. " Corporal " " | |
| | | | 51609 L/Cpl. Denton. V. " " " " | |
| | | | 50736 A/L/Cpl. Sissen. J.J. " " 21.10.17 | |
| | | | " " " " Paid Lance Corpl " 21.10.17. | |
| | | | M.C.E. Halliday having been transferred to M.G.C. | |
| | | | Lieut. M.C.E. Halliday struck off the strength of the Squadron from 22.10.17. | |
| Do. | 22nd | | In billets. Training (cav) continues. | |
| Do | 23rd | | In billets. Health Inspection by Medical Officer in charge 9th Machine | |
| Do. | 24th | | " Gun Squadron. | |
| Do. | 25th | | In billets. An 8 days refresher Course in Machine Gunnery commences. | |
| Do | 26th | | " 1 Rider evacuated to Base Veterinary Hospital and struck | |
| | | | off the strength of the Squadron from 25.10.17. | |
| Do | 27th | | In billets | |

Army Form C. 2118.

# WAR DIARY
## or
## INTELLIGENCE SUMMARY.
*(Erase heading not required.)*

Instructions regarding War Diaries and Intelligence Summaries are contained in F. S. Regs., Part II. and the Staff Manual respectively. Title pages will be prepared in manuscript.

| Place | Date | Hour | Summary of Events and Information | Remarks and references to Appendices |
|---|---|---|---|---|
| MONTCAVREL | 28th | | In billets. | |
| Do | 29th | | " Inspection of horses by O/C. 89th Mobile Veterinary Section. | |
| Do | 30th | | Gun bde takes part in a Brigade Tactical Exercise. In billets. | |
| Do | 31st | | " | |
| | | | Strength of Squadron. (On Oct 31st 1917.) | |
| | | | Personnel. Horses. | |
| | | | Officers 9 Riders 183. | |
| | | | Warrant Officer 1 Draught 66. | |
| | | | Sergeants 16. Pack. 42. | |
| | | | O/Ranks. 204. Total 291. | |
| | | | Do. (Attached) 6. | |

R.H. Settle
Major.
Commanding 9th Machine Gun Squadron.

Vol 22

CONFIDENTIAL

WAR DIARY

of

9th MACHINE GUN SQUADRON

Vol: 20.

Nov. 1917

CONFIDENTIAL

**Army Form C. 2118**

Oct ? active Service Records
November 1917
Volume ?

# WAR DIARY
## or
## INTELLIGENCE SUMMARY
*(Erase heading not required).*

Instructions regarding War Diaries and Intelligence Summaries are contained in F.S. Regs., Part II. and the Staff Manual respectively. Title Pages will be prepared in manuscript.

| Place | Date Nov | Hour | Summary of Events and Information | Remarks and references to Appendices |
|---|---|---|---|---|
| MONTCAVREL | 1. | | In Billets | CALAIS 13 |
| | 2. | | " | |
| | 3. | | " | |
| | 4. | | " | |
| | 5. | | " | |
| | 6. | | " | |
| | 7. | | " | |
| | 8. | | " | |
| | 9. | | Brigade Route March through a Defile | |
| | 10. | | In Billets | |
| | 11. | | Brigade marched Squadron billeted the night 10/11 at CAPRON + CONTES | ABBEVILLE |
| | 12. | | Brigade marched Continued Squadron billets at AUTHIEUX ST GRATIEN | LENS 11 |
| | 13. | | " do do 11/12 : CHIPILLY | AMIENS 1 |
| | 14. | | " do do 12/13 : do : LE MESNIL | AMIENS V |
| | 15. | | Squadron billeted in Lubricants | |
| LE MESNIL | 16. | | " | |
| | 17. | | " | |
| | 18. | | Marched | |
| | 19. | | Brigade to Bivouacked Greenchilita area N.W of FINS | ENEMY REAR |
| | 20. | | Arrived at day break at Greenchilita area, off saddled + breakfasted, about 11 a.m. moved to METZ EN COUTURE in a succession of Bounds, where Squadron passed the night, sleeping to until 11p.m. Raining heavily | ORGANIZATION SHEET 2. |
| | 21. | | Brigade moved to a Ravine between METZ EN COUTURE and TRESCAULT 15'Hussars C.O. (Advance Regiment.) + the 1 & 2 Sub-Sections M.G.S moved at 1 p.m to MARCOING. At dusk Brigade moved up West of MARCOING where horse were 'off' + dismounted Pah. of Brigade relieved 2d Cavalry Brigade, holding line from Lod. 5.9 & 6.24 a cables all four of Squadron in action. Squadron Gun withdrew at 10 a.m. + Squadron moved back to METZ EN COUTURE where they Bivouacked for the night. | |
| | 22. | | | |
| | 23. | | Moved up at 8.30 to FLESQUIERES to exploit the success of the 40th and 62nd Infantry Divisions which were attacking BOIS DE BOURLON and FONTAINE NOTRE DAME respectively. At 4 p.m. horses were sent to South Eastern Outskirts of FLESQUIERES | |

# WAR DIARY or INTELLIGENCE SUMMARY

Army Form C. 2118

| Place | Date | Hour | Summary of Events and Information | Remarks and references to Appendices |
|---|---|---|---|---|
| | 23 | | And the Dismounted Party of the Brigade were sent up as reserves to 40th Division. No 1 & 2 Sub-Sections M.G.S. with 18th Hussars were attached to 119th Infantry Brigade. Remainder of Squadron with Remainder of Brigade to 121st Infantry Brigade. The Squadron less the 1 & 2 Sub Sections spent the night in still Gulch on high ground. No 1 & 3 Sub Sections in Quarry in F.20.a. | E.29.a |
| | 24 | | The Squadron less No 1 & 2 Sub Sections received information that the Enemy was massing for a Counter Attack. Same were ourselves at 8.30 a.m. At 9.30 a.m. the Guns were brought forward & dug in field shells E.23.d West of BOURLON WOOD. Indirect fire was opened. Rul. heavy Enemy shelling necessitating moving to a more covered position & rapt. road through felled E.23.a - E.24.c. A trench was dug to sub-section shelter to high ground Position (10.R killed 1.0.R wounded). At 10 p.m. moved to dir behind SUGAR FACTORY (with ment. Gauntlets attached to 15th Hussars) took up a defensive position along the No 1 & 2 Sub Sections (attached to 15th Hussars) took up a defensive position along the Sunk Eastern Corner of BOURLON WOOD. Working in connection with the 119th M.G. Coy at 3 p.m. the Battalion of the ROYAL WELSH FUSILIERS who were holding RIGHT FLANK of BOURLON WOOD retired in a disorderly fashion through the line of Guns. Two Guns of No 1 Sub Section retired to high ground 300 yards EAST of ANNEUX to cover retreat of the 2 Sub Section in case of their retirement. Enemy Aeroplanes flying very low engaged the Retiring Infantry with M.G. fire & directed Enemy's artillery barrage between BOURLON WOOD and ANNEUX. Shelling now became more intensive. At 3.30 p.m. the 3rd Coldstream Guards relieved their left flank had been left unsupported owing to retirement of ROYAL WELSH FUSILIERS and asked for the support of 2 Sub Section to protect their flank. The 3rd Coldstream Guards were extended their line from F.14.C.8.0 - Troads at E.20.A.H.6 Stragglers of the ROYAL WELSH FUSILIERS were collected and together with a gun of the 119th M.G. Coy took out the line which was extended from E.20.a.4.6 to road Junctions at ANNEUX CHAPEL. At 4.45 p.m. the 3rd Coldstream Guards received a warning order that they intended to advance to their former positions & orders for to 2 Sub Section | |

# WAR DIARY or INTELLIGENCE SUMMARY

Army Form C. 2118

| Place | Date | Hour | Summary of Events and Information | Remarks and references to Appendices |
|---|---|---|---|---|
| | 25. | | To advance with their line up to the Southern edge of BOURLON WOOD and then take up positions to cover their further advance. At 5:30 am the above position was commenced and at 6 pm a report was received from the 36 Ulsterian Guards that they were re-established in their former line. There was intermittent shelling during the night - otherwise quiet. Casualties during these operations were - Kia: SHOTKING 12 wounded 1 OR killed E.O.Katzenel Lieuts. the same. Quiet day. No 1 & 2 Sub Sections withdrew at 6hrs & were billeted at RIBECOURT where they billeted. Nos 3,4,5 & 6 Sub Sections were withdrawn, relieved by a M.G. Coy at 9 pm and marched to FLESQUIERES when they billeted for the night. | A.A.A. Kiwi RY. ARANCLIFFES killed & Kiwi BELFORD HS wounded at SUGAR FACTORY at 4 p.m. |
| | 26 | | The Squadron moved to METZ EN COUTURE | |
| | 27 | | At METZ EN COUTURE | |
| | 28 | | The Brigade moved to MERICOURT area the Squadron billeted at FROISSY. | |
| | 29. | | Billet at FROISSY. | |
| | 30. | | Squadron ordered to stand to at 12 midday, at 2:30 pm Brigade moved to ROISEL and bivouacked for the night. | |

Chas. S. MacAndrew Capt.
Commanding 9th Motor Gun Squadron

CONFIDENTIAL

War Diary
of
9th Machine Gun Squadron
December 1917.

Volume No 22

Army Form C. 2118.

# WAR DIARY
## or
## INTELLIGENCE SUMMARY.
*(Erase heading not required.)*

Instructions regarding War Diaries and Intelligence Summaries are contained in F.S. Regs., Part II. and the Staff Manual respectively. Title pages will be prepared in manuscript.

| Place | Date | Hour | Summary of Events and Information | Remarks and references to Appendices |
|---|---|---|---|---|
| | DECEMBER | | | |
| ROISEL | 1st | | Squadron standing to at ROISEL. Bivouacked for night in field. | Map 62c. Reference |
| " | | 2.0. | Brigade Dismounted Battalion rendezvoused at 5 p.m. and proceeded to the Railway. | |
| | | | Embarkment in W.24.d. arrived at midnight, awaiting daybreak in shell sidings on the railway. | |
| | | | 2nd Lieut Mount A.C. M.H. 18 other ranks arrived at the Squadron "B" Echelon | |
| ※ | | | from M.G.C. Base Depot. | |
| W.24.d. | 2nd. | | At daybreak the Squadron was subdivided into three, 4 gun Batteries. | |
| (RLY. EMBKT) | | | Battery positioned here "A" Battery = W.24.d.3.8.   "B" Battery = W.23.b.9.9. | |
| | | | "C" Battery W.11.c. Central.  Squadron H.Qrs W.17.d.85.22. | |
| | | | An S.O.S. barrage was fired as follows :- "A" Battery of 4 guns = X.8.d.9.5. to X.15.c. Central. | |
| | | | "B" Battery of 2 guns = X.8.c. 0.9. to X.1st.d.99.60 | |
| | | | "B" Battery of 2 guns = X.1st.d. 7.6. to X.1st.d. 99.40 | |
| | | | "C" Battery of 4 guns = X.2.a.9.4. to X.8.b.3.7. | |
| | | | Furthermore all guns were prepared to concentrate on any of the following map squares | |
| | | | X.8.N. X.8.d. X.1st.d. X.1st.b. X.8.a. X.2.c. X.1st.a. X.1st.c. | |
| | | | The Squadron spent a quiet time in these positions | |
| " | 4th | | The Squadron were relieved by the S.R. Machine Gun Squadron and marched to ROISEL after dark. | J.M. |

Army Form C. 2118.

# WAR DIARY
## or
## INTELLIGENCE SUMMARY.
(Erase heading not required.)

Instructions regarding War Diaries and Intelligence Summaries are contained in F. S. Regs., Part II. and the Staff Manual respectively. Title pages will be prepared in manuscript.

| Place | Date | Hour | Summary of Events and Information | Remarks and references to Appendices |
|---|---|---|---|---|
| | DECEMBER | | | |
| ROISEL | 5th | | In Bivouac. Squadron spent the day in Inspections, cleaning of Arms, ammunition &c. | |
| " | 6th | | In Bivouac. Major R. H. Settle M.C. proceeded to join 10th Battalion K.O.Y.L.I. as second in command. (Authority A.G. 157/143 dated 11.12.17.) Authority 9th Cavalry Bde. wire dated 5.12.17. Capt. to G. MacAndrew assumed Command 9th Machine Gun Squadron. | |
| " | 7th | | In Bivouac. 9th Cavalry Battalion formed. Lieut Belford N.B. and Lieut Suckling F. struck off the strength of the | |
| " | 8th | | Squadron from the 2.12.17. The former evacuated to BASIS Hospital and the latter to ENGLAND. H.Qrs. 1st Cavalry Dismounted Brigade established in the H.Qrs. of LONGAVESNES. | |
| " | 9th | | In Bivouac. | |
| " | 10th | | " Brigade ready to move at ½ an hours notice from 6am to 9am, and from 3pm to dark, at other times, 1 hours notice. The 16th Division has a call on the 9th Cavalry Battalion, when moved assembly section is in P. 14. Central. | |
| " | 11th | | In Bivouac. Horses returned to FROISSY. | |
| " | 12th | | In Bivouac. | |
| " | 13th | | In Bivouac. Dismounted party digging Gun positions. | |
| " | 14th | | In Bivouac. 2nd Lieut: R. Insley admitted Camp 54 Hospital and Struck off Strength of Squadron. | O.W. |

Army Form C. 2118.

# WAR DIARY
## or
## INTELLIGENCE SUMMARY.
(Erase heading not required.)

Instructions regarding War Diaries and Intelligence Summaries are contained in F. S. Regs., Part II. and the Staff Manual respectively. Title pages will be prepared in manuscript.

| Place | Date | Hour | Summary of Events and Information | Remarks and references to Appendices |
|---|---|---|---|---|
| | DECEMBER | | | |
| ROISEL | 15th | | In Bivouac. Inspection of horses by O/c Bgh Mobile Veterinary Section | |
| " | 16th | | In Bivouac. Dismounted party returned by train arriving at FROISSY 11.30 p.m in heavy snowstorm. 2nd Reinforcements arrived from M.G. Base Depot | |
| FROISSY | 17th | | In billets. Squadron bathed. | |
| " | 18th | | " | |
| " | 19th | | " | |
| " | 20th | | Capt. M.E.A. Jones arrived from the M.G. Machine Gun Squadron to act as Second in Command this Unit. Lieut. L. Gates and one L/cpl to S.A. School | |
| " | 21st | | In billets. Brigade moved to the LE MESNIL-BRUNTEL area. Squadron moved independently via CHUIGNES – FOUCAUCOURT – ESTREES – BRIE. Keeping hard roads very slippery. No casualties | |
| LE MESNIL | 22nd | | In billets. Working on hutments and stabling. | |
| " | 23rd | | " | |
| " | 24th | | " | |
| " | 25th | | Squadron mounted a parade of six Armed for protection from hostile aircraft. The Commanding Officer inspected Mens Christmas Dinner | |

# WAR DIARY
## or
## INTELLIGENCE SUMMARY.

Army Form C. 2118.

| Place | Date | Hour | Summary of Events and Information | Remarks and references to Appendices |
|---|---|---|---|---|
| | DECEMBER | | | |
| LE MESNIL | 26th | | In billets. 9th Cavalry Brigade acts as duty Brigade from 12-1 am to midnight | |
| " | | | same day | |
| " | 27th | | In billets. Refitting horsemeat and stabling | |
| " | 28th | | " " | |
| " | 29th | | Refitted clothing 2nd class kit to Smithy and 6 other ranks aircraft from No 4 Corps Base Depot | |
| " | 30th | | In billets | |
| " | 31st | | In billets. Working in stables | |
| | | | Chas. Mere Lindley | |

WM 24

"Confidential"

WAR DIARY.
of
9th Machine Gun Squadron.
January 1918

(Volume No 23)

Army Form C. 2118

# WAR DIARY
## or
## INTELLIGENCE SUMMARY
*(Erase heading not required.)*

Instructions regarding War Diaries and Intelligence Summaries are contained in F.S. Regs., Part II. and the Staff Manual respectively. Title Pages will be prepared in manuscript.

| Place | Date | Hour | Summary of Events and Information | Remarks and references to Appendices |
|---|---|---|---|---|
| LE MESNIL | JANUARY 1918 1st. | | In billets. Inspection of horses by O/C 39th Mobile Veterinary Section | |
| " | 2nd. | | In billets. Repairing of hutments and stabling. The Brigade under 1 hour's notice to move mounted. | |
| " | 3rd. | | In billets. Repairing of hutments and stabling. The G.O.C. 9th Cavalry Bde inspected hutments and stabling of this Unit. | |
| " | 4th. | | " " | |
| " | 5th. | | " " | |
| " | 6th. | | " " Capt. L.L. MacAndrew and No 50719 Sergt. Sellbrook F. proceeded to S.A. School G.H.Q. Lieut. L. Eade and No 50749 Pte Beacham W. rejoined from S.A. School. Capt. M.O.H. Jones and 2nd Lieut W. Linsley proceeded to join 14th Machine Gun Squadron and struck off the strength of this Unit. Lieut H.B. Belford arrived from BASE DEPOT and taken on the strength of the Squadron. | |
| " | 7th. | | In billets. No 105263 L/Cpl. Gardner Ls. to School of Cookery 5th Army. No 101407 Pte Johnson L. returned to BASE DEPOT (under age.) | |
| " | 8th. | | In billets. 9 other ranks joined this Unit from M.G.C. BASE DEPOT. | |
| " | 9th. | | " " | |
| " | 10th. | | " " Health Inspection by Medical Officer i/c 9th Machine Gun Squadron. | |
| " | 11th. | | " " | |

**Army Form C. 2118**

# WAR DIARY
## or
## INTELLIGENCE SUMMARY
*(Erase heading not required.)*

Instructions regarding War Diaries and Intelligence Summaries are contained in F.S. Regs., Part II. and the Staff Manual respectively. Title Pages will be prepared in manuscript.

| Place | Date | Hour | Summary of Events and Information | Remarks and references to Appendices |
|---|---|---|---|---|
| LE VERGUIER | JANUARY 1918 12th | | In billets. The Corps Commander presented medal ribbons recently awarded to O.R. Cavalry Bde. No 50767 Sergt. Aylwyn A.J. represented this Squadron. | |
| " | 13th | | In billets. Inspection of horses by O/C 39th Mobile Veterinary Section. Preparing for trenches. Capt R.P. Nicol proceeded to relieve the 8th Machine Gun Sqn. in line. | |
| " | 14th | | In billets. Trench Party paraded at 1.45am en route to trenches. | |
| " | 15th | " | Trench party in trenches at LE VERGUIER. Both sides very quiet. | |
| " | 16th | " | Nothing important to report from Trench Party. | |
| " | 17th | " | No 50741 S.S.M. Hall E.G. awarded the Distinguished Conduct Medal for "Gallantry in the field". Lieut. G. Bade and No 51889 Pte Lethury W.B. "mentioned in Dispatches." | |
| " | 18th | 1+1.18 | In billets. | |
| " | 19th | " | " | |
| " | 20th | " | " | |
| " | 21st | " | Health Inspection on Back Party by Medical Officer i/c this Unit. | |
| " | 22nd | " | Inspection of horses by O/C 39th Mobile Veterinary Section. | |
| " | 23rd | " | | |
| " | 24th | " | Trench party relieved by Canadian M.G. Squadron. 2 Officers and 45 other ranks from Trench Party proceeded to VERMAND, remainder of Trench Party proceeded to Back party of this Unit. | R.M. |
| " | 25th | " | | |

Army Form C. 2118

# WAR DIARY
## or
## INTELLIGENCE SUMMARY
*(Erase heading not required.)*

Instructions regarding War Diaries and Intelligence Summaries are contained in F. S. Regs., Part II. and the Staff Manual respectively. Title Pages will be prepared in manuscript.

| Place | Date | Hour | Summary of Events and Information | Remarks and references to Appendices |
|---|---|---|---|---|
| | January 1918 | | | |
| VERMAND | 26th | | In billets. Party sent up to relieve gun teams at VERMAND. | |
| " | 27th | | The party at VERMAND relieved the 11th Machine Gun Squadron in Battery positions at R.5.c.9.0. at 10 a.m. Back party resumed work on hutments and stabling. In billets. | |
| " | 28th | " | " | |
| " | 29th | " | " | |
| " | 30th | " | Inspection of horses by the Divisional Commander. | |
| " | 31st | " | Strength of Squadron | |

PERSONNEL
Officers. 9
Other ranks. 230.

HORSES
Riders
Light Draught.
Pack.

146
61
42
―――
249

R.R. West Capt.
Comm'g 9th C.K. Machine Gun Squadron

February 1st 1918.

WA 25

CONFIDENTIAL

War Diary

of

9th Machine Gun Squadron.

February 1918.

Volume No. 24.

# WAR DIARY or INTELLIGENCE SUMMARY

Army Form C. 2118

Of Machine Gun S.M. Squadron 1915
Of Squadron of Secunderabad Cav. Bde.

| Place | Date FEBRUARY | Hour | Summary of Events and Information | Remarks and references to Appendices |
|---|---|---|---|---|
| LE MESNIL | 1st. | | In billets. Trench Party at portland at R.S.C.9.0. | |
| " | 2nd. | | The Divisional Commander inspected the Squadron dismounted at 2.30 pm. In conjunction with the 15th Hussars a hollow square was formed and the Divisional Commander addressed all ranks. In billets. | |
| " | 3rd. | | Horses of the squadron proceeded to VERMETZ to be clipped. Work done on revetting, hutments and stabling. | |
| " | 4th. | | The O.C. Cavalry Brigade inspected the hutments, cook houses and stabling of the Squadron. | |
| " | 5th. | | The squadron was employed on a General Fatigue building an ablution hut and making baths. 1st Cavalry Divs. Light Horse Battery drawn from units of the Division were attached to the Squadron for rations and accommodation from the 4th inst. Officers & and 69 other ranks of billets. | |
| " | 6th. | | Squadron and light trench Mortar Battery bathed. | |
| " | 7th. | | Lieut H.D. Bedford left for ENGLAND to attend a Board for admission to the Indian Army. Sale of athing 11.2.18. Authority A.M.S. Cas Cap.S. 320/398. Two other ranks proceeded to the 1st Cav. Div. Working Party. In billets. the Divisional Gas N.C.O. inspected the box respirators of the Squadron | Q.S. |
| " | 8th. | | At 2.30 pm. Gas Drill was carried out. Lieut Mount H.C. discharged temporary Hospital and joined Brick Party. | |

Army Form C. 2118

# WAR DIARY
## or
## INTELLIGENCE SUMMARY
*(Erase heading not required.)*

| Place | Date | Hour | Summary of Events and Information | Remarks and references to Appendices |
|---|---|---|---|---|
| LE MESNIL | FEBRUARY 9th | | In billets. Repairing stabling, and working on revetting of hutments. | |
| " | 10th | | " A minute inspection of equipment of the Squadrons carried out at 10 a.m. Site for gun chosen. | |
| " | 11th | | In billets. Revetting continued. Lieut. D.H. Clifford arrived from 3rd Machine Gun Squadron and taken on the strength of this Unit from this date. | |
| " | 12th | | In billets. Inspection of clothing at 2 p.m. Continuation of work on huts. | |
| " | 13th | | " Personnel from 1st Cavalry Divisional Working Party returned. | |
| " | 14th | | " The use of meteorological telegrams came into use with our French Party. | |
| " | 15th | | " | |
| " | 16th | | " Health Inspection by M.O. i/c of Squadron | |
| " | 17th | | " | |
| " | 18th | | " | |
| " | 19th | | " Preparing grounds for Jumping. | |
| " | 20th | | " " No. 62032 Corpl. J. Cochrane to ENGLAND | |
| " | 21st | | In billets. Working on revetting huts and preparing ground for Jumping. | |
| " | 22nd | | " Lieut. R.S. Belford struck off the strength of the Squadron. Authority D.A. & Q.M.G. 1st Cav Divis: No. 50145 Pte Bennett B. died of wounds 55th C.C.S. 19.2.'18. | |

# WAR DIARY
## or
## INTELLIGENCE SUMMARY

Army Form C. 2118

| Place | Date | Hour | Summary of Events and Information | Remarks and references to Appendices |
|---|---|---|---|---|
| LE MESNIL | FEBRUARY 23rd | | In billets. Working on the protection of huts. | |
| " | 24th | | " S.O.S. fire was put up by guns of the French Party. | |
| " | 25th | | " Inspection of the Squadron Arms, the Armourer Staff Sergeant present. | |
| " | 26th | | " Inspection of the horses of the Squadron by the O/C Sqn. Horses. | |
| " | 27th | | Veterinary Section at 10.30 a.m. In billets. Road Routine. The 1st Cavalry Division Light Trench Mortar Battery, temporary disbanded, and personnel returned to units. "Stand to" alarm given out at 8 p.m. Observation Post manned at 0.18.a.8.4. "Stand Down" received at 10.45 p.m. | |
| " | 28th | | In billets. Troops confined to billeting area. Two Gun teams with guns and equipment sent up to H.Qrs 9th Dismounted Brigade to man post at PARKERS POST. | |

Strength of Squadron.

PERSONNEL.
Officers  9.
Other ranks  226.

HORSES.
Riding  140.
Light Draught  61
Pack  42.

Eagleton Capt.
Commd'g. 9th Machine Gun Squadron.

Vol 26

WAR DIARY
of
9th Machine Gun Squadron.
Month of MARCH 1918.
Volume 24.

**Army Form C. 2118.**

# WAR DIARY
## or
## INTELLIGENCE SUMMARY.
*(Erase heading not required.)*

Instructions regarding War Diaries and Intelligence Summaries are contained in F. S. Regs., Part II. and the Staff Manual respectively. Title pages will be prepared in manuscript.

| Place | Date | Hour | Summary of Events and Information | Remarks and references to Appendices |
|---|---|---|---|---|
| LE MESNIL-BRUNTEL | MARCH 1st | | In billets. French Party at LE MERGUIER. | 62 C. |
| " | 2nd | | " 2nd Lieut. C.E. Boles and 2 other ranks to Cavalry Corps Signal School. | |
| " | 3rd | | 11 Riders arrived | |
| " | 4th | | In billets. Usual routine. | |
| " | 5th | | " One other rank arrived from M.G.C. Base depot. 3 L.D. horses arrived | |
| " | 6th | | " 2 L.D. horses arrived. | |
| " | 7th | | " Usual routine. | |
| " | 8th | | " " | |
| " | 9th | | " No 50060 Pte Perrin W. slightly wounded at duty | |
| " | 10th | | " Summer time in force. | |
| " | 11th | | " Usual routine. | |
| " | 12th | | " French Party relieved night 11/12th March. | |
| " | 13th | | " Usual routine. Guns and Gun equipment overhauled. | |
| " | | | 1 L.D. died. | |
| " | 14th | | In billets. Usual routine | |
| " | | | " F.G.C.M. on No 41824 S.Q.M.S. McGinn R. | |

# WAR DIARY or INTELLIGENCE SUMMARY

Army Form C. 2118.

| Place | Date | Hour | Summary of Events and Information | Remarks and references to Appendices |
|---|---|---|---|---|
| LE-MESNIL-BRUNTEL | MARCH 15th | | In billets. Inspection of Transport by L.O.C. 9th Cavalry Bde. and O/C. A.S.C. Health Inspection at 2 p.m. | |
| | | At 6 a.m. | 1st Cavalry Division became part of 18th Corps to serve at three hours notice. Squadron was held ready to move at three hours notice. R.A.M.C. personnel for water duties returned to Divisional Fld. Amb. Two other ranks from Bde. | |
| " | 16th | | In billets. Sentence on No H1824. S.Q.M.S. McGinn R. duly promulgated. No. H1824. Pte McGinn R. handed over to A.P.M. 1st Cavalry Division. | |
| " | 17th | | 1 other rank rejoined from S.A. School, G.H.Q. 1 other rank Water cart and two L.D. horses proceeded with 9th Cavalry Bde. Squadron Battalion. | |
| " | 18th | | In billets. | |
| " | 19th | | " | |
| " | 20th | | At 7.45 a.m. a Brigade warning test move to BERNES received print) and then to BERNES at 9 a.m. Brigade marching | |

# WAR DIARY or INTELLIGENCE SUMMARY.

Army Form C. 2118.

| Place | Date MARCH | Hour | Summary of Events and Information | Remarks and references to Appendices |
|---|---|---|---|---|
| LE MESNIL-BRUNTEL | 21st | | In billets. Warning wire received at 6.10 a.m. to expect an order from Division to move to BERNES within an hour. Squadron saddled up ready to move at 7.10 a.m. Order to move received at 1 p.m. moved to P.8.a. by 2 p.m. and from there in open order to BERNES. | |
| BERNES | 22nd | | Nos 1 and 2 Hub sections joined the 15th Hussars at 9.15 p.m. Remainder of Squadron "shoot to" up to 1 a.m. and then moved to MONTIGNY FARM. Horses were parked over with the exception of pack horses. The guns on pack with complete team left MONTIGNY FARM at 3 a.m. and proceeded to BOIS-DU-CROIX, A. [actual H.S.Mount 15th 2 gunt with escort of 9th Hussars moved to JEANCOURT] At 9 a.m. enemy shelled the wood and adjacent fields vigorously and the Squadron hill on until orders were received from the 9th Cavalry Bde. to make a detour and form up for a counter attack with active Gun consolidation on the village of HERVILLY. Guns were disposed in conjunction with the attacking forces, with the exception of one gun which commanded the high ground. During this counter attack one gun was lost to the enemy after the whole team were killed or wounded. | |

# WAR DIARY or INTELLIGENCE SUMMARY

Army Form C. 2118.

(Erase heading not required.)

| Place | Date MARCH | Hour | Summary of Events and Information | Remarks and references to Appendices |
|---|---|---|---|---|
| VERMILLY | 22nd | | With the exception of two men who put the Gun out of action. One other Gun was destroyed by shell fire. Late the Squadron retired through the Brown line to the Green line where the Guns teams dug themselves into position. This line was held until 4 pm. when a retirement was forced by the enemy swinging back the flank held by the Infantry the guns were carried away under heavy machine gun and rifle average fire to BOUVINCOURT. An enemy aeroplane centering low was brought down in flames by rifle fire and the pilot captured. The Squadron retreated and retired to ATHIES. by 9.30 pm. No news received of the two guns attached to the 15th Hussars or of Lieut. Bridges M.C. who was in command of these two guns. The Squadron left ATHIES at 11 pm and went the night with 'B' Echelon on roadside near MARCHÉLPOT. | |
| MARCHÉLPOT | 23rd | | Continued the march to CURCHY. Squadron remained for the night. | |
| CURCHY | 24th | | Left CURCHY at 8 am and proceeded under Brigade arrangements to FROISSY. In the afternoon Lt Guns under Lieut Bade were sent to | |

Army Form C. 2118.

# WAR DIARY
or
## INTELLIGENCE SUMMARY.
*(Erase heading not required.)*

| Place | Date | Hour | Summary of Events and Information | Remarks and references to Appendices |
|---|---|---|---|---|
| | MARCH | | | |
| FROISSY | 25th | | MONTAUBAN. Two Guns were in forward positions and helped to beat off a counter attack. The guns were heavily shelled and seven casualties occurred. The remainder of the Squadron left FROISSY at 8.30 pm for CERISY | |
| CERISY | 26th | | Left Cerisy and proceeded to BUSSY-LES-DAOURS. | |
| BUSSY-LES-DAOURS | 26th | | Re-organised gun teams. Lent bade and 4 guns returned. One gun and two other tanks returned from Lieut Bridges battery. Marched at 5 am to BONNAY. Lieut Clifford with 2 guns went forward with the 19th Hussars. | |
| BONNAY | 28th | | Returned to BUSSY-LES-DAOURS | |
| BUSSY-LES-DAOURS | 29th | | Squadron re-organising. | |
| " | 30th | | 2nd Lieut H.S. Howett and 2nd Lieut G.C. Millard proceeded with personel of the gun teams to WARFUSSEE-ANANCOURT to relieve the gun teams of the 2nd Machine Gun Squadron | |
| " | 31st | | Lieut H.D. Clifford and two gun teams were relieved by gun teams sent up early in evening. | |

Charles W. Anley Capt.
Commanding 9th Machine Gun Squadron

War Diary of the
9th Machine Gun Squadron
for the month of
APRIL. 1918
Volumne. No. 26.

CONFIDENTIAL

Army Form C. 2118.

# WAR DIARY
## INTELLIGENCE SUMMARY
*(Erase heading not required.)*

| Place | Date | Hour | Summary of Events and Information | Remarks and references to Appendices |
|---|---|---|---|---|
| BUSSY LES DAOURS | 1/4/18 | | Lieut. D. H. CLIFFORDS from Reinforcements. 1 O.R. to Hospital | |
| | 2/4/18 | | No. 32905 Pte. MOUNT MASAIRD & Trans. returned to MARIFUSES. LAYNOCK at Inspection of WARIFUSES. No. 31905 Pte. CORNHILL'S dead in No 13 Ambulance Hospital | |
| FOUILLY | 3/4/18 | | Move to FOUILLY at 6pm. Squadron marching through the village shortly after 15th Fusiliers passing 1/2 hour earlier | AMIENS ? |
| | | 12 Noon | Reinforcements joined | |
| | 4/4/18 | | Orders to turn out saddled & to see the Commander Battery 52nd Res. Inspected Guns & prepared to fall in ready for going into the line | |
| AMIENS | 5/4/18 | 01.F.30 am | Squadron left FOUILLY. Some shelling 2 ORs wounded. Proceeded to BUSSY LES DAOURS. ORs saddled had Billets at 4pm. Orders to move received. Left BUSSY at 5.30am. Proceeded to AMIENS across Country. Billeted men in Farm + Horses in a Paddock N. of AMIEN N.S. | |
| | 6/4/18 | | Reorganising Squadron | |
| | 7/4/18 | | 6r. Grand Anvil do | |
| | 8/4/18 | | Reorganisation Continued | |
| | 9/4/18 | | do | |
| PERNNINEL | 10/4/18 | | G.O.C. 9th Corps Inspected Remounts. Left AMIENS 2.30pm Proceeded to PERNINEL arriving there 10.10 pm. 14 Riding + 9 Pack Horses through from Remount Depot. | |
| | 11/4/18 | | Left Remounts & marched to GRAND BOURST arrived midday. 2 Officers + 14 O.Rs arrived from 13 M.G.Sqn. Viz. 2/Lieut. N.G. AYLOTT + 2/Lieut. J.J. PINKER 28 OR Joined 12n 11-13 Midday. | |
| BUCHY AU BOS | 12/4/18 | | Rev. GRAND BOURST and marched to BUCHY AU BOIS arriving 8pm and Billeted in Barns + Outhouses | |
| | | | Picked up Billets by List. Crossfield + marched with the Supply. The Reinforcements were composed of Bays, the Squadron mobile as it could not possibly be in order. 12 Regs at - the King Under 1/2 Hours notice to move. These men at BAZE N Awarded the MILITARY MEDAL 8.4.18 | |

Army Form C. 2118.

# WAR DIARY
## or
## INTELLIGENCE SUMMARY.
*(Erase heading not required.)*

Instructions regarding War Diaries and Intelligence Summaries are contained in F. S. Regs., Part II. and the Staff Manual respectively. Title pages will be prepared in manuscript.

**Army Machine Gun Squadron**
No. ..........
Date ..........

| Place | Date | Hour | Summary of Events and Information | Remarks and references to Appendices |
|---|---|---|---|---|
| AUBY-AU-BOIS | APRIL 10/4/18 | - | R.S.M. & Orderly returned to 6' Co Field Ambulance when G.R.O. | HAZEBROUCK 5.2 |
| | 11/4/18 | - | S.M. Bell on 6 Riders | |
| | 12/4/18 | - | Sp Riding Horse through T.M. Conveyance sent to rear left with Supply Column | |
| | 13/4/18 | - | Jn. Sergt. M'BURKE F.H. D.C.M. awarded a BAR to his D.C.M. 15.4.18 No. 30473 | |
| | 14/4/18 | - | I.O.R. joined from Base | |
| | 15/4/18 | - | In Billets | |
| | 16/4/18 | - | 6. O. R.s. (5 Sgt — 1 Cpl.) joined from Base | |
| | 17/4/18 | - | S.Q.M.S. BARCLAY No. 41/98 awarded 2nd M.G. Star | |
| | 18/4/18 | - | In Billets | |
| | 19/4/18 | - | 5. O.R.s. also awarded 1914-18 Star — also 2nd M.G.C. Bar Star — Battn. 1 of Bath | |
| | 20/4/18 | - | I.O.R. rejoined from Cav Corps D.R. Station | |
| | 21/4/18 | - | Inspection of Squadron in Mounted Marching Order by Divisional Commander at 12 pm | |
| | 22/4/18 | - | Pte C.E. BOWLES rejoined from Cav Corps Repelling School — also No. 245 Pte 2 Ridley Horace | |
| | 23/4/18 | - | In Billets | |
| | 24/4/18 | - | | |
| | 25/4/18 | - | 2/Lieut A.C. MOUNT awarded the MILITARY CROSS No. 51 95 Sergeant H.F. TOMLINSON awarded D.C.M. J 27.4.18 | |
| | 26/4/18 | - | Parade Service at HQ H.Q. attended by G. O. C. 9 Cav. Bde. Inspect. By Squadron in Mounted Marching Order at 10 a.m. | |
| | 27/4/18 | - | | |
| | 28/4/18 | - | O/C A.S.C. reported to Squadron in Wagons at HQ Squadron at 3.30 pm | |
| | 29/4/18 | - | | |
| | 30/4/18 | - | In Billets 5.O.R.s joined from Base | |

Chas. F. MacAndrew Capt.
Commanding 9th M.G. Sqn.

CONFIDENTIAL

War Diary.
of
9th Machine Gun Squadron
for
month of MAY 1918.

Volume No. 27

Army Form C. 2118.

# WAR DIARY
## or
## INTELLIGENCE SUMMARY.
(Erase heading not required.)

| Place | Date MAY | Hour | Summary of Events and Information | Remarks and references to Appendices |
|---|---|---|---|---|
| AUCHY-AU-BOIS | 1st | | In billets. Course for No's. 1. on the gun commences under Lieut. C. Eade. | HRK Sheet 5.A |
| " | 2nd | | " Squadron training. | |
| " | 3rd | | " " | |
| " | 4th | | " Squadron "Stood to" saddled up from 6am. to 8am. at half an hours notice. The 9th Cavalry Brigade at disposal of XI Corps. After 8 a.m. Brigade reverts to 3½ hours notice. | |
| " | 5th | | In billets. Routine as on May 4th. | |
| " | 6th | | " " " Course for No's. 2. on the gun commences under Lieut. C. Eade. | |
| " | 7th | | In billets. "Stood to" as above. 10t. Cavalry Bde. relieves 9thCavalry Bde on duty at disposal of XI Corps at midnight. Lieut B. R. Clifford admitted temporary hospital squadron on 3½ hours notice. | |
| " | 8th | | In billets. Firing on long range. 2nd Lieut wounds 2nd Lieut. life In Cavalry Corps Equitation School. 2nd Lieut Mount A.C. and sent to In billets. Squadron training Cavalry Corps Equitation School to undergo a course. Lecture to Gas N.C.O.'s by the Divisional Gas Officer. | |
| " | 9th | | | EW |

Army Form C. 2118.

# WAR DIARY
## or
## INTELLIGENCE SUMMARY.

(Erase heading not required.)

Instructions regarding War Diaries and Intelligence Summaries are contained in F. S. Regs., Part II. and the Staff Manual respectively. Title pages will be prepared in manuscript.

| Place | Date | Hour | Summary of Events and Information | Remarks and references to Appendices |
|---|---|---|---|---|
| AUCHY-AU-BOIS | MAY 10th | 10A | In billets. Squadron training | MAPS 36B NW & S.A. |
| | 11th | 11A | " Lieut. D.H. Clifford struck off the strength. |  |
| | 12th | | Re Squadron. 20 other ranks inoculated |  |
| | | | In billets Squadron training. 2/Lieut. A.V. Piggott arrived |  |
| | 13th | | " D Squadron tactical exercise without troops. |  |
| | 14th | | Buried camp. 3 hrs notice. |  |
| | | | " Brigade Scheme |  |
| | 15th | | " Squadron Drill |  |
| | 16th | | " Inter Brigade Scheme |  |
| | 17th | | " Squadron training |  |
| | 18th | | " " |  |
| | 19th | | " Squadron moved billets to NEDONCHELLE to gain better |  |
| NEDONCHELLE | 20th | | watering facilities. Move completed by 10 a.m. |  |
| | | | In billets. Arranging res squadron. |  |
| | 21st | | Bought horses billeted for night MONCHY-CAYEUX. |  |
| MONCHY-CAYEUX | 22nd | | Brigade marches to an area about QUOEUX. Squadron billets at LES PONCHEL. LENS H |  |
| LE PONCHEL | 23rd | | In billets. Arranging billets. inspects 2/N Forkes and H.A tanks arrived from M.G.C. Depot |  |

Army Form C. 2118

# WAR DIARY
## or
## INTELLIGENCE SUMMARY.
*(Erase heading not required.)*

Instructions regarding War Diaries and Intelligence Summaries are contained in F. S. Regs., Part II. and the Staff Manual respectively. Title pages will be prepared in manuscript.

| Place | Date | Hour | Summary of Events and Information | Remarks and references to Appendices |
|---|---|---|---|---|
| LE PONCHEL | MAY 24th | | Squadron training. | 4.5.18 II. |
| " | 25th | | Inspection of Guns, Gun equipment, saddlery and arms. | |
| " | 26th | | Church parade. 2nd Lieut W. N. Neill arrived from M.G.C. Base Depôt | |
| " | 27th | | Squadron training. "A" Section firing table C. 2nd Lieut W.G.Aylot to 16th Sqn. G. Coy | |
| " | 28th | | " " " "B" " | |
| " | 29th | | Squadrons BoxRespirators tested in gas chamber "C" section | |
| " | | | firing table "C". | |
| " | 30th | | 11 bles Squadron visited at CAUMONT. | |
| " | 31st | | Squadron training. Brigade Tactical Exercise (short hours). | |

Chas MacAndres Capt.
Comm'g 9th Machine Gun Squadron. (M.G.C. Cav.)

WR 29

"CONFIDENTIAL"

WAR. DIARY.

9th MACHINE GUN SQUADRON

JUNE. 1918.

Volume No. 28.

Army Form C. 2118.

# WAR DIARY
## or
## INTELLIGENCE SUMMARY.
*(Erase heading not required.)*

9th MACHINE GUN SQUADRON

Instructions regarding War Diaries and Intelligence Summaries are contained in F.S. Regs., Part II. and the Staff Manual respectively. Title pages will be prepared in manuscript.

| Place | Date | Hour | Summary of Events and Information | Remarks and references to Appendices |
|---|---|---|---|---|
| LE PONCHEL | JUNE 1 | | In Billets. Squadron Training | Lens II |
| | 2. | | do 3 O.Rs arrived from M.G.C. Base Depot | |
| | 3. | | do "A" Section FIRING on Range | |
| | 4. | | do "B" " " " " | |
| | 5. | | do "C" " " " " | |
| | 6. | | MAJOR J.R. MONCREIFFE. M.C. assumed Command of Squadron vice Capt. C.G. MacANDREW | |
| | | | Capt. C.G. MacANDREW to M.G.C. BASE DEPOT. BOX RESPIRATOR DRILL at 9.30 pm | |
| | 7. | | In Billets. Squadron Training | |
| | 8. | | do D.D.R. + G.O.C 9th Cav.Bde. Paid the Official Visit at 2.30 p.m. | |
| | 9. | | do Signalling Officer Inspected the Signallers of the Squadron. | |
| | 10. | | Voluntary CHURCH OF ENGLAND parade service. | |
| | 11. | | Squadron Training. Lecture by Divisional Gas Officer at 9.30 a.m. | |
| | 12. | | "A" Section Inspected by the Commanding Officer at 6.30 a.m. Games + Physical Exercises at 2 p.m. | |
| | 13. | | "B" do do do do with Box Respirator Inspection. | |
| | 14. | | 1. OFFICER + 5 men sent to the Range to act as MARKERS at A.R.A Competition. | |
| | 15. | | "C" Section Inspected by the Commanding Officer | |
| | 16. | | No. 50716. Sergt. STUART. H. accidentally injured returning from Leave. 10 O.Rs arrived from M.G.C. Base Depot. | |
| | 17. | | Voluntary CHURCH SERVICE. FIELD KITCHEN 12.0 Noon. Visit Inspected by Medical Officer | |
| | 18. | | Squadron Training. Divisional A.R.A. Meeting. Health Inspection | |
| | 19. | | Lecture by Commanding Officer on "ALLOCATION OF DUTIES" 2.Pdr A.C.MOUNT Inspected by Lt Col Innes | |
| | | | "A" Section Shipped Saddlery Inspection by the C.O. at 2.15 p.m. | |
| | 20. | | G.O.C 9 Cav.Bde Inspects at a demonstration of DRILL afterwards Inspected the Squadron Transport in full Marching Order. | |
| | 21. | | Squadron Training —— Box Resp. notes Drill at 9.p.m. | |
| | 22. | | "B" Section Review Coincided + Ordinary training Carried out. | |
| | 23. | | "A" Section field FIRING. Games in afternoon. Precautions against P.U.O taken. | |
| | 24. | | In Billets. Squadron Training. "B" Section Shipped Saddlery Inspection at 2.15 p.m. by | |
| M.G.245 | | | the C.O. No. 51693 Sergt. S.R. WAKEFIELD to ENGLAND on Commission this day. | |
| 30.6.18 | | | To 60 Industrial Classes commenced this day. Signal Class Commenced this day. | |

A.7092  Wt. W.1128 g/M.1293 750,000. 1/17. D.D. & L. Ltd. Forms/C.2118/14.

Army Form C. 2118.

# WAR DIARY
## or
## INTELLIGENCE SUMMARY.

(Erase heading not required.)

9th MACHINE GUN SQUADRON

| Place | Date | Hour | Summary of Events and Information | Remarks and references to Appendices |
|---|---|---|---|---|
| LE PONCHEL | JUNE 25. | | Jackals Ride under the C.O for all Officers and Sergeants. | F.S.R. vol II. |
| | 26. | | Squadron to-day. Games & Physical Exercises in the Afternoon including Swimming | |
| | 27. | | Manning of Pack Horses. No 5050H Sergt HADLEY.C to 1/1 Batt A.P.C on Commission 2/Lieut. H. C. MOUNT M.G. | |
| | | | BATHS. Two Hour Riding Horses under 2/Lieut. H. C. MOUNT M.G. | |
| | 28. | | "B" Section Field FIRING "C" Section Shipped Saddlery Inspection by C.O. | |
| | 29. | | Squadron Drill. Games & Exercises Swimming. 3 ORs from M.G.C Base Depot. | |
| | 30. | | Voluntary CHURCH PARADE. | |
| | | | Strength = { OFFICERS. 11 | |
| | | | O.Rs. 241 | |
| | | | R. 184 | |
| | | | L.D. 66 | |
| | | | Pack 42 | |

J.A.Moncreiffe
Major
Commanding 9th Machine Gun Squadron.

Vol 30

"CONFIDENTIAL"

WAR DIARY
of
9th Machine Gun Squadron

July - 1918.

Volume No. 29

# WAR DIARY
## or
## INTELLIGENCE SUMMARY.

(Erase heading not required.)

Army Form C.-2118.

9th MACHINE GUN SQUADRON

| Place | Date | Hour | Summary of Events and Information | Remarks and references to Appendices |
|---|---|---|---|---|
| LE PONCHEL | July 1 | | Squadron Training | LENS. 11. |
| | 2 | | Squadron Training. Bridging & Rafting. Demonstration given to Officers & N.C.O's by 9th Signal Troop R.E. | |
| | 3 | | Training | |
| | 4 | | G.O.C. 9 Cav Bde Inspects the Squadron in marching order. | |
| | 5,6,7,8 | | Training 5th PINTER SECTION left for Course at Cav arm Gas School. B.I.R. | |
| | 9 | | Training 2/Lieut PIGGOTT & Indian proceed at NEUILLY L'EDSEN Church for Medical Examination with 5th Hussars | |
| | 10 | | Programme of Training Cancelled owing to P.U.O. | |
| | 11 | | D.A.D.O.S's Representative Inspects Squadron linen. 14 O.Rs arrive from M.G.C. Base | |
| | 12 | | 10. O.Rs Horses & 4 h.D. arrived from 3rd M.G. Sqn. | |
| | 13 | | Inspection of Squadron Horses by C.O. D.R. Paid a surprise visit. Lieut BAILEY R.W. & 2/Lieut NEIL W.H.E. & LAMBE H.A. admitted temporary Hospital | |
| | 14 | | Brigade marched to DOULLENS - ORVILLE area. Squadron Bivouacked in fields at THIEVRES | |
| THIEVRES | 15 | | In Bivouacs. 2/Lieut W.N. FORBES attended F.G.C.M. as Subaltern Member at 15th Hussars H.Q. | |
| | 16 | | do 5. O.Rs from M.G.C BASE DEPOT | |
| | 17 | | do B/Lieut H.S. PINKER from Cav Corps Gas School. | |
| | 18 | | do | |
| | 19 | | do 2. O.Rs from M.G.C Base DEPOT | |
| | 20 | | Brigade marched to occupies area. Squadron billeted at MEZEROLLES. Lieut. S.J. PINKER left at THIEVRES to carry out Reconnaissance Duties in IV, V, VI & VII Corps areas. | |
| MEZEROLLES | 21 | | I.O.R from M.G.C BASE DEPOT. | |
| | 22 | | Lorry arrived to Charge Eye-Pieces of Inner/Box Respirators | |
| | 23 | | 2/Lieut W.H.E. NEIL accidentally injured - Kicks | |
| | 24 | | W.H.E. NEIL | |
| | 25 | | Lieut. C. EADE M.C. & LIEUT BAILEY Reconnoitered VI Corps area 2/Lieut W.H. LAMBE believed Lieut S.J. PINKER at THIEVRES. | |

Army Form C. 2118.

No. 11.4.24.
Date M.A. 7.18.

## WAR DIARY
or
## INTELLIGENCE SUMMARY.
*(Erase heading not required.)*

9th Machine Gun Sqdn.

| Place | Date | Hour | Summary of Events and Information | Remarks and references to Appendices |
|---|---|---|---|---|
| MEZEROLLES | July 26. | | In Billets | LENS. 11. |
| | 27. | | do. | |
| LE MEILLARD | 28. | | Squadron Bathed at OUTRE BOIS. Moved at 2/pm to new billeting area at LE MEILLARD, settling into Billets. | |
| | 29. | | 9th C.F. Ambulance moved into LE MEILLARD & took over Northern half of village | |
| | 30. | | Capt. R. P. NICOL relieved Lieut. M.A. LANGE at THIEVRES. | |
| | 31. | | C.O reconnoitered VI. Corps Area with a Party of Officers. | |

OFFICERS = 11
O.Rs   258 + 5 (attached)

Strength

R.    204
L.D    71
PACK  42

[Signature] Major,
COMMANDING 9th M. G. SQUADRON.

Army Form C. 2118.

# WAR DIARY
## or
## INTELLIGENCE SUMMARY.

9ᵗʰ MACHINE GUN SQUADRON

(Erase heading not required.)

| Place | Date 1918 | Hour | Summary of Events and Information | Remarks and references to Appendices |
|---|---|---|---|---|
| LE MEILLARD | AUGUST 1ˢᵗ | | In billets. Stopped holding Inspection by the Commanding Officer. | REFERENCE ARMY CENTRE |
| do | 2ⁿᵈ | | In billets. | |
| do | 3ʳᵈ | | In billets. Rear H.Q. Packs and 'A' Echelon transport proceeded to St Ickbac M.G. Branch CANIERS. | |
| do | 4ᵗʰ | | In billets. | |
| do | 5ᵗʰ | | In billets. 9ᵗʰ Cavalry Brigade under one hours notice to move. The Squadron ready to move from LE MEILLARD at 11 am and marched to Brigade concentration at PERNOIS. Arrived at 2.45 am, and bivouacked for night. | |
| PERNOIS | 6ᵗʰ | | In bivouac. Marched at 9.30 pm under Brigade arrangements to LONGPRÉ arriving 2 am. | |
| LONGPRÉ | 7ᵗʰ | | Marched off at 10.30 pm to concentration point in triangle South side of LONGEAU. ATHIES. | |
| LONGEAU | 8ᵗʰ | | No 1 Section was attached to the 15ᵗʰ Hussars, who were the leading Regiment, and during the advance Lt Wade located good targets, and inflicted considerable casualties on the enemy. By great dash and pluck the brigade in an enemy machine gun nest along the HARBONIERES - ROSIERES road, which hung to fight, and became involved. A Section took part in the mellé. also took an action to cover the advance of the Squadron of the 8ᵗʰ Hussars on the right flank of the brigade. C Section in reserve got into action at long range to toue. | |

Army Form C. 2118.

# WAR DIARY
## or
## INTELLIGENCE SUMMARY.
*(Erase heading not required.)*

9th MACHINE GUN SQUADRON

| Place | Date | Hour | Summary of Events and Information | Remarks and references to Appendices |
|---|---|---|---|---|
| | | | Whole of Squadron were in action to the 1914 Hallyers. | |
| | | | On the 3rd Sqdn hit a signaller & himself both wounded | |
| | | | In the scrap held by the Regiment which they recaptured | |
| | | | in the evening. Distichon was brought back wd, with | |
| | | | 6 Indian infantry. Their group shown greatly by 6th | |
| | | | and 7th Gurkha infantry. | |
| | | | During the day this half sqd. 1.O.R. seems not too greater | |
| | | | 6 Indes killed and 8 wounded. They also had some wore | |
| | | | Ventions unhorsed by a bullet through its pannier case of | |
| | | | him at trotting next day up to our own | |
| GUILLAUCOURT | | | On the strength of the 9th sqn of the Indian infantry was not sent | |
| | | | Brigade what had been concentrated in valley E.K. of | |
| | | | Cailling, not took with & GUILLAUCOURT. | |
| | | | "C" section were attached to the 7th hussars who were in reserve | |
| | | | Regt and advanced at a trot from GUILLAUCOURT onto VRELY to | |
| | | | MEHARICOURT where half the Regt deployed in right to L. Wh [?] being in the | |
| | | | line and No 6 in support. | |
| | | | "A" section also in support were well up but the Austrian machine 1.O.R. killed 1.O.R. | |
| | | | gunners opened fire 1.O.R. killed and 12 wounded killed and wounded | |

Army Form C. 2118.

# WAR DIARY
## or
## INTELLIGENCE SUMMARY.
(Erase heading not required.)

9th MACHINE GUN SQUADRON

| Place | Date 1918 | Hour | Summary of Events and Information | Remarks and references to Appendices |
|---|---|---|---|---|
| CAIX | August 10th | 10h | In the course of the attack the Brigade were to take part in REFERENCE AMIENS | REFERENCE AMIENS |
| CAIX | 11th |  | The Squadron lived with the Brigade. The Squadron and Brigade marched to the right and remained there till the afternoon of the 12th. |  |
| CAMON | 12th | PM | The Squadron marched to RIVERY. |  |
| RIVERY | 13th |  |  |  |
|  | 14th |  | The Commander looked at the MG School and were round the Brigade lines but did not have time to visit the hut. |  |
|  | 15th | 16h | Marched from RIVERY at 9pm to LONGUEVILLETTE arriving there at 2 am. | REFERENCE PARIS 11 |
| LONGUEVILLETTE |  |  |  |  |
| THIEVRES | 19th |  | The Brigade moved at 1.30 pm to THIEVRES arriving at 8 pm. 11.15 pm |  |
|  | 20th |  | In the night of the 19th posts marched at 11 pm and arrived at 2 am at the concentration point 3 kilometres East of SOUASTRE. |  |
|  | 21st |  | On the 21st at 6.45 am the Brigade attacked from FONQUEVILLERS (which is a point 6 km West of BUCQUOY, remaining there till 6 pm when the Brigade advanced by THIEVRES & AMPLIERS, reaching ABLAIN-ST-NAZAIRE by 1 am on 19th. Squadron and proceeded to full North of BICQUOY (F.21.C.5) where they remained for two days. Then went to the Western edge of LONGEAST WOOD, where they remained till 4.30 am and returned to the 19th Division and rejoined the Squadron at AMPLIERS. During these operations Lieut A E Knott MC was slightly wounded but remained at duty. Or Rank killed and 3 wounded |  |

Army Form C. 2118.

# WAR DIARY
## or
## INTELLIGENCE SUMMARY.
(Erase heading not required.)

9th MACHINE GUN SQUADRON

Reference Map: SENS 1k

| Place | Date | Hour | Summary of Events and Information | Remarks and references to Appendices |
|---|---|---|---|---|
| AMPLIERS | August 22nd | | In billets. At 6 p.m. the Machine Gun Officer 1/1 Cav. Bde. held a conference re ORVILLE as Gen H.Q. defence. | |
| ORVILLE | 23rd | | Squadron 1/1 Bde. marching to move at 5 p.m. to point near. At 5.30 p.m. order received to remain at Amplier, moved to bivouac to rest at a moment's notice. | |
| Do | 24th | | At bivouac. Yet to move standing to and prepared to move at a moments notice from 5 a.m. | |
| Do | 25th | | At bivouac. Moves which were cancelled. | |
| Do | 26th | | Orders received at 2 p.m. to saddle up & move. The Squadron marched with Brigade and arrived at LEMCOURT arriving at 10 p.m. | |
| LEMCOURT | 27th | | In billets. Received orders to hold the 1st cavalry lines from 10 a.m. which was always to 3 horse sorties 1st Bgd. 3 sqdns. to hold the line, the other 3 sqdns to move at 2 hours notice. | |
| Do | 28th | | | |
| Do | 29th | | This unit to be supposed ready at 6 hours notice. | |
| Do | 30th | | | |
| Do | 31st | | | |

Officers: 10
O.R.: 253 + 4 (attached)
R's: 196
L.D.: 69
P.C.K.: 38

Skeagh
Major
Commanding 9th M.G. SQUADRON

CONFIDENTIAL.

9 Bde / 1 Cav Div

War Diary

of the

9th Machine Gun Squadron.

September 1918.

Volume 32.

Army Form C. 2118.

# WAR DIARY
## or
## INTELLIGENCE SUMMARY.
(Erase heading not required.)

9th MACHINE GUN SQUADRON

| Place | Date Sept 1918 | Hour | Summary of Events and Information | Remarks and references to Appendices |
|---|---|---|---|---|
| LEINCOURT | 1st | | In billets. The Squadron report to meet at 5 hours notice. 2nd Lieut F. TWIST M.C. taken to | LENS 11 |
| Do | 2nd | | At 9 am the strength of the Squadron from the M.G.C. Base Depot. At 9 am the Squadron was detailed to move at a moments notice, which had later altered to "stand to" not "stand down", ready to move at once. Orders received at 9.30 pm to stand down, and be prepared to move at 5 hours notice. | |
| Do | 3rd | | In billets. At 5 hours notice to move. At 11 am orders were received 1½ hours notice. At 6.30 pm at 5 hours notice to move which was altered at 9.15 pm to 1 hours notice. | |
| Do | 4th | | In billets. At 12.40 am the Squadron were under orders to move at 6 hours notice. Training as usual. | |
| Do | 5th | | " " " | |
| Do | 6th | | "A" Section fired on Range. | |
| Do | 7th | | "B" " " " | |
| Do | 8th | | The Squadron took part in a Cavalry Corps Scheme. | |
| Do | 9th | | Training as usual. | |
| Do | 10th | | " " " | |
| Do | 11th | | " " " | |
| Do | 12th | | "B" Section firing on Range. | |
| Do | 13th | | "C" " " " | |
| Do | 14th | | " " " | |
| Do | 15th | | Usual Routine. Training as per programme. | |

# WAR DIARY or INTELLIGENCE SUMMARY

Army Form C. 2118.

(Erase heading not required.)

**"A" Machine Gun Squadron.**

| Place | Date Sept 1918 | Hour | Summary of Events and Information | Remarks and references to Appendices |
|---|---|---|---|---|
| LEINCOURT | 16th | | In billets. The Squadron marched from LEINCOURT at 9 am and returned for the night at MONCHEL. | MAP REFERENCE LENS. 1. |
| MONCHEL | 17th | | In billets. The Squadron took part in a tactical exercise held by the Cavalry Corps, which was attended by the Commander-in-Chief and the Inspector General of Cavalry. The object was the co-operation of Infantry, Cavalry, Motor Machine Guns and armoured cars in the securing and holding of river crossings. After this exercise the Commander-in-chief held a conference at AUXI-LE-CHATEAU in which many tactical points were brought out. The Squadron bivouacked for the night at LE PONCHEL. In the afternoon the Squadron marched from LE PONCHEL at 10 am, arriving at LE QUESNEL FARM at 1.30 pm. | [signature] |
| LE PONCHEL | 18th | | | |
| LE QUESNEL FM | 19th | | The Squadron moved to BOIS BERGUES at 3 pm. | |
| BOIS BERGUES | 20th | | In billets. Arranging of kits etc. | |
| Do | 21st | | " training as usual. | |
| Do | 22nd | | " " " " | |
| Do | 23rd | | " " O. Mackenzie firing on Range, remainder Action Off Pack etc. | |
| Do | 24th | | Orders the Squadron moved with Brigade to an area about AUTHIE. Billeted for the night at ST LEGER-LES-AUTHIE. | |

Army Form C. 2118.

# WAR DIARY
## or
## INTELLIGENCE SUMMARY.
(Erase heading not required.)

of "A" Machine Gun Squadron.

| Place | Date Sept 1918 | Hour 1918 | Summary of Events and Information | Remarks and references to Appendices |
|---|---|---|---|---|
| SPIEGEL-LES-AUTHIE | 25th | | In billets. The Squadron moved at 5.45 p.m. to MEAULTE, arriving 11 p.m. | MAP REFERENCE LENS 11. |
| MEAULTE | 26th | | The Squadron moved at 8 p.m. to an area near MAMANCOURT, arrived about 3 a.m. 27th and bivouacked in N.E. corner of BOIS ST. MARTIN. | AMIENS 11 LENS 11 |
| B. S. ST. MARTIN | 27th | | In bivouac | |
| " | 28th | | " | |
| " | 29th | | The Squadron moved at 2 p.m. arriving at HERVILLY about 4 p.m. and bivouaced for the night. | |
| | | | In bivouac. The Squadron afford No "ready to move at 10 a.m. Orders received at 1.30 p.m. | |
| HERVILLY | 30th | | to off battle, and stand to ready to move at 3 hours notice. | ST. QUENTIN 11 |

Strength of Squadron.

PERSONNEL

OFFICERS   11.
OTHER RANKS   245

HORSES
RIDERS              146
LIGHT DRAUGHT   10
PACK                  24

[signature]

CONFIDENTIAL.

# War Diary
## of the
## 9th Machine Gun Squadron.

### October 1918.

### Volume 33.

Army Form C. 2118.

# WAR DIARY
## or
## INTELLIGENCE SUMMARY.
(Erase heading not required.)

| Place | Date | Hour | Summary of Events and Information | Remarks and references to Appendices |
|---|---|---|---|---|
| HERVILLY | | | | ST QUENTIN 18 |

# WAR DIARY
## or
## INTELLIGENCE SUMMARY.

Army Form C. 2118.

of 9th Essex Regt Gun [?]

| Place | Date | Hour | Summary of Events and Information | Remarks and references to Appendices |
|---|---|---|---|---|
| BUISSON GUILLAINE RIDGE. | 1918 Oct 23 | | The Brigade moved 04.00 to MAIRON. "A" + "B" Squadrons and "C" [?] section under Lieut F.M.S.T. M.C. were attached to the 19th Hussars. "B" + "C" Squadrons 9/17th Lancers B/Hrs S.S. & RHA The Brigade under 9th KHC moved N.C. to move northwards at 5.5 A.M. At 6.23 A.M. H.Q. and "B" Squadron moved on to 6.26 & H.Q. "C" [?] Squadron at 6.40. but enemy MG fire forced the infantry move forward to reach N.E. of village at 5.59 A.M. "B" Squadron 19th Hussars received orders to establish touch "C" Squadron 19th Hussars and a troop about 5.20. "B" Squadron moved forward through the village to EAINBOURT in the N.E. limits of the village and enemy position from EAINBOURT through AVELU to MAIR "LE CATEAU ro[?]" One gun team rode to command tank. O. EAINCOURT to silence the MGs. The position was unable to come up. The two MGs and team rode grew unable to come up. Ran no casualties in trying to get touch with C Squadron as 19th Hussars since they had Miles to [?] Avelu 20 is joining with reinforcement. Enemy MGs about 5 minutes later. All opened fire by a Maxim [?] by the retreat of Capt MASSEY 1630 Hussars were forced to withdraw rapidly by the force of enemy fire. The remains of Squadron reported that remains of Squadron returned to RV at Lillieres At about 12.00 this squadron reported Ret. rapid [?] [?] | ST QUENTIN NKL Nov 5/18. " 6.2.3. VALENTINE -sd 12. |

# WAR DIARY or INTELLIGENCE SUMMARY

Army Form C. 2118

(Erase heading not required.)

| Place | Date | Hour | Summary of Events and Information | Remarks and references to Appendices |
|---|---|---|---|---|
| | 8 (continued) | | No 2 sub section (under 2 Lieut F. Taribs M.C.) moved with the main body of the 19th Hussars and took up a position at C.5 & H.3. and engaged enemy cavalry, including enemy M.Gs at C.12 & 9.H., C.12 & 5.6 and C.6 a 5.y. Two guns at this limits and lost much direction respectively were silenced and some of the gunners were observed running towards the road. During the 15 minutes these guns were in action 2000 rounds were fired. Engaging was then created a squadron 19th Hussars Mounting to get round to the right, making towards BUSIGNY. The led horses, under Sergt Sunderland, were sent back to the village of PREMONT but were shelled en route, having 5 horses killed and 5 wounded. The sub section moved from here to C.17. b.5.2. where enemy M.Gs. in C.18. c.6.3. and C.18.a.0.1 were engaged. His position was seen for 10 minutes and 1000 rounds fired. Aero marks had to be worn the whole time as the enemy was firing many gas shells. Later owing to the rapid attempts of the 19th Hussars again made progress to the right attempting to get forward to BUSIGNY. Eventually the followed this squadron of which two troops charged the enemy - Colonel FRANKS being killed and he two troop commanders wounded. On the situation repairing the remainder Hqrs. the whole Rectification 18 N of BRAH COURT. A brass horse was then sent to Brigade reserve for a supply of ammunition. The marks had to be | ST QUENTIN 18. and SHEET 57B. " 62B. VALENCIENN- ES. 12. |

**Army Form C. 2118**

**WAR DIARY**
or
**INTELLIGENCE SUMMARY**
(Erase heading not required.)

On Machine Gun Operations

| Place | Date | Hour | Summary of Events and Information | Remarks and references to Appendices |
|---|---|---|---|---|
| | 1918 Oct | 8 (continued) | worry in short intervals three times during the day. No.5 Subsection (under Lieut. B.J. PINKER) was ordered at 12.00 to report to 19th Hussars and found 1 Squadron at C29a central. The Subsection stayed with this Squadron until reaching Brigade Bivouac Area at BEAUREVOIR, when they rejoined the Squadron. No.6 Subsection (under Lieut. H.A. LAMBE) receiving orders at 11.20 to report to B.G.S. "B" Squadron 15th Hussars, from whom Lieut LAMBE received orders to dislodge an enemy M.G. in sunken lane running E from SERAIN through U15 and 16., the two guns taking up positions in U21a and U22c. The left gun got into action at U21 a 80.70 and was in charge of Sergt. KEEBLE. This gun was in position at 11.55 where it remained for about 2 hours. While reconnoitering for another position Sergt KEEBLE was wounded in the arm by an enemy M.G. bullet at 12.50. L/Cpl AMIS took charge of the gun and at 13.20 moved to a position in U21 a 80.30 where he was able to bring fire to bear upon an enemy M.G. in position in U16 b central. This enemy gun was forced to retire owing to position by our fire. Great credit is due to L/Cpl AMIS for his handling of this gun. The right gun was throughout in action at U22 d 20.50 and brought fire to bear upon an enemy M.G. in position at U16 c 80.30. Enemy gun was forced by our fire to retire to a position along sunken track running W from this | 1st QUENTIN 18 (new) SHEET 57B ,, 62B VALENCIENN ES 12. |

Army Form C. 2118

# WAR DIARY or INTELLIGENCE SUMMARY   9th Machine Gun Squadron
(Erase heading not required.)

| Place | Date | Hour | Summary of Events and Information | Remarks and references to Appendices |
|---|---|---|---|---|
| | 10/18 October | 8 (continued) | Original position. The right gun was then moved to a position about U.22.a.70.40, bringing oblique fire to bear upon wicket that 4 enemy M.Gs. were seen to retire from this direct to a position S.W. of MARETZ. One troop of "C" Squadron 15th Hussars occupied an event to this gun. While these guns were in action one pack horse was wounded by enemy air Snipes and on coming out of action one packhorse was wounded by shell fire. Ammunition expended approximately 2000 rounds. At 15.20 this Squadron received orders to withdraw and rejoin the Squadron in Brigade reserve. The remainder of the Squadron (in Brigade reserve) moved to be with Sgt SERAIN where they remained until Squadron withdrawn. Casualties during the above operation — Officers NIL. Other ranks, wounded 12 (including 2 remaining to duty). Horses killed 6, wounded 11, missing 1. About 1800 the Brigade moved back to the valley at BEAUREVOIR. Four sweeps and most parts of the night enemy airmen bombed the actions made by our own advance. No casualties were inflicted on the Squadron whilst in bivouac. At 11am of 9th WHEAT and Cpl CHRISTIE (Early Room Corporal) on cycle, proceeding to join the Squadron were both killed by bomb. Sergt 950 MILE being wounded at the same time. | VALENCIENNES- 12. ST QUENTIN 18. SHEET 62.C. 573. |
| BEAUREVOIR | 9th | | The Brigade (in Corps Reserve) remained in bivouac until 10.00, when | |

1875   Wt. W593/826   1,000,000   4/15   J.B.C. & A.   A.D.S.S./Forms/C. 2118.

Army Form C. 2118.

# WAR DIARY
## or
## INTELLIGENCE SUMMARY.
(Erase heading not required.)

Of Machine Gun Squadron

| Place | Date | Hour | Summary of Events and Information | Remarks and references to Appendices |
|---|---|---|---|---|
| BEAUREVOIR. | 9th | (Continued) | Orders were received to move to valley S. of VIEMAIN. At 14.30 orders were received to move to N.W. edge of village of PREMONT - received here until 18.00 and then moved into valley W. of MARETZ arriving about 23.00. In bivouac for the night.  14 other ranks (Reinforcements) taken on the strength.  Casualties - Officers nil. Other ranks - nil. Horses, wounded 1. | VIOLEN-VIOLEN- NEST 12. SHEET 62.B. |
| MARETZ. | 10th |  | The Squadron received orders that the Division was moving forward and left MARETZ valley at 06.00 and marched to concentration point N. of REUMONT arriving about 08.00. Here the Brigade stood to and halted until 15.30 when the order was received to return past to MARETZ valley and arrived here at 17.00. The Squadron bivouacked for the night and was under ½ hours notice to move. 3 other ranks struck off the strength. |  |
| MARETZ. | 11th |  | In bivouac. Under ½ hours notice to move which was later altered to 4 hours. At 15.00 the Squadron received orders to be ready to move at 3½ hours notice.  3½ horses mange. 1 O.R. admitted hospital. 1 L.D. to B.W.H. each struck off the strength. |  |
| " | 12th |  | In bivouac. Orders were received that the Brigade was moving back to an area about the river OMIGNON. The Brigade moved at 0950 and marched | |

/to

Army Form C. 2118.

# WAR DIARY
## or
## INTELLIGENCE SUMMARY.

(Erase heading not required.)

| Place | Date 1916 | Hour | Summary of Events and Information | Remarks and references to Appendices |
|---|---|---|---|---|
| TREFCON | 13. | (continued) | 16 TREFCON arriving about 15.00. | REQUEST 18. |
| " | 14. | | In billets. 1 2nd Lt 16 Bn. sent. sick & struck off strength. | SHEET 62C. |
| " | 15. | | The C.O. 6. 1st Can. Div. accompanied by the G.O.C. 9th Can. Bn. inspected the billets of the Battalion at 10.30. 2 Officers rank & file taken on strength. That was taken during the operations same enum this at close of phase:— |  |
|  |  |  | Officers. Nil. Other Ranks. Killed 4, wounded 13 (including two remaining at duty). Killed 6, wounded 15, missing 1. In total 7. |  |
| " |  | 16.50 | 1 Other rank taken on strength. 1 L.D. 2 men transferred on strength. 1 L.D. 16 Bn. struck off strength. |  |
| " |  | 17.40 | The following Officers are reported killed at [illegible] as found buried. Pre Regim[ental] numbers in yards 6 by the Divisional Burial Officer. T.R.W. struck off the strength. |  |
| " | 18 |  | In billets. C.W.S.[?] running. 9 men wounded & two admitted to [illegible] hospital. |  |
| " | 19. |  | Nothing to report. |  |
| " | 20. |  | In billets. 4 parcels were taken on strength. Twenty [illegible] Lewis Gunners. |  |
| " | 21. |  | In billets. Wing O.C. Bombers, admitted to hospital. Eng. [illegible] reported. |  |

| Place | Date | Hour | Summary of Events and Information | Remarks and references to Appendices |
|---|---|---|---|---|
| TREFCON | 22 | | [illegible handwritten entry] 1 truck from 19th Division their position in hills. 1 O.R. admitted to hospital. | ST QUENTIN [illegible] SHEET 62c |
| " | 23 | | 20 Grenadiers had to push on a Brigade house & some WWs. Recd B Coy. 2/Lt [illegible] joined. The 15th Division across the starting lines. | |
| " | 24 | | The morning was broken whenever enemy movement was [illegible]. Shown Cambrai Battn [illegible] Summary taken on Strength. 1. O.R. rejoined [illegible] 2 B 16 B.W. 1. O.R. admitted to hospital. 5 truck wire telephones &c. in hill. | |
| TREFCON | 24H 25 | | The Grenadiers took [illegible] to those [illegible] of [illegible] the 15. Division [illegible] attacking [illegible] and action on ground very difficult and of such like and a bog 15. 2 B 16 B.W. and truck to strength. | |
| " | 26 | | 1 killed. 1 O.R. discharged to hospital. 5 O.R. from town & Ln on strength. | |
| " | 27 | | In Billets. Relieve in Enemy of Infantry War. 1 O.R. Gunner taken on strength. | |
| " | 28 | | In Billets. Grenadiers had on a [illegible] Division. O.R. [illegible] and Cushion were the attacking force, and the [illegible]. 1 O.R. admitted [illegible] | |

Army Form C. 2118.

# WAR DIARY
## INTELLIGENCE SUMMARY.
(Erase heading not required.)

| Place | Date | Hour | Summary of Events and Information | Remarks and references to Appendices |
|---|---|---|---|---|
| TREFCON | 29 | | In hills. A and C sections took part in a Stokes defence in which the 4th Dragoon Guards were the attacking force. The 8 guns of A and C sections representing machine guns. | |
| " | 30 | | In hills. 1 O.R. transferred to M.E.E. Riantspirant. Reduction of strength. | |
| " | 31 | | In hills. Instead of being carried out by the 9th Cavalry Brigade in which the squadron with the Lighty Division took part, B section was attached to the 6th Division. The Divisional Squadron 2nd Cavalry Division supplied 12 machine guns that present the 2nd machine gun squadron and the Corps Commander was present. In hills. This unit supplied 12 machine guns and 3 reserves. 1 section also sent out, to represent the machine gun squadron. A similar scheme carried out by the 2nd Cavalry Brigade. The Corps Commander was present. | |

Strength of the Squadron.

Personnel.                          Horses.
Officers.  Other Ranks.       R.   L.D.   Pack.  Mules.
  10         252              210   41    44      1
              3
Attached      —

J.M.Moore  Major
COMMANDING 9th M.G. SQUADRON

Confidential.

# War Diary
## of the
## 9th Machine Gun Squadron.

### November 1918.

### Volume XXXIV.

SECRET.

I.

Army Form C. 2118.

# WAR DIARY
## INTELLIGENCE SUMMARY.
(Erase heading not required.)

Ok Machine Gun Squadron

| Place | Date | Hour | Summary of Events and Information | Remarks and references to Appendices |
|---|---|---|---|---|
| TREFCON. | 1st Nov | | In billets. | ST QUENTIN. |
| " | 2nd | | 4 Riders & 1 Pack struck off the strength. | |
| " | 3rd | | Squadron Drill. 1 rider taken on to strength. | |
| " | 4th | | Instruction of N.C.O.'s & men by the brigade officer. 12 O.R's taken on the strength. | |
| " | 5th | | Firing on the range at HANCOURT. | |
| | | | At 13.30 orders were received to be ready to move at 2½ hours notice. Off. O.R.'s Horses and Y.O.'s struck off the strength. | |
| " | 6th | | The Brigade moved north via HANCOURT, ROISEL, EPEHY, to an area about BANTOUZELLE, arriving about 15.00. | ST QUENTIN and |
| BANTOUZELLE | 7th | 09.00 | The Squadron marched with the Brigade to the area BRUNEMONT - ARLEUX. The Squadron billeted for the night at ARLEUX, arriving at 14.30. 2 Riders struck off the strength. | VALENCIE-NNES 1/100,000 |
| ARLEUX. | 8th | 08.00 | The Brigade moved to the area PONT A MARCQ - EMIEVELIN. The Squadron arrived at PONT A MARCQ about 15.00 & was in billets for the night. | TOURNAI |
| PONT A MARCQ | 9th | | Orders received for 1 section to be attached to 8th Hussars. "C" Section was detailed for this duty. The Squadron, less "C" Section, marched via North of GENECH - south of LA CROIX Troads, north of LAVERRE RUE, to RUMÉS, arriving about 11.30. On arrival orders were received to move. Arrived at GAURAM RAMECROIX about 17.00. The "C" Section, under Lieut L.J. PINKER, moved | |

Army Form C. 2118.

# WAR DIARY
# INTELLIGENCE SUMMARY.
*(Erase heading not required.)*

9K Machine Gun Squadron

| Place | Date | Hour | Summary of Events and Information | Remarks and references to Appendices |
|---|---|---|---|---|
| GAURAIN RAMECROIX | 9/K Nov | 06.00 | with the 8th Hussars to MOUCHIN, arriving about 14.00. The Brigade moved through LEUZE along the ATH road. A section was attached to the leading regiment i.e. 15th Hussars. 1st Squadron under Capt. M.G. MOUNT M.C. moved forward with the advanced squadron of 15th Hussars. At 08.00 Patrols encountered the enemy East of LIGNE and the two guns with an escort of 1 N.C.O. and 4 men were ordered forward to assist in the attack. An enemy gun was located on main road 400 yds. W. of the village. By creating a diversion to the right the guns were able to bring fire to bear on this enemy gun, and the enemy were seen to retire through the village. Both guns kept in touch with the enemy and brought fire to bear on them as they crossed the railway crossing E. of LIGNE. They eventually retired towards VILLERS ST ARMAND. The led horses were sent for & rejoined these two guntiams [guntiams] at level crossing E. of LIGNE. Gunfire was again ordered forward to engage the enemy M.G.s which were holding up our patrols in VILLERS ST ARMAND, and got in touch with an enemy M.G. 100' about 1/2 mile E.N.E. of VILLERS ST ARMAND. This enemy position was taken with little difficulty and finally a position was taken up covering the crossing over the river DENDRE 1/2 mile S.E. of ATH. From this position troops were engaged in ATH until nightfall, when the guns were withdrawn, and rejoined the remainder of the squadron at VILLERS ST ARMAND where they were billeted for the night. During these operations No. 51077 | TOURNAI. |

Army Form C. 2118.

# WAR DIARY
## —of—
## INTELLIGENCE SUMMARY.
(Erase heading not required.)

of No 2 Machine Gun Squadron

| Place | Date | Hour | Summary of Events and Information | Remarks and references to Appendices |
|---|---|---|---|---|
| | 1918 Nov 2 | 10 (continued) | Pte Arthur Knight, proved exceptionally useful as scout, showing great courage and nerve. No.2 Subsection, under Pte F. TWIST M.G.M. moved with the 15^th Hussars towards ATH, and on reaching VIKERS ST ARMAND Reinforced "B" Squadron 15^th Hussars) and a position taken up at N9.b.69, and enemy targets at farms at N3.d.89 and N4.e.89 were engaged exceedingly, and the enemy were seen to retire from Fire the two guns got into action in Sewerin Road at N4.d. The left gun engaged enemy M.Gs. an farm houses at 133 and N34, two belts were expended and the enemy was seen to retire behind the buildings and after 10 minutes the action from that direction the right gun gave covering fire whilst a troop of 15^th Hussars attempted to reach ATH the way of N4 and N5. Our enemy M.Gs. were located in N5.c. and their fire kept down. As the 15^th Hussars were held up in N5.c. by fire from direction of main road N11.5.59. The two guns were then moved to a position at N4.d.15 and gave covering fire to troops of 15^th Hussars who attacked a party of horses at N5.b. tactics by enemy MGs. Our guns remained in this position until 16.45, when they were withdrawn, and | SHEETS 44 and 5 |

# WAR DIARY
## INTELLIGENCE SUMMARY

Army Form C. 2118.

Ot. Machine Gun Squadron

| Place | Date Hour | Summary of Events and Information | Remarks and references to Appendices |
|---|---|---|---|
| | 10th (continued) | Rejoined the Squadron on hills at VILLERS ST ARMAND. No. of rounds expended by the sub-section during the day 4,000. | TOURNAI! |
| | 08.00 | B. Section under Lieut. C. Sale R.C. was ordered to join K.E. Horse to tell them of opposition in LIGNE, but this had disbanded before the Section arrived. At 12.00 no 2 sub-section with a Squadron of 15th Hussars, endeavoured to capture an enemy M.G. north of ATH – TOURNAI road. The led horses were left in the yard and gun positions taken up about 200 yards in front. From this position enemy M.Gs. were engaged, but the position remained unchanged. The led horses were heavily shelled and sustained the following casualties:— Officers Nil. O.Ranks. Killed 1. Wounded 5 O.Rs. Horses. Killed 8. Wounded 6. Pack Killed 4. Wounded 2. At dusk this sub-section was withdrawn and rejoined the Squadron at VILLERS ST ARMAND. | |
| | 08.30 | C. Section with the 8th Hussars, marched to PERUWELZ, arriving at 14.00. | |

Army Form C. 2118.

# WAR DIARY
## INTELLIGENCE SUMMARY.
(Erase heading not required.)

O.C. Machine Gun Squadron

| Place | Date | Hour | Summary of Events and Information | Remarks and references to Appendices |
|---|---|---|---|---|
| VILLERS ST PRIMA. | 1918 Nov 11th | | Orders received that the Squadron was to be ready to move at 2 hours notice from 07.00 but not saddled up. Orders were then received that the Brigade would move at 09.00 to a position E of River DENDRE about the M of MAFFLE. The infantry having reached the iron Bridge south of ATH, Squadron marched 14.30. Off saddled until 11.00 and crossed at 11.00 and troops asked to remain in present positions with outpost precautions. At 04.45 C Squadron marched from PERUWELZ and rejoined the Squadron at MAFFLE at 12.00. At 15.00 Squadron moved into billets for the night, and was ordered to be ready to move at 2 hours notice. | TOURNAI |
| MAFFLE. | 12th | 09.00 | The Squadron marched with the 1 Brigade to an area about CALLENELLE, the Squadron being billeted at LA GARENNE. | |
| LA GARENNE | 13th 14th | | 6. O.R.s struck of strength. 1.L.D.E. Sgt. struck of strength. 5 O.R.s. 4 2 O.R. B.V.R. and struck of strength. 1 O.R. struck of strength. 1 O.R. taken on strength. Officers and other ranks of the Squadron attended a Thanksgiving service | |

Army Form C. 2118.

# WAR DIARY
## or
## INTELLIGENCE SUMMARY.
(Erase heading not required.)

Of Machine Gun Squadron

| Place | Date | Hour | Summary of Events and Information | Remarks and references to Appendices |
|---|---|---|---|---|
| La GARENNE | 1916 15th | | In billets. | TOURNAI and BRUSSELS. 1/100,000 |
| " | 16th | | Reinforcements 10 O.R's. taken on strength. 1 O.R. taken on strength. | |
| " | 17th | 04/30 | The Brigade marched to BAGENRIEUX, arriving about 15.00. 'C' Section marched into billets at BAGENRIEUX and the leading Squadron ('9th Hussars') being billeted with that regiment for the night. | |
| BAGENRIEUX | 18th | 08.00 | The Squadron marched with the Brigade to ECAUSSINES D'ENGHIEN, and 'C' Section rejoined while on the march. 2/Lt W.H.B. Neil taken on strength. Under Authority granted by the Field Marshal Commanding in Chief, No. 6948 Pte Arthur Knight has awarded the Military Medal to 5711 O.R. Pte Arthur Knight. | |
| ECAUSSINES D'ENGHIEN | 19th | | In billets. 1 O.R. struck off the strength. 2 riders taken on strength. | |
| " | 20th | | 1 L.O. to B.O.K. and struck of the strength. | |
| " | 21st | | The Squadron moved at 08.00, arriving at MELLERY at 14.30. In billets for the night. | |

Army Form C. 2118.

# WAR DIARY
## or
## INTELLIGENCE SUMMARY.
(Erase heading not required.)

Of Machine Gun Squadron.

| Place | Date | Hour | Summary of Events and Information | Remarks and references to Appendices |
|---|---|---|---|---|
| MELLERY. | 22nd Nov 1918 | 07:45 | The Brigade moved to the area TILLIER - SART D'AVRIL. The Squadron arrived at SART D'AVRIL at 14.30 and billeted there for the night. | BRUSSELS. |
| SART D'AVRIL | 23rd | | In billets. 1 O.R. to 1 K.D.G. 1 O.R. to B.O.R. returned of the strength. 1 O.R. struck off the strength. | |
| " | 24th | | The Brigade continued the march to the line 2 miles east of the East suburbs allotted to 3rd Cav. Div. The Squadron reached HUCCORNE at 13.30 where they billeted for the night. | LIÉGE. |
| HUCCORGNE | 25th | | In billets. | |
| " | 26th | | " | |
| " | 27th | 08.00 | The Brigade continued the march to the main SPRIMONT - LIÉGE Road, the Squadron arriving at ESNEUX at about 14.20 | |
| ESNEUX. | 28th | | In billets. | |
| " | 29th | | The Brigade continued the march to the frontier via FRAMPONT - PEPINSTER - VERVIERS. The Squadron arrived at DOLHAIN (LIMBOURG) and was billeted there for the night. | |

Army Form C. 2118.

# WAR DIARY
## INTELLIGENCE SUMMARY
Of the Machine Gun Squadron

(Erase heading not required.)

VIII.

Instructions regarding War Diaries and Intelligence Summaries are contained in F. S. Regs., Part II. and the Staff Manual respectively. Title pages will be prepared in manuscript.

| Place | Date | Hour | Summary of Events and Information | Remarks and references to Appendices |
|---|---|---|---|---|
| DOLHAIN (LIMBOURG). | 30th Nov | In billets. | Strength of the Squadron :- <br><br> Personnel     Horses. <br> Officers. O.Ranks.   R.   L.D.   Pack. Mules. <br> 10.    252    174   64   34    5. <br><br> Attached -   3 <br><br><br> J.Morris. Major. <br> Commanding 9th Machine Gun Squadron. | LIEGE. <br> 1/100,000 |

Confidential.

War Diary
of
9th Machine Gun Squadron.

December 1918.

VOLUME XXXV.

Confidential.

Army Form C. 2118.

# WAR DIARY
## INTELLIGENCE SUMMARY.
(Erase heading not required.)

Of Machine Gun Squadron

| Place | Date | Hour | Summary of Events and Information | Remarks and references to Appendices |
|---|---|---|---|---|
| BELGIUM. DOLHAIN. (LIMBOURG) | 1918 Dec. 1st | 08.30 | The Brigade crossed the frontier and marched to the area of ROTGEN. The Squadron arrived at ROTT at 14.30 and was in billets for the night. (Horses in the open). | GERMANY. I.L. 10000 |
| GERMANY. ROTT. | 2nd | | In billets. | |
| " | 3rd | 08.00 | In billets. | |
| " | 4th | 08.30 | The Brigade marched to the line DROVE – KREUZAU – DUREN – SULGERSDORF. The Squadron arriving at GURZENICH at 14.00 where they billeted for the night. | |
| GURZENICH | 5th | 09.00 | The Brigade marched to the line MODRATH – East Bank ERFT Canal – MOKKEN. The Squadron arrived at GIESENDORF at 12.00 and was billeted for the night. | |
| GIESENDORF | 6th | | In billets. 1 O.R. to England for transfer, strength of strength. | |
| " | 7th | 09.00 | The Brigade moved to an area west of the Rhine. The Squadron being billeted in STRABERG and arrived here at 14.30 in billets. | |
| STRABERG | 8th | | | |
| " | 9th | 08.30 | The Brigade marched to the North-Western outskirts of COLOGNE, arrived at 15.00, the Squadron being billeted at the PIONEER BARRACKS, COLOGNE. | |

Army Form C. 2118.

# WAR DIARY
# or
# INTELLIGENCE SUMMARY.
(Erase heading not required.)

II.

Instructions regarding War Diaries and Intelligence Summaries are contained in F.S. Regs. Part II. and the Staff Manual respectively. Title pages will be prepared in manuscript.

Of Machine Gun Squadron

| Place | Date | Hour | Summary of Events and Information | Remarks and references to Appendices |
|---|---|---|---|---|
| PIONEER BARRACKS, COLOGNE | 10/12/18 | 10th | In Barracks. | Summary I.K. |
| " | | 11th | " | |
| " | | 12th | June 10th. J. HALLWELL joined from 6th M.G. Squadron. The Division crossed the Rhine, marching via Cologne Cathedral, Hohenzollern Bridge, thence N. of MULHEIM, and formed a bridgehead from ODENTHAL – NEUKIRCHEN – HITDORF. The Division being the first to cross the Rhine, marched past General Sir Herbert Plumer, G.C.B., G.C.M.G., G.C.V.O., A.D.C., Commanding 2nd Army. The G.O.C. Cav. Corps was present and a large staff. Escort, trumpeters etc. The R.H.G. Band played, and the Union Jack was broken on the arrival of the G.O.C. 2nd Army at the Hohenzollern Bridge. The Brigade arrived at WIESDORF at 14.00 & the Squadron billeted for the night at LEVERKUSEN. | |
| LEVERKUSEN | 13th | 08.30 | The Brigade marched to the final Bridgehead to BIRSCHEIT. The Squadron marching to Hillers at OHLIGS, arriving at 12.30. | |
| OHLIGS | | 14th | In Billets. | |
| " | | 15th | Lt. HOTWARD and 1 O.R. arrived from Base. The Brigade marched to COLOGNE area, the Squadron being billeted to-night at the Artillery Depot, Cologne. | |
| WIDENER | | 16th | The Brigade marched to a wooded area ISEDBURG–MONKEN, the Squadron being billeted in CASTER. | |

Army Form C. 2118.

# WAR DIARY
# INTELLIGENCE SUMMARY.

(Erase heading not required.)

9th Madras Guard......

| Place | Date 1/18 | Hour | Summary of Events and Information | Remarks and references to Appendices |
|---|---|---|---|---|
| KASTER | 17th | | In billets. | General I.K. |
| " | 18th | | " | |
| " | 19th | | " | |
| " | 20th | | " | |
| " | 21st | | " | |
| " | 22nd | | " 5 O.Rs struck off the strength. | |
| " | 23rd | | " | |
| " | 24th | | " | |
| " | 25th | | " | |
| " | 26th | | " 1 O.R. from Hospital taken on strength. 5 O.Rs to England for tour of duty, struck off the strength. | JM |
| " | 27th | | In billets. | |
| " | 28th | | " | |
| " | 29th | | " 15 O.Rs taken on the strength. | |
| " | 30th | | In billets. 12 O.Rs struck off the strength. | |

Army Form C. 2118.

# WAR DIARY
## or
## INTELLIGENCE SUMMARY.
(Erase heading not required.)

9th Machine Gun Squadron.

Instructions regarding War Diaries and Intelligence Summaries are contained in F.S. Regs., Part II. and the Staff Manual respectively. Title pages will be prepared in manuscript.

IV.

| Place | Date | Hour | Summary of Events and Information | Remarks and references to Appendices |
|---|---|---|---|---|
| KASTER Jn. | 1918 | | In Billets. Lieut H.O.Fortain transferred to 1st Machine Gun Squadron. | |
| | | | Strength of the squadron. | |
| | | |          Riding   Horses  L.D.  Pack  Mules | |
| | | | Officers  O.R.s     174     70    34    1 | |
| | | | 11.    287 | |
| | | | Attached        1 | |
| | | | | |
| | | | J.Moncrieff Maj. | |
| | | | Commanding 9th Machine Gun Squadron. | |

Confidential.

War Diary
of
9th Machine Gun Squadron.
January 1919.
Volume XXXVI

Army Form C. 2118.

# WAR DIARY
## INTELLIGENCE SUMMARY.
*(Erase heading not required.)*

Instructions regarding War Diaries and Intelligence Summaries are contained in F. S. Regs., Part II. and the Staff Manual respectively. Title pages will be prepared in manuscript.

| Place | Date | Hour | Summary of Events and Information | Remarks and references to Appendices |
|---|---|---|---|---|
| MASTER | May 1 | | | |
| | | | | |
| | | | | |
| | | | | |
| | | | | |
| | 6 | | | |
| | 7 | | | |
| | 8 | | | |
| | 9 | | | |
| | | | | |
| | 10 | | | |
| | 11 | | | |
| | 12 | | | |

Army Form C. 2118.

# WAR DIARY
# or
# INTELLIGENCE SUMMARY.

*(Erase heading not required.)*

O. Machine Gun Sanction

Instructions regarding War Diaries and Intelligence Summaries are contained in F. S. Regs., Part II. and the Staff Manual respectively. Title pages will be prepared in manuscript.

| Place | Date | Hour | Summary of Events and Information | Remarks and references to Appendices |
|---|---|---|---|---|
| MASTER | Jany 13th | | On Lines of March | Rennes |
| " | 14th | | " | Rennes IV |
| " | 15th | | Return strength of the strength in the Brigade line | |
| " | | | Trial of No 2 Air Compressor by the Chief Officer | |
| " | | | 1st Batty R.H.A. were to be shown round & commenced | |
| " | | | on a visit for the Garrison Gunners 14 noon to 2 | |
| " | 16th | M 8/1/43 | " | |
| " | 17th | | | |
| " | 18th | | Corps Commander Col. G.E. Brigade Stan between | JMB |
| " | | | 1 Gunner & 9th H.L.I.B. which was played on the | |
| " | | | 18 Hussars Ground at BERBURG Permitted the | |
| " | 19th | | Motor van vice by Gnr G. | |
| " | 20th | c 4/1/43 | | |
| " | 21st | | | |
| " | 22nd | | | |

Army Form C. 2118.

# WAR DIARY
## — of —
## INTELLIGENCE SUMMARY
*(Erase heading not required.)*

Of Machine Gun Sqdn Div

Instructions regarding War Diaries and Intelligence Summaries are contained in F.S. Regs., Part II. and the Staff Manual respectively. Title pages will be prepared in manuscript.

| Place | Date | Hour | Summary of Events and Information | Remarks and references to Appendices |
|---|---|---|---|---|
| KASTER | Aug 23rd | | In billets | Reconnaissance Scout Off |
| " | 24th | | " | |
| " | 25th | | 3985.y Private Oxley Cyril Cheshire Regt. wounded Ac. | |
| " | | | N.S.M. since been evacuated. (Supp. Orders Gazette | |
| " | | | Arkel 18th February 1919 | |
| " | 26th | | In billets | |
| " | 27th | | " | |
| " | 28th | 11.30am | The G.O.C. 1st Cavalry Division inspected the Squadron | ODn |
| " | | 14.30 | A whole Parade was given by the G.O.C. to the Officer and a | |
| " | 29th | | N.C.O.'s & O.R. Block of the billets. | |
| DUREN | 30th | | The squadron entrained for Duren, 3rd Squadron of Lancers on the Divisional | |
| " | | | reconnaissance of the 61/18 Cavalcanious Rgt. at DUREN took the place of Machine | |
| " | | | Gun Squadron 2. 13 Squadron 9 Lancers | |
| KASTER | 31st | | In billets | |
| | | | Strength:— Officers 10  OR's 276  L.D. 69  R. 166  PACK 33 | |

O.R's 276 / O/P/2118/1/H1ed 1

A6945  Wt. W11422/M1160  350,000  12/16  D. D. & L.  Forms/C/2118/1/H1ed

J. Moncrieff
Major
Commanding of Machine Gun Squadron

Confidential

War Diary
of
9th Machine Gun Squadron.
February 1919.
Volume XXXVII

Army Form C. 2118.

# WAR DIARY
## or
## INTELLIGENCE SUMMARY.  Of Machine Gun Squadron

(Erase heading not required.)

| Place | Date 1919 Feby. | Hour | Summary of Events and Information | Remarks and references to Appendices |
|---|---|---|---|---|
| Germany EASTER | 1 | | In billets. 30 Officers + Other ranks attended a most interesting lecture by Mr. [illegible] on "ALSACE LORRAINE and the German Revolution" delivered by Mr. [illegible] [illegible]. 1st O.R's church of army. | General 1 K |
| " | 2 | | Ch[urch] [illegible] | |
| " | 3 | | "B" Squadron football team played "B" Squadron [illegible] [illegible] and the latter squadron won their [illegible] cup [illegible] [illegible] [illegible] [illegible] B.E.F. In billets. | |
| " | 4 | | | |
| " | 5 | | [illegible] Sunrise today and was quite [illegible] heavy showers. Ran during later in the evening and [illegible] [illegible] to Brigade [illegible] and cleared for the rest of the day. Educational Cinema screenings in "A" Subsector. Boxing type P.T. tests 1 O.R sent off strength | |
| " | 6 | | 3 Riding classes of [illegible] | 5 |
| " | 7 | | In billets. 3 O.R's struck off strength. All troops marked "Y" were relieved by Persons [illegible] Board and [illegible] were re-marked as "X" also Pack Horse Lines are here re-marked "Z" | |

A6945   Wt. W14422/M1160 350,000   12/16   D. D. & L.   Forms/C./2118/14.

Army Form C. 2118.

# WAR DIARY
## INTELLIGENCE SUMMARY.
(Erase heading not required.)

Instructions regarding War Diaries and Intelligence Summaries are contained in F. S. Regs., Part II. and the Staff Manual respectively. Title pages will be prepared in manuscript.

O.K. Machine Gun Instruction

| Place | Date | Hour | Summary of Events and Information | Remarks and references to Appendices |
|---|---|---|---|---|
| KASTER | 7/1/19 | | Very hard frost. Roads bad for exercising. | Germany |
| " | 8 | | All horses originally marked "X" were re-examined by the M.O. above 50 officers & other ranks had to be exercised. Dane is an interesting lecture at BEDBURG on "Life at Windhoek" and interesting Lecture on "Life at a long distance wireless Station" delivered by Captain HARLOW Intelligence Corps, late of 2nd Brigade R.A.F. | I.K. |
| " | 9 | | As at 8. | |
| " | 10 | | | |
| " | 11 | | | |
| " | 12 | | Lieut. Lewisham to be Medical Officer. 1 OR returned off the strength. | |
| " | 13 | | Gave rendezvous to ½ Brigade Machine Guns Officers. Mr Capt Ritchie lectures on small arms and | |
| " | 14 | | received ammunition delivered an address hereto to the Squadron & to Newcastle Regt. Gave Inspection by Lt. Col. M Donne, Officer | |

A6945. Wt. W14122/M1160 350,000 12/16 D. D. & L. Forms/C.2118/14.

# WAR DIARY
## or
## INTELLIGENCE SUMMARY.

Army Form C. 2118.

| Place | Date | Hour | Summary of Events and Information | Remarks and references to Appendices |
|---|---|---|---|---|
| MASTRICHT | 15 | | In Billets | Germany |
| " | 16 | | 2 Riding Horses on Strength | |
| " | 17 | | | |
| " | 18 | | The A.D.M.S. at Ian Div. inspected transport vehicles | |
| " | 19 | | 50 Ameri: 98 lbs attended service at BEDBURG R.C. Church billets show huts &c. "Billeted" and "in Billets with Buck Brigade" | |
| " | 20 | | stables, 2 R with D destroyed | |
| " | 21 | | | |
| " | 22 | | | |
| " | 23 | | Voluntary Church Parade Sunday Service as usual. The Brigade Band. 2 O.R. struck off strength & sent to be to field ambulance | |
| " | 24 | | rifles. Inoculation complete Party sent to BEDBURG Church to fetch altar. Extra routine as usual | |
| | | | A.W. 1 Brigadier Gen 1 O.R. Other Ranks struck | |
| " | 25 | | w.o.&s.b.s | |

Army Form C. 2118.

# WAR DIARY
## or
## INTELLIGENCE SUMMARY.
*(Erase heading not required.)*

Instructions regarding War Diaries and Intelligence Summaries are contained in F. S. Regs., Part II. and the Staff Manual respectively. Title pages will be prepared in manuscript.

| Place | Date | Hour | Summary of Events and Information | Remarks and references to Appendices |
|---|---|---|---|---|
| KASSIK | 26 | In billets | | Command |
| " | 27 | " | One attempt at strength to Kidwa's post carried on | I.K. |
| " | 28 | In billets | | |
| | | | Strength of the squadron | |
| | | | Officers & others | |
| | | | Riding B.D. Pack mule | |
| | | | 10 249 160 68 31 | |
| | | | Attached 1 1 | |

Moneypts Major
Command ? Machine Gun Squadron

A6945 Wt. W14422/M1160 350,000 12/16 D. D. & L. Forms/C/2118/14.

No 38

Confidential V.E.

WAR DIARY
of
Capt. Maurice Cullen RN Squadron
MARCH 1919

# WAR DIARY or INTELLIGENCE SUMMARY

9th Machine Gun Squadron

Army Form C. 2118.

| Place | Date 1919 March | Hour | Summary of Events and Information | Remarks and references to Appendices |
|---|---|---|---|---|
| KASTER | 1 | | In billets. No. 50960. Pte W. Mears died in Hospital. | Germany 1.K. |
| " | 2 | | " | |
| " | 3 | | " | |
| " | 4 | | " | |
| " | 5 | | Health Inspection by the Medical Officer. No. 41166 Cpl Amidien in Hospital. | |
| " | 6 | | 3 Other Ranks struck off strength. | |
| " | 7 | | In billets. 50 Officers & O.Rs attended a very interesting Lecture by Archdeacon Wakeford at Beeburg. | |
| " | 8 | | In billets. No. 10058 Pte. A.B. Smith died in Hospital. | |
| " | 9 | | " 2 Riders & 1 L.D. struck off. 41 Z. Class horses | |
| " | 10 | | 2 T. Moves & 1 M. Move with covering party of 1 Officer & 51 O.R.s proceeded to 1st Dragoon Bgds. The horses as follows have been struck off: 5 T. & O. 3 | |
| " | 11 | | In billets. A Composite Football Team made up from 1st, 2nd & 9th M.G. Sqdns. played the 5 Dragoon Guards. Result M.G. Sqdns 4 | |
| " | 12 | | " Health Inspection by the Medical Officer. | |
| " | 13 | | " Lieut. W.J. Hallinwell struck off the strength. | |
| " | 14 | | " 1 O.R. struck off strength. | |
| " | 15 | | " 3 Officers & 20 O.Rs attended Cavalry Sports Sheepleduce 4 L.D. struck off strength | |

Confidential  II

Army Form C. 2118.

**WAR DIARY**
or
**INTELLIGENCE SUMMARY.**
(Erase heading not required.)

9th Machine Gun Squadron

| Place | Date 1919 March | Hour | Summary of Events and Information | Remarks and references to Appendices |
|---|---|---|---|---|
| KASTER | 16. | | In billets. R.C. Church service at 10 a.m. No. 50890. Sgt. P.R. Ede accidentally killed. | Germany |
| " | 17. | | In billets. 6 Riders, 55 Light Draught and 17 Pack struck off the strength. | |
| " | 18. | | In billets. | |
| " | 19. | | 1 Officer & 14 O.Rs taken on strength from 4 m.g. Sqdn. 25 ORs attached from 4 m.g. Sqn. 50 Riders, 11 Light Draught and 17 Pack and 1 Mule taken on strength. | 1 K. |
| " | 20. | | In billets. 21 other Pack struck off strength. | |
| " | 21. | | " 1 Light Draught & 1 Pack struck off the strength | |
| " | 22. | | In billets. | |
| " | 23. | | " 1 mule struck off the strength. Cinema Show in Recreation Room. | |
| " | 24. | | In billets. 35 O.Rs attended demonstration on army Footbce at Cologne between 5th Dragoon Guards & 9th K Highlanders. Lieut. S.J. Dunker transferred to 3rd D.G. Sqn, struck off strength. 3 ORs to Watford for duty. 1 Officer taken on strength. | |
| " | 26. | | In billets. | |
| " | 26. | | " Health Inspection by the Medical Officer. 1 Other Rank off the strength. 1 Officer & 2 ORs from 9th L.G. Sqn taken on the strength. | |
| " | 29. | | | |

Confidential III

Army Form C. 2118.

# WAR DIARY
## or
## INTELLIGENCE SUMMARY.

(Erase heading not required.) 9th Machine Gun Squadron

| Place | Date 1919 March | Hour | Summary of Events and Information | Remarks and references to Appendices |
|---|---|---|---|---|
| KASTER | 28 | | En billets. 83 Other Ranks to U.K. for Demobilisation | Germany |
| " | 29 | | 58 Light Draught & 5 Pack Horses of Strength. | |
| | | | En billets. Owing to shortage of personnel Horses | |
| | | | divided into two parties. 25 Other Ranks to U.K. for | |
| | | | Demobilisation. 63 Riders taken off the strength. | 1.K. |
| " | 30 | | In billets. Voluntary Divine Service in the | |
| | | | Recreation Room at 09.00. Baden Show 21 16 30. | |
| " | 31 | | En billets. | |

Strength of the Squadron

| | Officers | O.Ranks | Horses Riding | L.D. | Pack | Mules |
|---|---|---|---|---|---|---|
| | 11 | 238 | 193 | 40 | 42 | 1 |
| Attached | | 12 | | | | |

J. Moncy Major,
Commanding 9th Machine Gun Squadron.

600 q5/1116/5

## 1917
## 1ST CAVALRY DIVISION
## 9TH CAVALRY BRIGADE

9TH CAV. PIONEER BATTN
MAY - JLY 1917

9th Bde. Pioneer Battalion. War Diary    9 Cav. Bde. Pioneer Bn.

| Hour Date Place | Summary of events & information | Remarks & references to |
|---|---|---|
| 17/5/17. | 9th Cav Bde Pioneer Battalion was formed as under. | Vol 1 |
| NINE ELMS | 15th Hussars Coy Strength 1 Of. 4 Capt & Sub Alterns including 1 Q.M. | |
| | 19 " " " 95 1 " 4 " xx including Staff | |
| | Bedfordshire Yeomanry " 193 1 " 3 " | |
| | The Battalion was commanded by Major Tanner (19th Royal Hussars) & proceeded from ARRAS to NINE ELMS Camp. | May 1917 – , 1917 |
| 18/5/17 | This day was spent in filling in shell holes around the Camp, & clearing up the ground around; also building a track for horse traffic from the Camp to the main Arras road | |

# WAR DIARY or INTELLIGENCE SUMMARY

Army Form C. 2118.

9th Pioneer Battn
9th Cav. Bde. Pioneer Battn.

| Hour, Date, Place | Summary of Events and Information | Remarks and References to Appendices |
|---|---|---|
| 7 AM to 5 PM 19/5/17 at Pts T.14.6.4.5 to Pts Sheet 51 NWL B7a.1.9 to h.5 Green Line | A trench of about 200x was commenced by the 19th Hussars. Coy of the 9th Pioneer Battalion 1st Cav Div. Two parties of 80 men & two others working two hours each dug an average depth of 3'6" in hard and chalky soil. Casualties amounted to one man killed by shell fire, which on the whole was very slight. The trench is to be a fire trench with traverses #6ft wide with bays to hold 8 men. Breadth of trench to be two feet to start. Stretcher parties to work. The trench faces NE parallel to the Farbus line. A party drawn as ist of 15 men were attached to work of the 6th Div. to search for German Cables between Arras near the Ry due west of Bailleul. | TYPE of Trench [sketch of trench profile with measurements 5'6", 3', 2'6", Slope (1 in 5), "firing position"] |
| 8.30 AM to 4 PM 19/5/17 near Bailleul | | |

| Hour Date | Place | Summary of events & information | Remarks |
|---|---|---|---|
| 20/5/17 | | On the morning of the 20th much shelling occurred on the railway & in the neighbourhood of THÉLUS. Nine & this camp was also shelled causing the following casualties | |

Regiment — Killed — Wounded
15th Hussars — 1 — 3
19th Hussars — 5 — 20
Bedfordshire Yeomanry — — 3

Total 5 — 26

At about 12 noon the shelling ceased and at 9 pm the Camp was struck & moved to ECURIE.

# WAR DIARY
## or
## INTELLIGENCE SUMMARY.
*(Erase heading not required.)*

Army Form C. 2118.

| Hour, Date, Place | Summary of Events and Information | Remarks and References to Appendices |
|---|---|---|
| from 8.30 p.m 20/5/17. Place as for 19th | A working party of 172 OB relieved party of 3 hour continued their work on the trench started the previous day. A mean depth of 3 foot was reached. Though several bays were dug to the required depth of 5ft, the breadth of the trench is (also being solved) gives to 5" with 4-4gap, 6" width, 1" high. In the height of the mint was badly damaged. 1.50 of apron wire was laid by 60 men, 1 officer of the 15th Hy. Coy working in parties of 20 men to 1 NCO. 14 more is now NW to SE (with the MG emplacement at SE about to the parallel to wire (not not doubt.) | |
| 21/5/17 9.50 p.m — 22/5/17 3.30 a.m | Work on the same trench was continued in two reliefs @ 9.30pm - 12.30am & 3.30am. Average pace was 2 feet 3" long x deep an average width of 3'. Original depth of the trench was obtained to 5" with 4-4gap, 6" width, 1" high. | Rain interfered the progress of working party. Insufficient wire carried up. Bent Coy was came to wire also to return early. |

# WAR DIARY or INTELLIGENCE SUMMARY.

Army Form C. 2118.

| Hour, Date, Place | Summary of Events and Information | Remarks and References to Appendices |
|---|---|---|
| 22/5/17 Green Line<br>8.15pm to 3.45am (23/5/17) | No. 4 Coy of 15 men continued work on their original party of Green line Trench, which was completed to the required depth. Also a small part of the Gt Jerusalem trench was filled in.<br><br>Wiring parties were NB: Lieut Edwards (ARB) Reserve No.6, in 3 parties of 2 men & NCO, supported by 1 officer. About 10pm was completed.<br><br>An MG emplacement is to be constructed to short along the wire towards Jerusalem.<br>This line is being constructed by the B Coy.<br><br>The 15 H. Coy supplied another 6 men & 1 officer who worked in parties of 2 men under 1 NCO & continued their wiring of the previous night making a further 160ft of apron fence and 80ft of 3 wire also interior piquet for a further 80'. | Work on the whole line certainly continues was rendered extremely difficult for the follow<br><br>(i) Complete clearance of the night, & the mud, causing<br><br>(ii) The long (angle iron) German wire Pickets were purposely making movement impossible except by narrow lanes, & certainly making it very difficult + tiring for the officers to ensure that their own wire lines were running straight<br><br>(iii) The damage by much shell fire during the day along the whole line displacing the parapet in places + causing much damage to the parapet + traverses of the new part of the right Green line. |

Army Form C. 2118.

# WAR DIARY
## or
## INTELLIGENCE SUMMARY.
(Erase heading not required.)

Instructions regarding War Diaries and Intelligence
Summaries are contained in F. S. Regs., Part II.
and the Staff Manual respectively. Title pages
will be prepared in manuscript.

| Hour, Date, Place | Summary of Events and Information | Remarks and References to Appendices |
|---|---|---|
| 4 AM – 9 AM 24/5/17 (GREEN line) | The 9th Cav. Btn Pioneer Battn continued their work just at dawn on the front line & were digging in saunders. The 'D' Coy 9th Btn have completed the first part of the trench all below the region of war with exception of unconnected fire & Lps in the Range. The new part given to them has been dug to a depth of about 4' throughout. The parapet & parados have been sandbagged and are nearly complete.<br><br>The Batt 'F' Coy have practically finished the 275ft of Barb(?) wire (5 lines of Pickets) & reached the end of the Fries of Capt ............ all adding their own by 6 a.m. After this the Coy continued the line East of the 13th Hussars their particular part of the trench being soon shelled on the night of the 24/25. This was repaired – See above the trench 3' × 3' The 15th Coy have prolonged their wire & tunnels about ............ So ft of the trench apron wire completed since '22nd ×25............' | Strength Estd for 'D' of 9th O.R. Digging took place 6 to 9 A.M. |

(9 29 6) W 2794 100,000 8/14 H W V Forms/C. 2118/11.

# WAR DIARY or INTELLIGENCE SUMMARY

Army Form C. 2118.

| Hour, Date, Place | Summary of Events and Information | Remarks and References to Appendices |
|---|---|---|
| 25/6/17 GREEN Line 4 AM & 9 AM | 1 9/pro Coy supplied 89 men working on (6) 7 T Heads of BAYER & NE 9 French Trys; achieving an acc aye depth of 3ft x 3' wide Two of these T Heads are nearly completed for probable intake by tonite. No tamping as yet. There as no head traps. Seven of Auxilaries Shafts were cleaned out & tops of these put to the Coy Shaft depth. For the most part an Aeroplane hovered over at a high altitude. It appears that there works were carried on (mainly for instance Shelling Occured more intermittent went a while. Int were compar'd. in front & behind all 50* of O.D famen Trench appears an original trench was putted in & another 40* partially filled in. The moment Artz Battn 15 Aero Coy 141 STA 9 2 pro. The times were deepend throt on the way home came giving an average dpt in the center of 4' 6" 8 o* of Dorsets & memb'ld was boiled out & rand trips. briots while firm  I firing bay was completed 3 traps 3/4 finished & 5 Bags of trieed frequently. No casualties A further 130* was prepared to an average of 6' & width occurred An average of 64 of the Dorsets |  Form 7.15 AM anxiety the trench was made intangible by topside air reconnaissance |

**Army Form C. 2118.**

# WAR DIARY
## or
## INTELLIGENCE SUMMARY.
*(Erase heading not required.)*

Instructions regarding War Diaries and Intelligence Summaries are contained in F. S. Regs., Part II. and the Staff Manual respectively. Title pages will be prepared in manuscript.

| Hour, Date, Place | Summary of Events and Information | Remarks and References to Appendices |
|---|---|---|
| 25/5/17 Greenland<br>3.45AM - 9AM | Bays for coy. 70' x 3' of trench was dug down to 5' widened from 3' at bottom to 5' at Surface. Bays firing steps & throw outs were well adapted - should be finished on the 26th. Parados was sand bagged to about 2/3 of its distance.<br>30" demilion to the above was also done in trench on part of the 15th H.Q. Corps allotted trench.<br>60' of altering started on Jack E of Jack Trench was widened and deepened to about 4' x 3'6 | Strength 102 O.R. 3 Officers |

# WAR DIARY
## or
## INTELLIGENCE SUMMARY.
(Erase heading not required.)

Army Form C. 2118.

Instructions regarding War Diaries and Intelligence Summaries are contained in F. S. Regs., Part II. and the Staff Manual respectively. Title pages will be prepared in manuscript.

| Hour, Date, Place | Summary of Events and Information | Remarks and References to Appendices |
|---|---|---|
| 4 AM to 9 AM 26/5/17<br><br>Green Lane<br>Row Bois<br>9th Pioneer Battn<br>Saxon | The 19th Coy dug a dog leg communication trench forward Bayern Weg 30' x long to a depth of 3'6".<br><br>The German trench just opposite and parallel to the rear of our line has now been completely filled in with the exception of about 15" which is practically rendered useless for men to take cover or throw bombs from it. 3 of the T heads commenced yesterday are completed with the exception of sand bags, the remaining one ?? are about three quarters finished.<br><br>The parapet and parados of the Gun Line trench dug by the Coy have been covered with dark earth to make this trench invisible for air craft photography. Their colors continued ??<br><br>The 15th Coy 102 strong completed their section of trench FG (about 130') by deepening throughout to 5' 6" widening to about 4'3", 1 Bay was completed by Huns? 3 finished which to? Sources ? + 32 bays completed, all bays are lined with sandbags. 6 of trench is lined on both Parapet & parados with earth to make the whole trench invisible | Strength of this company 82 men<br><br>A shortage of sandbags too hold up all this Corps<br><br>Their parapets + parados of these Bays were partly dug + then destroyed by enemy shell fire hence their ?? state. |

Army Form C. 2118.

# WAR DIARY
## or
## INTELLIGENCE SUMMARY.
(Erase heading not required.)

| Hour, Date, Place | Summary of Events and Information | Remarks and References to Appendices |
|---|---|---|
| 4 AM till 9 AM 26/5/17 (Continued) | B.35 fea. Coy 105 strong worked along the 135" of trench allotted to them — all the 7 in bags were brought to a state of immediate readiness for use in case of emergency along the whole line should they be required. 20 men worked on a stop up communication trench to BAYERN W.C.R. but owing to the tapes being wrongly laid, the work of the 20 men for 2 hrs was miss applied & the trench confirmed | The work carried have been most improved & there been more sandbags |

## WAR Diary

| Hour Date Place | Summary of events & information | Remarks |
|---|---|---|
| 1.0 pm - 26/6/17 to 2.30 am - 27/5/17 Tommy Trench | The Batt. Bos. Strong Parties under Capt Hargreaves To continue assist retains Tommy Trench. The alloted task was best which was along & an average depth of 4'6" - 3'6" wide at the surface 2'6" at the bottom | Ref Map: France 57B NW B.5 c 9.5 |
| 11 pm - 27/5/17 to 3.30 am 28/5/17 Tommy Trench | The Battn. Bos. Strong dug a further 60 ft of Tommy Trench. An average depth of 5' being dug. | |

# WAR DIARY
## or
## INTELLIGENCE SUMMARY.
*(Erase heading not required.)*

Army Form C. 2118.

| Hour, Date, Place | Summary of Events and Information | Remarks and References to Appendices |
|---|---|---|
| 15/7/17 Green Line. 3 AM to 8 AM | The 19th/Hro Coy supplied 50 OR to carry to these with in the Green Line. The T head themselves were completed for use & for the most part the communication trenches had been completed, though they are not yet sandbagged in these areas. The dug as communication trenches commenced by the 19 Hro Coy has now been completed though a certain amount of trimming up is required such as Camouflage.

The 15 Hro Coy & the Bed's Yeomanry dug 30 6 40 yards each of a dog leg trench. Leading to Bayern W.E. This Trench is to be called Curly But & have a few fire bays made. | |

Army Form C. 2118.

# WAR DIARY
## or
## INTELLIGENCE SUMMARY.
*(Erase heading not required.)*

| Hour, Date, Place | Summary of Events and Information | Remarks and References to Appendices |
|---|---|---|
| 29/5/17 GREEN Line 3 AM to 8 AM. | 19th Aus Coy completed the 7 T Heads & found ad. mine in their seats partly blown. Thus they completed sandbags & it is now ready for use. 150° of BAY&RN was dug to an average depth of 5'. A German French loophole was discovered & found true is not repair. The 15 Hrs Coy & B.S.O. yet by have now joined the N.S. & tails of curly Rib & dug to the required depth. Rifling in this post was particularly heavy & gallop & but the men worked with vigour. There now only a few yards at the forks end of curly but remain to complete, the whole new &c of 2HB &w & Coop | Trench Heads require deepening to 4'6" below the parapet also in certain cases. Steps at in birrah [?] went buildings also in case where tren is used. 3. The German artillery have apparently [?] On most of T heads 65 lbs trench morty small shells about 2"× in front of the T.S |

War Diary or Intelligence Summary

A.F. C.2118

| Hour. Date. Place. | Summary of Events and Information | Remarks & Refs to Appendices |
|---|---|---|
| 3 am to 8 am. 31.5.17 Green Line | The 19th Hussars Coy dug and completed 150'x of BAYERN WEG a further 60'x long & finished. The 15th Hussars Coy completed 75'x of CURLY BIT & 5 fire bays of MAIN ST. 3 fire steps & 4 traverses which had been blown in were revetted with sandbags & 60 yds wire entanglement completed. The Beds. Yeo. Coy. completed & deepened 130'x wire, also began & finished 70 yds new wire. 30'x of communication trench was dug & revetted and practically finished. 100'x of communication trench was dug 4' wide at top, 2'6" at bottom & 5' deep for nearly the whole length. | |
| 9.45 pm 31.5.17 to 1.30 am. 1.6.17. TOMMY TRENCH. | The Bed. Yeo. Coy. 70 strong dug 22 lunt pits in TOMMY TRENCH. The Coy was divided into parties of 3 or 4 men, each party working on one pit. Digging did not cease until the pits had reached the necessary measurements and were passed by an R.E. representative | Lieut Shrail rendered great assistance by his thorough marking out of the ground. |

G. Hanmer Lieut & Adjt. for Major.
Commanding 9th Bn. Beds. Queen Battalion.

"C" Batt⁻ Cavalry Pioneer Brigade.

Army Form C. 2118.

**WAR DIARY**
or
**INTELLIGENCE SUMMARY.**
(Erase heading not required.)

Map Ref = 51 B, N.W. 1/20,000

Instructions regarding War Diaries and Intelligence Summaries are contained in F.S. Regs., Part II. and the Staff Manual respectively. Title pages will be prepared in manuscript.

| Place | Date | Hour | Summary of Events and Information | Remarks and references to Appendices |
|---|---|---|---|---|
| | 1917 | | | |
| ECURIE | 13/6 | | Batt⁻ under Major S.T. Green, Beds. Yeo., marched into camp, (A.21.d.05), composed as under:— | |
| | | | Batt⁻ H.Q. 3 officers, 17 O.R., 5 horses. | |
| | | | XV Hrs. Coy. 5 —, 187 —, 8 — | |
| | | | XIX Hrs. Coy. 5 —, 186 —, 10 — | |
| | | | Beds Yeo Coy. 5 —, 181 —, 10 — | |
| | | | R.E. 1 —, 17 —, 3 — | |
| | | | R.A.M.C. 1 —, 9 —, 0 — | |
| | | | Total Strength. 20 Officers, 597 O.R., 36 horses. | |
| do. | 14/6 | | Consolidation of camp proceeded. — G.O.C. 1st Cav. Div. inspected camp. | |
| | | 8.30 pm | Batt⁻ less XIX Hrs. Coy. began work on sector of Town C.T., from 13.27.c.6.1. running E. to ARRAS – GAVRELLE road, about A.4.b.8.5. — Nature of work: deepening trench, widening berms, indenting floor etc. 70 duckboards and tools were taken to the trench by Batt⁻ Transport. | |
| do | 15/6 | 8.30 pm | Batt⁻ less B.Y. Coy. continued work as before. — 70 duckboards dumped. (Transport were slightly wounded) | M |

Army Form C. 2118.

# WAR DIARY
## or
## INTELLIGENCE SUMMARY.
*(Erase heading not required.)*

Instructions regarding War Diaries and Intelligence Summaries are contained in F. S. Regs., Part II. and the Staff Manual respectively. Title pages will be prepared in manuscript.

| Place | Date | Hour | Summary of Events and Information | Remarks and references to Appendices |
|---|---|---|---|---|
| ECURIE | 16/6 | 9 a.m. | Duck-boarding party, 1 Off[r] and 26 O.R., in TOWY C.T. | |
| | | 8.30pm | Batt[n], less XV th Coy, continued work of previous night. Lorries were provided to take Batt[n] from ECURIE to Rly crossing at B.26.c.2.2., and to fetch it back at 3.30 a.m. – Two sump pits begun on TOWY C.T., duckboards (from GREEN LINE eastwards, were fixed) and 80 duckboards dumped by transport. | |
| do. | 17/6 | 4 a.m. | Coy Duckboarding party as before on TOWY C.T. | |
| | | 10.30 am | G.O.C. Cav. Bde. inspected camp. | |
| | | 12 noon | Kit-inspection by companies | |
| | | 3.30pm | Batt[n] less XIX th Coy, continued work on TOWY C.T. The sector allotted to Batt[n] being increased by addition of THAMES C.T., from its junction with TOWY C.T. (H.4.a.7.9.) to ~~AVION-GAVRELLE~~ DITCH POST (H.4.b.6.7.). | |
| do. | 18/6 | 8.45pm | Batt[n] continued work on TOWY & THAMES C.T's. – Some shelling of GAVRELLE road. M.O. and 1 man XV th Coy slightly wounded. | |

T2134. Wt. W708—776. 500000. 4/15. Sir J. C. & S.

Army Form C. 2118.

# WAR DIARY
## or
## INTELLIGENCE SUMMARY.
*(Erase heading not required.)*

Instructions regarding War Diaries and Intelligence Summaries are contained in F.S. Regs., Part II. and the Staff Manual respectively. Title pages will be prepared in manuscript.

| Place | Date | Hour | Summary of Events and Information | Remarks and references to Appendices |
|---|---|---|---|---|
| ECURIE | 19/6 | 4 a.m. | Duckboarding party of 191st and 60 O.R., continued boarding of TONY and THAMES, C.Ts. | |
| | | 8.45 p.m. | Batt" continued work of previous night. | |
| | 20/6 | 4 a.m. | Duckboarding party as before. | |
| | | 8.0 p.m. | Party of 2 officers and 16 O.R. erected camouflage on ARRAS-GAVRELLE road. Batt" parade cancelled by G.O.C. owing to very heavy rain. | |
| | 21/6 | 4 a.m. | Duckboarding party, less B.Y. contingent, working as before. | |
| | | 10.30 a.m. | G.O.C. Corps Pioneer Bde inspected camp | |
| | | 8.45 p.m. | Batt" worked on sector of RED LINE (from B.17.c.2.4. to B.23.cent.). Nature of work: widening and deepening the trench, which was in parts about 1/3 dug, in parts only just begun. — One man XV Bn., slightly wounded by M.G. fire. | |
| | 22/6 | 4 a.m. | Duckboarding party, less XV Bn. contingent, continued work on TONY and THAMES, C.Ts. Remainder of Batt" in rear. | |
| | 23/6 | 2 a.m. | Batt" at work on TONY and THAMES, C.Ts. | |

Army Form C. 2118.

# WAR DIARY
## or
## INTELLIGENCE SUMMARY.
*(Erase heading not required.)*

Instructions regarding War Diaries and Intelligence Summaries are contained in F. S. Regs., Part II. and the Staff Manual respectively. Title pages will be prepared in manuscript.

| Place | Date | Hour | Summary of Events and Information | Remarks and references to Appendices |
|---|---|---|---|---|
| ECURIE | 23/6 (cont'd) | 4 am | Duckboarding party, less XIX Bn contingent, continued work on THAMES C.T. | |
| | | 8.45 pm | Batt'n continued work on RED LINE. | |
| | 24/6 | 4 am | Duckboarding party, less B.Y. contingent, (which paraded later with Batt'n) finished boarding of THAMES C.T. up to 1800 yards from GREEN LINE. | |
| | | 8.45 pm | Batt'n continued work on RED LINE. | |
| | 25/6 | 8 am | Maintenance party of 1 corp'l and 6 men, on TOWY and THAMES C.T's. Supervision of sump-pits, drainage, signal-wires, and general upkeep of trench. 240 duckboards carried to RED LINE in G.S. wagons after dark. 1 man and 1 wagon injured, latter abandoned on RED LINE. | |
| | 26/6 | 5.30 am | Duckboarding party, 1 Off'r and 90 O.R. on RED LINE. | |
| | | 6 am | Maintenance party, as before, on TOWY and THAMES C.T's. | |
| | | 3 pm | Duckboarding party, 1 Off'r and 90 O.R. on RED LINE. 45 duckboards carried from RIDGE DUMP. | |
| | | 12 mid't | Derelict wagon salved on RED LINE. | |

Army Form C. 2118.

# WAR DIARY
## or
## INTELLIGENCE SUMMARY.
*(Erase heading not required.)*

| Place | Date | Hour | Summary of Events and Information | Remarks and references to Appendices |
|---|---|---|---|---|
| ECURIE | 27/6 | 4 am | Duck-boarding party, 10ff.Y and 75 O.R., continued work on THAMES C.T. Sump pits, funked sally ports, and stretcher-rests built. | |
| | | 6 am | Maintenance party, as before, on TOWY C.T. | |
| | 28/6 | 6 am | Maintenance party, as before, on TOWY and THAMES C.T. | |
| | | 7.10 pm | Most officers in the Batt.n witnessed successful attack by 5th & 31st Div.s on OPPY and CADORNA trenches. | |
| | 29/6 | | LT. SELBY-LOWNDES XV th.Y, relieved LT. HAY, XIX th.Y, as O.C. XIX th. Coy. | |
| | | | LT. HORTON, XIX th. Coy, transferred to "A" Batt.n | |
| | | 8.0 pm | 280 duckboards carried in G.S. wagons to junction of TOWY C.T. with ARRAS-GAVRELLE Rd. | |
| | | 9.0 pm | XV th. Coy and 1 Platoon Beds. Coy began excavation of CLYDE C.T., a new trench (to run from TIRED ALLEY (at B.9.d.9.9.) to RED LINE (at B.10.c.9.5.) | |
| | | | - 1 man XV th.Y severely wounded, since died. 3 men XV th.Y slightly wounded | |
| | | 10.0 pm | XIX th. Coy and Beds. Coy less 1 Platoon, at work on E. end of TOWY C.T. from its junction with THAMES C.T. to about H.5.a cent. - Drainage, sump pits, etc. | |

JA

Army Form C. 2118.

# WAR DIARY
## or
## INTELLIGENCE SUMMARY.
(Erase heading not required.)

| Place | Date | Hour | Summary of Events and Information | Remarks and references to Appendices |
|---|---|---|---|---|
| ECURIE | 30/6 | 4 a.m. | Duck board party of 1 Off. and 60 O.R. on TONY C.T. | |
| | | 9.0 pm | XIII th Co. and 1 platoon of Beds Yeo Coy continued work on CLYDE C.T. | |
| | | 10.0 pm | XIX th Coy and Beds Yeo Coy as one platoon — TONY & THAMES C.T. | |
| | 1/7 | | Work as on June 30th. | |
| | 2/7 | | Do. — 1 man, Beds Yeo, slightly wounded. | |
| | 3/7 | 4 a.m. | Duck board party of 1 Off. and 80 O.R. on TONY and THAMES C.T's. Rem'r of Batt'n rested. | |
| | 4/7 | 10.30 am | G.O.C. Corr R. Bde. inspected camp | |
| | | 7.30 pm | XIX th Coy and Beds Yeo Coy worked on extn. of TONY C.T. from the ARRAS - GAVRELLE road to the RED LINE (H.S. a cent) — Drainage sump pits, widening French etc. | |
| | | | XV th Coy worked on RED LINE N. of DITCH POST, starting from about I.B.28.d.8.4. and continuing the excavation of the trench for 300 yds. | |

T2134. Wt. W708—776. 500000. 4/15. Sir J. C. & S.

Army Form C. 2118.

# WAR DIARY
## or
## INTELLIGENCE SUMMARY.
*(Erase heading not required.)*

Instructions regarding War Diaries and Intelligence Summaries are contained in F. S. Regs., Part II. and the Staff Manual respectively. Title pages will be prepared in manuscript.

| Place | Date | Hour | Summary of Events and Information | Remarks and references to Appendices |
|---|---|---|---|---|
| ECURIE | 5/7 | 5am | Duckboarding party of 1 Officer and 100 O.R. on T.U.W. C.T. E of ARRAS-GAVRELLE road. | |
| | | 8am | Maintenance party of 1 corporal and 6 O.R. on N end of TOWY C.T. and THAMES C.T. | |
| | | 7·30pm | Batt'ns worked as on July 4th | |
| | 6/7 | | Work as before. I saw that of night 5/6 on left the RED LINE and works on TOWY C.T. beyond the Hun line were completed. | |
| | 7/7 | 4pm | Work as before | |
| | | | G.O.C. 4th Can Div. inspected camp. | |
| | 8/7 | 5am | Duckboarding party on TOWY C.T. beyond GAVRELLE road. | |
| | | 6am | Maintenance party on N end of TOWY C.T. and THAMES C.T. | |
| | | | Rem'r of Batt'ns on rest. | |
| | 9/7 | 2·0pm | Batt'n marched out of camp and returned to night billets in town. | |

Signed Capt & Adjt
for Major S.T. Green commanding O. Batt'n